Enlightenment and Genocide, Contradictions of Modernity

P.I.E.-Peter Lang

Bruxelles · Bern · Berlin · Frankfurt/M · New York · Oxford · Wien

This book was produced in the framework of the research project *The Cultural Construction of Community in Modernisation Processes in Comparison* in co-operation between the European University Institute in Florence and Humboldt University in Berlin. The project is sponsored by the *Bank of Sweden Tercentenary Foundation*.

James KAYE & Bo STRÅTH (eds)

Enlightenment
and Genocide,
Contradictions of Modernity

Series Philosophy & Politics
No.5

Die Deutsche Bibliothek – CIP-Einheitsaufnahme

Enlightenment and genocide, contradictions of modernity /
James Kaye & Bo Stråth (eds). – Bruxelles ; Bern ; Berlin ;
Frankfurt/M. ; New York ; Oxford; Wien : PIE Lang, 2000
(Series philosophy & politics ; No. 5)
ISBN 90-5201-919-3

*CIP available from the British Library, GB
and the Library of Congress, USA.*

ISBN 0-8204-4657-2

© P.I.E.-Peter Lang s.a.
Presses Interuniversitaires Européennes
Brussels, 2000
E-mail : info@peterlang.com

ISBN 90-5201-919-3
D/2000/5678/10

Contents

Preface

On the threshold to the 21st century the cry "never again" seems illusory, even absurd. Did it ever harbour credibility? Were we so naive? The Holocaust was not a finality, not the end of "final solutions" in Europe. Genocide has continued to emerge as an active element in European politics and policies. Kosovo and Bosnia provide testament. This book presents the concept genocide as a political and social tool in modern Europe, not only reconciled with modernity, but as what may be an integral component. Modernity, however, is also closely linked with the Enlightenment and its concepts of tolerance, equality and liberty. This volume sheds light upon the inherent contradictions of modernity between Enlightenment and genocide, and on how this ambivalent European heritage is confronted.

In addition to the Holocaust and Yugoslavia, Stalinist terror has been newly documented as another of the colossal horrors of our century. The extent to which mass executions can be considered to be genocide as well as, of all things, a forced sterilisation campaign in Sweden is also discussed.

A uniting factor may be the "good" or "higher" intentions of the perpetrators; the goal of a scientifically better or even ideal society. Another problem raised addresses the connection between these disastrous expressions of modernity in more general terms and specific historical developments. This anticipates the question of why the Holocaust was engineered in a cultural and intellectual centre of Europe and not elsewhere.

When societies create community through an emphasis on demarcation from the Other, purification programmes based on concepts like race and *ethnos* easily emerge. The connection to genocide from such developments is clear, but how can we understand eugenics in this context? The link to modernity becomes evident in this question, but can we call the prevention of reproduction of certain genes genocide?

The questions of this book were first discussed at a workshop at the European University Institute in Florence in November 1998. The contributions have since been revised in the wake of the discussions. Two of the participants have published their contributions elsewhere.

9

Janina Bauman confronted the persecution of the Roma. Her contribution was published as "Demons of Other Peoples Fear: The Plight of the Gypsies" in *Thesis Eleven*, Number 54 (1998). Bernd Giesen discussed the role of Holocaust in the collective memory in Germany. His contribution is being published in Neil Smelster and Jeffrey C. Alexander's forthcoming volume *Cultural Trauma* and Giesen's own *Triumph and Trauma* (both University of California Press, 2000).

This book was produced in the framework of the research project *The Cultural Construction of Community in Modernisation Processes in Comparison* in co-operation between the European University Institute in Florence and Humboldt University in Berlin. The project is sponsored by the *Bank of Sweden Tercentenary Foundation*. We want to express a special thanks to its Director Dan Brändström for all his support and encouragement.

Florence, in October, 1999

James Kaye and Bo Stråth

Enlightenment and Genocide, Contradictions of Modernity

James KAYE and Bo STRÅTH

The concepts Modernity and Enlightenment have often and plausibly been linked in causal historical narratives. Reinhart Koselleck, for example, in his doctoral thesis *Kritik und Krise* argued, during the Cold War, that the Enlightenment provoked critique which, in turn, provoked crisis and adjustment.[1] Ideas of freedom and equality, which were vehemently voiced as maxims of the French and American Revolutions, would later be cleaved into the ideologies of liberalism and socialism, which by the 1950s held the globe in check through a balance of terror. Social criticism based on the Enlightenment, in this view, paved the way for modernity through the introduction of a belief in an evolutionary development towards an ever better society, an evolution made possible by the conscious application of logic, and science to the environment. Attempts at "social engineering" illustrate this concept. Confidence in the capacity of social and economic sciences to contribute to the improvement of society has been an important component of this view, which exist both in Marxist and liberal functionalist versions. Social criticism and the belief in progress through human action proved to be an explosive mixture insofar as they took the world to the brink of atomic war which challenged the right to life itself. Beliefs in technology based progress merged with a fear of technology based extinction, utopian images of the future uncannily became dystopian. This is the essence of modernity. There are both optimistic and pessimistic views on modernity.

The recognition that both Hitler and Stalin were disciples of this faith in progress provoked a novel interpretation of the relationship

---

[1] KOSELLECK, R., 1959.

11

between the Enlightenment and modernity. Civilisation's critique of modern technique, capitalism, socialism and a pluralistic society, provoked a conception of modernity as atomistic, which in turn, paved the way for totalitarianism and fascism/Nazism through attempts to realise idealistic dreams of *Volksgemeinschaft*, holistic community and "back to nature". This tension between experienced atomism and an exaggerated desire for holistic communities was one significant factor in the process that had a crescendo, but did not terminate in the Holocaust. Genocide continues as a factor in civilisation. A key element in the construction of holistic communities is the invention of Others, they underpin this project.

Weber's modernisation view exhibits elements of a clearly evolutionary element, although not necessarily towards ever higher stages in an optimistic scenario. Works by Detlev Peukert and, quite recently, Arpád Szakolczai, emphasise similarities between Weber and Nietzsche. Modernity is a permanent process of mystification and de-mystification.[2] From his "post-modern" standpoint Zygmunt Bauman ascribes to Weber's pessimistic view in an explanation of the Holocaust as little more than a banal consequence of modernity and its *Zweckrationalität* (*i.e.* instrumental rationality).

The aim of this book is to problematise interdependence within the confines of the tripolar field Enlightenment-Modernity-Genocide, and then inherently the tension between the optimistic and the pessimistic scenarios of modernity.

The tension between the optimistic and the pessimistic views of progress hold this volume together and will be discussed and problematised by asking whether there are elements of the Enlightenment project, or even its precursor the Renaissance, that still could be of importance as responses to technical developments. This raises the questions: "Can technology be controlled and Jacobinism domesticated? And if yes, then under what conditions?"

This volume emphasises the contradictory qualities of Enlightenment in the mirror of genocide, adding to what may be an uncanny genre of academic literature, which offers a number of contemporary and hopefully original perspectives of two landscapes that are infinitely intriguing and as such have been investigated in the most minute detail. This process is undertaken at a very specific time. Its production was contemporary to the introduction of the Euro, ethnic cleansing in

---

[2] PEUKERT, D., 1989.

Bosnia, war and genocide in Rwanda, the publication of Adolf Eichmann's memoirs, and the elimination of the theory of evolution from the curriculum of the state of Kansas, as well as numerous anniversaries that fell on 8 and 9 November 1998. Central to the inspiration or motivation of this volume is to emphasise what we perceive as the relevance of Enlightenment and genocide in the present and near future.

Additionally although every time is liminal in the sense that it lies perpetually between newly redefined pasts and futures, this work may be more the product of a time at the turn of a century, or the end of a double century according to Göran Rosenberg, in the concluding chapter of this volume. Its most prominent product in this view is doubt. A doubt particularly of the very foundations of the Enlightenment which ironically new little or no doubt.

In essence the challenge this volume poses can be delineated in two questions, neither of which is very new and both of which have been hotly contested: *i.e.* their formulation and response have been habitually revised since they were first probed and will most probably continue to be contested in the foreseeable future. The questions, implied in this volume's title, are "What is Enlightenment?" and "What is genocide?". The juxtaposition of these concepts is novel, although it finds its foundations in Horkheimer, Adorno, Arendt and most recently Zygmunt Bauman's seminal work *Modernity and the Holocaust*.[3] It implies that the simultaneous shift of focus from modernity to Enlightenment and the Holocaust to genocide, both specifications and generalisations, may incite new positions or perspectives as well as provoke or broaden a reflexive, self questioning debate within the tripolar field.

Of course, the Holocaust is central to this undertaking. In a recent contribution to the debate Daniel Goldhagen interprets the Holocaust as a consequence of the German *Volk* and their very unique exterminatory anti-Semitism during the 19th and first half of the 20th century. He has been characterised as extreme in the development of his thesis, and has met many objections. The thrust of the German *Historikerstreit* some ten years ago claimed that the Holocaust was unique and as such could not be compared with any other event. However in this interpretation, not the German *Volk*, but a specific German historical trajectory, the *Sonderweg* paved the way to disaster. Goldhagen has

---

[3]   HORKHEIMER, M. and ADORNO T. W., 1947 [1944]; ARENDT, H., 1963; BAUMAN, Z., 1989.

in a sense shifted the focus from an exceptional (abnormal) history to an exceptional (abnormal) *Volk*.

The outcome of this German *Historikerstreit*, the emphasis upon a German uniqueness, as opposed to Bauman's universal view should be seen within the framework of Ernst Nolte's provocative thesis, which proposed Hitler as a European Anti-Lenin and Germany as an Anti-Bolshevist bulwark. Like Goldhagen, although for contrary reasons, Nolte until the publication of the *Livre noir*[4] was more or less exiled from the academic agenda as extreme and biased. Ten years after the German debate the *Livre noir* in France documented the terror and "genocide" of Communist practice. The Algerian and the Yugoslavian civil wars present other cases of "genocide". Without disputing the uniqueness of the Holocaust, modernity and genocide can be convincingly associated.

What remains relevant however is the tension between Bauman's view and a more historical view, that questions why the Holocaust was engineered by Germany? Is the answer similar to the one given by a directors of the firm *Topf und Söhne*, premier designers and builders of the crematoria for German death camps, "If we didn't build them someone else would have."?[5] Although the technical component in the form of instrumental rationality is obvious, the role of the Jacobin component must also be accounted for, and related to the *Zweckrationalität*. Who are the perpetrators and victims? And why do they occupy these roles?

In this respect it is necessary to ask, what is specific, to 20th century genocide when compared with general questions of violence and warfare. Were, for instance, witch-hunts or Napoleon's execution of 3,000 Turkish prisoners still "normal" historical atrocities in comparison to the practice of the Serbs?

The mutual strength of the two dominant positions on the connection Modernity-Enlightenment – the optimistic and the pessimistic – has varied over time in theoretical reflection on society. The optimistic scenario did not wane in the wake of knowledge of the Holocaust, but underpinned much of the social sciences in the 1960s and 1970s. It was reborn under a new label during the neoliberal 1980s and during the brief euphoric period in the wake of 1989. Develop-

---

[4]   COURTOIS, S. *et al.*, 1997.

[5]   Here we cite the recording of Zygmunt Bauman's contribution to the workshop "Modernity, Enlightenment and Genocide", Florence 9 November 1998.

ments in Yugoslavia and the exposure of the outrages in the name of Communism brought genocide once again to Europe and they reinforced its connection with modernity and the Enlightenment.

Zygmunt Bauman, in his contribution to this volume, reassess his seminal work *Modernity and the Holocaust* where he emphasised the importance of ceasing to view the Holocaust as a bizarre and aberrant episode in modern history and instead portrayed it as an integrated part of that history. The prevalent view of the Holocaust as a component of Germany's *Sonderweg*, is that of a deviation, an exception from the narrative of modernisation which is tied to progress. Bauman's argument is that the Holocaust was not a deviation or digression that is disassociated from modernity but in fact its consequence.

Modernity passionately declared war on passion and inscribed reason on its banners. Reason went hand in hand with abstraction. One of the most important abstracting efforts in the name of Enlightenment has been classification. A veritable obsession to categorise and classify emerged. Abstraction and classification effaced the face, when the owner of a category was transformed from being an individual to a specimen. In the next step the classified took on essential proportions. Two cases in point are race in biology and *ethnos* in anthropology. Classification was supported by all the technological tools modernity has provided and the idea of scientific management as embodied in bureaucratic organisation, the ability to co-ordinate actions of a great number of individuals and make the overall outcome independent of personal idiosyncrasies. Connected to the idea of constant improvement intrinsic in Enlightenment (*i.e.* modernity as a perpetually unfinished project, embedded in utopian ideas of some end goal, in constant need of critical scrutiny and revision) a potentially explosive mix has emerged. Here the contradictions of modernity become visible. Memory of suffering does not necessarily assure dedication in the fight against inhumanity. The equally probable outcome of martyrdom is the division of humankind into victims and victimisers. If you are the victim your task is to reverse the tables.

Bauman in this volume connects the Holocaust to today's situation of stone-throwing Palestinians against Israeli settlers. The cult of survival, in the process of victimisation contains dangers of tremendous dimensions, where ideas of "who strikes first, survives" and "the stronger lives" emerged and can easily be linked to Darwinian development theories and scientific classification. In Bauman's wording in this volume: the macabre paradox of being a hereditary victim is to develop vested interests in the hostility of the world, by fomenting and maintaining hostility of the world. The self anointed children of martyrs live in fortresses. Here Bauman approaches to Hannah Arendt's critical questions in connection with the Eichmann trial, where she coined the expression "the banality of evil".[6] The problem in the focus of Arendt's interest was somewhat different although still very close to Bauman's way of poseing the problem: questions of blind obedience and subsequent personal responsibility.

Against a view, which emphasises bureaucratic processes, where the executors emerge as more or less thoughtless cogs in the mass murder machinery, the German historian Götz Aly has recently argued that the role of hate feelings and terror should not be forgotten.[7] In this respect we refer to Arne Johan Vetlesen's chapter where he discusses Ernest Becker, Otto Rank, Elias Canetti and C. Fred Alford concerning the mechanisms at an individual and mass psychological level which broke through social and moral barriers against mass execution of fellow human beings. Here Vetlesen seems to become ambivalent between modernity and human conditions of a more anthropological nature in his view on such mechanisms thereby building a bridge to Robert Thurston's chapter, who sees organised mass murder and persecution, not only as a modern but also, as a pre-modern phenomenon.

Not only the self described martyrs in their fortress but also a more general fight against inhumanity and injustices for a better world contains a quest for a moral re-awakening or ethical purification. In the extension of such fundamentalism, with or without Jacobinism, claims for ethical purification are easily transformed into claims for ethnic purification. Modernity, understood as division of labour, science, technology, scientific management and rational calculation of costs and effects, provokes critical questions of right and wrong, questions which easily are transformed into orthodoxy versus heterodoxy, and promote fundamentalism. There is a connection between this view and Weber's pessimistic view on rationalisation as a process, which in the long run engulfs all enchantment, but where charisma retains the

---

[6] ARENDT, H., 1963; Cf. PAPPE, I., 1999.

[7] Lecture by Götz Aly at the conference *Zur Historiographie des Holocaust am Beispiel von Hannah Arendts Eichmann in Jerusalem* at the Potsdam Einstein Forum 19-22 June 1997; cf. DACHS G., "Hannah Arendt in Jerusalem" in *Die Zeit* No. 34, 19 August 1999; James Schmidt refers to BROWNING C., 1992, in this volume, arguing that the slaughter of human beings face to face must contain other elements, basically of a psychological nature, than a cool instrumental reason.

ability to produce new fascination. Weber could hardly imagine how this concept would be realised thirteen years after his death.

Arne Johan Vetlesen's contribution underpins Bauman's argument on a connection between genocide and modernity. The Holocaust was not unique. What has happened in Yugoslavia in the 1990s is a similar case of violence against a targeted group of people selected for collective execution performed before an audience called European civilisation that, again, was neither ignorant of nor undaunted in its effort to stop this crime. At first glance the similarity between Germany and Yugoslavia seems to be a link between genocide and a lack of political modernity. Vetlesen, however, in his thoughtful analysis provides well-founded arguments for seeing the similar obsession with external and internal enemies as expressions of modernity. Modern style genocide was in both cases contemplated, thought-out, planned, administered and carried out by a specific organised collective, a perpetrator group against a target group, where the target group did not exist as such before it was bundled together by the construction of the perpetrators. Genocide in this view is generic attribution transformed into an ideology and then turned into practice through collectivisation of agency.

Both the Holocaust and Yugoslavian ethnic cleansing can be seen as protests against, and negation of, the development of a political modernity where identity is increasingly rendered optional for each individual. Modernity in the sense, provokes tension between individualism and collectivism, between optionalism and essentialism. Feelings of atomism and meaninglessness of modern secularised mass societies reach a point where isolated and alienated individuals long to belong to some sort of organic community. Vetlesen also emphasises a parallel tension in the Enlightenment idea, first voiced by Kant, between the respect for the many in the name of tolerance and a keen eye for the universal leading to a lack of commitment and a reluctance to confront the particular. If ideals such as impartiality and neutrality are added to tolerance and pluralism, a cacophony of proud ideals emerges. They legitimise the diverting attention from phenomena such as events in Germany in the 1930s and the 1940s and in Yugoslavia in the 1990s.

Despite over two centuries of Enlightenment critique, a number of contemporary assessments of the Enlightenment exist that would make the paradoxical challenge that confronts contributors to this volume, the association of genocide and Enlightenment, into an absurd provocation. The Enlightenment in this view is characterised by a belief in the universality of rights and commonality of humanity distinct from and in opposition to the modern notion of a nation-state according to which a people partakes of human rights only by virtue of their shared nationality, not an Enlightenment idea but a French Revolutionary invention. In this view the rights of man are paramount. However, recent experiences learn us that when universal ideals are politically implemented, they supersede and nullify any claims of sovereignty that are anchored in international law, and justify military attack such as has been demonstrated recently in the NATO bombing of Yugoslavia.

In his contribution Wokler, one of the most gifted contemporary defenders of Enlightenment, clearly divorces modernity and Enlightenment, stating that the nation state may be modern, it is however by no stretch of the imagination Enlightened. He may be creating what could be termed the very short Enlightenment, a liberation from myth and tradition, or in Kant's definition the "liberation from self-incurred immaturity", without acknowledging the self-incurred responsibility of legal age. He proceeds to maintain that despite this separation "Enlightenment" has, over the last two centuries, been continuously almost programmatically betrayed and desecrated by modernity leading to the current state of affairs where its name is erroneously and deceitfully casually associated with its nemesis genocide.

It is not difficult to envision an argument that demonstrates the transformation of liberal ideas of universal human rights into those of national strength, and thus corroborates Wokler's account. Even before the French Revolution the Scottish moral philosopher Adam Smith published his *Wealth of Nations*. This "nationalisation" of universalism accelerated in the 19th century, when, armed with ideas inspired by Darwin, an existential competition was perceived as a real threat, not only to species and races but also nations which were endangered and destined to participate in an eternal quest for survival. Liberal universalism became a theoretical instrument which in the end provided national political projects with ideological muscles.[8] Opposing this partnership between the nation-state and *modernity* Wokler emphasises *tolerance* as the core of *Enlightenment* which, he does not hesitate to identify as a project, with all the strong connotations contained in the concept of project, an archetype for tolerance. Referring specifically to Ernst Cassirer he underpins his argument; not as many "post-modern" thinkers would, where Enlightenment loved

---

[8]   Cf. STRÅTH, B., 2000c.

the thing it killed, but where modernity endeavoured to kill the thing it loved. In Cassirer's view Enlightenment comprised an interconnected set of philosophies which sought not only to interpret the world but to change it on the basis of cosmopolitan and polytheistic tolerance. In this sense the concept of reason took shape in opposition to political and religious intolerance and superstition.

A new objective of the ability and goal to initiate change differentiated the Enlightened political philosophers of the 18th century from those of their 17th century colleagues. Through this belief classicism became modern. Referring to Kant, Cassirer argued (in 1932) that the true spirit of Germany was not nationalist and militarist but humanist, tolerant, pluralist and cosmopolitan, in the tradition of Goethe.[9] Seen in the shadow, not only of the Nazi ascent to power one year later which would culminate in the Holocaust, but also more recent carnage in Yugoslavia, this Enlightenment project seems to be little more than misguided and blighted hope. So the pessimistic conclusion by Wokler. It could perhaps be argued, with the growing emphasis on change, and the subsequent quest for improvement of the world, that new qualities were ascribed to the concept of reason, following its release from its earlier connotation of tolerance. As such it became *instrumental reason.*

Wokler's argument evokes the fundamental question as to whether Enlightenment can be divested from modernity. Is Enlightenment conceivable without modernity? The driving force of the Enlightenment project was not only criticism and tolerance but also, and particularly, the quest for absolute knowledge to the end of changing *i.e.* improving the world. The idea of changing the world through moral and social reconstruction encapsulated a totalitarian faith in the unity of all sciences. An obsession with classification promoted the instrumental dimension in the concepts of reason and rationality. Or, put in other words: a secularised polytheism which was promised by the tolerance rhetoric could not emerge from the monotheist prison which had been established over the preceding 3000 years. As Hegel put it, paraphrased in this volume by James Schmidt, "Enlightenment defeats faith, but in doing so it undermines itself by revealing that it is nothing more than faith of a different sort: a faith in reason."

A radically different conception of enlightenment (here with a lowercase "e") can be found in Horkheimer and Adorno's Dialectic of

---

[9] CASSIRER, E., 1932. For a critical discussion of Kant's use of the concept of cosmopolitan, see MALCOMSON, S. L., 1998.

Enlightenment. This is discussed in James Schmidt's contribution from the perspective that enlightenment is not a specific 18th century phenomenon founded upon specific principles including the *paroles* of universal freedom, equality and fraternity but in Horkheimer's words: "the process of enlightenment as it was marked out in the first thought a human being conceived, ..."[10] In this Hegelian understanding of enlightenment as irresistible and interminable process, the relationship to genocide is both significant and necessary. What indeed could be external to this process?

The questions addressed in this volume are ambiguous, insofar as they confront both perceptions Enlightenment and enlightenment. Questioning the relationship between these enlightenments is then inherent to this volume.

Transcending the argumentation of other thinkers Adorno and Horkheimer maintain that the grand project of freeing mankind from illusion need not ultimately conclude in nihilism. The "irresistibility of enlightenment" is based on "that most fundamental of impulses: fear". Mythology does not offer any help in this respect. The names of the gods are little more than the petrified sound of human fear. Enlightenment is nothing but the search for a world in which everything is repeatable and calculable, a world in which nothing need be feared. Human civilisation rests on the organised and rationalised control of mimesis. Therefore, it becomes increasingly aware of those who appear to revert to more primitive forms of mimetic behaviour. Modern society is defined less by what it achieves than what it struggles to efface. Iconoclasm is a powerful force. And still, the fear remains. The outcome is a withering capacity for self-reflection and the emergence of paranoiac projection. Practices of reflection, which in a society balance claims of identity and otherness, descend into the eternal sameness of totalitarian ideology.

James Schmidt takes this reading of *The Dialectic of Enlightenment* as his point of departure. He finds that in the view offered by Adorno and Horkheimer enlightenment is so broadly defined that it becomes equal to the effort to master nature through instrumental reasoning. Nevertheless, they do not suggest a direct link between instrumental reasoning and the mechanised extermination of Nazi Germany. Their discussion of pathological forms of projection emphasises the psychological costs when cognition is reduced to instrumental manipulation.

---

[10] HORKHEIMER, M., 1996 [1941-1948], p. 446.

Their category of pathological forms of projection is interesting, because it implies also the question of whether non-pathological forms can be imagined. Horkheimer was, as James Schmidt tells us, aware of the potential in this question and was already in 1941 nursing a plan to complement the negative account of the dialectic of enlightenment with a positive theory of saving Enlightenment, but he did not bring this plan to fruition. Questions of why he didn't have yet to be explored.

Schmidt perceives clear links between Adorno and Horkheimer's *Dialectic of Enlightenment* and Bauman's *Modernity and the Holocaust*. Both works argue that discussions of the Holocaust which confine their focus to the historical, political and cultural peculiarities in 19th and 20th century Germany imply a comforting strangeness to the events. The Holocaust may, in its specifics, have been singular but genocide is not. The two books differ primarily in their location of the "driving forces" of pathological modernity: the implementation of instrumental reason or more socio-psychological factors based on the vain struggle for extermination of fear. This difference should not be seen as an illustration of mutually exclusive but rather as augmentative views.

Stefan Elbe in his chapter emphasises a third compatible view. He addresses more systematically the role of nihilism implicit in enlightenment and modernity. The point of departure is Nietzsche. In Nietzsche's well-known view the (monotheistic) quest for meaning was transformed into the search for Truth, which in turn resulted in the murder of God. This triumph, in the name of science, over religion was of short lived and empty. The pursuit of absolute truth was transmuted into general nihilism. Science temporarily assumed the responsibility long held by religion as a producer of value and meaning. Man would regress to a valueless bestial stage but this understanding or conclusion was rejected. Intoxication replaced value, intoxication with drugs such as hero-worship, hatred, mysticism and fanaticism. This stage in Nietzsche's opinion was an era of meek sheep-like followers under a dominant animal-leader.

This view corresponds well with Weber's conceptualisation of *Entzauberung*, where instrumental reason, bureaucratisation, professionalisation and specialisation either blinded society to values or, made it perceive itself as blind to values. Only the outburst of charismatic leadership could break this iron chain of modernity. With the charismatic element Weber relativises a commonplace view on modernity which overcomes tradition through reason and progress.

Projections emerge where the pre-modern world is seen as offering wholeness and unity as opposed to a world irredeemably fragmented through progress and nihilism. Nietzsche did not see nihilism merely as a consequence of modernity and Enlightenment but refers to a much longer historical tradition with roots in the worlds of Socrates and Christ. Elbe is also keen to emphasise that the fact that the Holocaust was an expression of modernity does not mean that modernity is necessarily equitable with the Holocaust. Nihilism is ambivalent.

Arpád Szakolczai, in his chapter, emphasises the process of civilisation rather than Enlightenment. Nietzsche, Weber and Foucault are his points of reference. His focus is not so much on nihilism but antitheses of nihilism: obedience and discipline. Nietzsche, Weber and Foucault discern religious and philosophical bases which simultaneously harbour world-rejecting and world-changing elements. Both Elbe and Szakolczai emphasise the tension between obedience/control/management and nihilism in both the modernity and the Enlightenment concepts. Szakolczai recounts a scenario where monastic asceticism is transformed into ossification of military life by way of mathematical calculation and soulless discipline. Neo-Stoic ideals emerged in the wake of the great religious wars in the 17th century and provided the spiritual background for what would later be Prussian military reforms. Ireland and the Netherlands become in this historical scenario crucial transmitters of value. Education and utopian images of a better world played key roles in this process. Such images emerged in particular in situations of experienced crisis.[11] Szakolczai adds to this interactive process the outcome in the form of utilitarian moralism leading to the terror of dictatorship in another chain of events parallel to that civilisation process that often is identified with Norbert Elias.[12] In this new but not oppositional reading, modernity and Enlightenment constitute a utopian dualism, where various sorts of moralising, enlightening, reforming and revolutionary ideologies, of politics both left and right, and of science have lead to the contemporary conditions, supported by "political technologies" and "governmental rationalities". This development was, and is, all the more explosive as the secularised techniques did not simply gain dynamics on their own, based on instrumental reason, but became mobilised on a massive scale by secularised versions of apocalyptic, utopian and Gnostic movements with the aim to realise Paradise on Earth.

---

[11] KOSELLECK, R., 1959.

[12] ELIAS, N., 1939.

Paradise may be an ancient concept, genocide as a concept is undeniably modern, practically contemporary. The term was coined in 1944 by Rapheal Lemkin in his study *Axis Rule in Occupied Europe, Laws of Occupation, Analysis of Government, Proposals for Redress*[13] to describe, or construct, the Holocaust perpetuated by Nazis against Jews. Lemkin constructed "genocide" using two Greek elements, *geno(s)*: race and *cide*: the act of killing. Although this term was originally applied to a case of mass murder, the phenomenon ironically need not even necessitate the murder of individuals. It is not directed against individuals but groups both defined and made abstract as "races", "people", "nations", "classes" or "gene-pools", and while this destruction may be attempted by murderous means as like those used by the Nazi's against the Jews or handicapped, it certainly does not require murder merely the inhibition of the continued existence of a group. Using a contemporary definition of gene it might also be applied to attempts at the eradication of specific unwanted genes in a society for example through selective breeding in a programme to socially and biologically engineer healthier more productive members of society. Intrinsic in the former group-based definition, this reasoning is a belief in groups as essential categories that are perpetuated through inheritance. This belief is necessarily modern if the groups are conceived to be nations, or in the case of the Nazi definition of the Jews anti-nations, and the nation is an invention of the French Revolution. Nevertheless earlier examples of race and inheritance exist including the blood libel of the passion or blue blood, *sangre azul* which was claimed by certain noble families of Castile, as being uncontaminated by Moorish, Jewish or other admixture. Or the Jewish concept of the "chosen people" where being chosen was an inherited characteristic. In view of the latter two cases this appears to be a both in- and exclusive ennobling of the masses.

Older, and in general less "civilised", terms than genocide such as mass-murder, war, slaughter, carnage, butchery, massacre, holocaust and annihilation apparently did not fit Lemkin's needs nor those of the legions of subsequent users of the term genocide. This phenomenon, the invention of a concept, has two most probable explanations: The employers of the descriptor "genocide" perceived a totally new phenomenon more accurately presented through the term, *i.e.* that something was perceived to have changed and it required a new classification; or they thought that the employment of a new jargon

---

[13] LEMKIN, R., 1944.

would promote and justify political or personal goals by describing an event as qualitatively without precedent which is almost requisite within the framework of a policy study.

In any case the word genocide landed on fertile soil. Within five years the concept progressed from obscurity to international illegality. On 9 December 1948 United Nations Resolution 260 (III) *Convention on the Prevention and Punishment of the Crime of Genocide* was adopted. The convention placed this crime in a far larger practically infinite context. "Recognizing that at all periods of history genocide has inflicted great losses on humanity."[14] Something unchanging and eternal that has never been a part of humanity and as such always attacked it from without. Now humanity had progressed to the point where it had taken the first step and recognised this ill and set out to eliminate it. The association of a new term with an ancient practice should raise a certain degree of scepticism. This irony may be a sign of denial or repression among the politicians of the victorious powers who set the agenda at that time. This justification was of a special order, it involved the redemption of civilisation from events that could not be explained within the image that they held of Western civilisation. It corroborates Zygmunt Bauman's diagnosis of the Nürenberg Trials as an effort of western civilisation to reassert itself in

---

[14] Resolution 260 (III) continued to define the concept that was to be prevented and punished as follows:
"Art. 2. genocide means any of the following acts committed with intent to destroy, in whole or in part, a national, ethnical, racial or religious group, as such:
(a) Killing members of the group;
(b) Causing serious bodily or mental harm to members of the group;
(c) Deliberately inflicting on the group conditions of life calculated to bring about its physical destruction in whole or in part;
(d) Imposing measures intended to prevent births within the group;
(e) Forcibly transferring children of the group to another group."
Cf. U.N.T.S., 1951, p. 277
Here two elements that require very modern awarenesses seem to distinguish this crime from other. Firstly it belongs to mass phenomena, and this not only on the receiving but also the giving end; it is not a crime perpetrated against an individual by an individual. It should be added that beyond the definition of what is genocide the resolution to "Prevent and Punish the Crime of Genocide" does not specify punishment or go much further than to say it should be done regardless of the public or private status of the perpetrator, legislation should be enacted, it shall not be considered a political crime for purposes of extradition etc.

the face of what was a terrible challenge.[15] Bauman illustrated the strategy employed in the selection of evidence by the self proclaimed representatives of humanity and civilisation to exonerate themselves.

The only two visual exhibits presented by civilisation, "the complaining party" at the Trials, were a shrunken head (produced in Buchenwald) from the sitting-room of Ilse Koch, "The Witch of Buchenwald", and a film entitled *Original German 8mm Film of Atrocities Against the Jews*. This was evidence of how the Nazis were presented by the victors as a primitive barbaric regression from civilisation.[16] The head from the sitting room associated the practices in Buchenwald with those of "brutal" and "primitive" tribes such as the South American Jívaro, who were known to shrink heads, and the 90 second film contained images of frenzied mob violence against Jews but not industrial killing. The selection of this evidence is telling. It presented or misrepresented the Holocaust as a re-emergence of awful unprepossessing aspects of human nature which civilisation was to polish away, even eradicate or annihilate. This metanarrative of the Nürenberg Trials under a hermeneutic analysis points to a double intention of the trial, first to reassert the superiority of civilisation, a successful undertaking, it emerges intact, unscathed from any experiences and does not cast any shadows upon what we think of ourselves. It is not a story about us. We are still superior, civilisation is the real "complaining party". The Other in the mirror of whom we could see ourselves and our superiority was a criminal band of Nazis who had seduced the German people. The second intention was exclusion of the entire terrible event by relegating it as insignificant to the sidelines of an enlightened narrative of progress. The abolition from history of everything that did not conform to it. Genocide as a timeless phenomenon which, separate from historical, change has inflicted great losses on humanity.

However, in another reading genocide can be seen as the fulfilment of, if not an Enlightened, than most certainly an 18th century notion. Fascist style was in reality the climax of a "new politics" a new

---

[15] Here we refer to the tapes of the workshop "Modernity, Enlightenment and Genocide", Florence 9 November 1998.

[16] The use of this narrative was even adapted in post-war Germany. "[...] the Nazi rulers, and Hitler in particular, were depicted as insane barbarians, as wild beasts, as satanic seducers who had approached the good an innocent German people from outside and deprived them of their common sense like a drug, disease or diabolic obsession." GIESEN, B., 1999, p. 242.

understanding of the significance of democracy based upon the emerging eighteenth-century idea of popular sovereignty. This concept of popular sovereignty was given possession by the "general will", as Rousseau has expressed it, by the belief that only when all are acting together does man's nature as a citizen come into existence.[17] As such the idea of people against people emerged.

[This is made very clear by the UN Resolution where genocide is a question of action taken against a "group", the word group is used six times in the description. Secondly, although this is inherent as the crime is against a group, the usage of "intent" implies that it is not genocide if the heinous crimes are committed without an awareness of a mass of Others and the will to eliminate the group but not necessarily the individual. It would appear that this dichotomy points to a problem inherent in Enlightenment. The division of humans into groups in the name of people's sovereignty and self-determination (or democracy) is antithetical to the enlightenment conception of the individual. Robert Wokler emphasises, in his chapter, the role played by the idea of political *representation* in the inception of this contradictory tension. The Enlightenment project, as a whole, has been plagued by perpetual tension between claims of individual freedom and the will to create a better collective order, a better society, a better community] This tension between the devices of the French Revolution, *liberté* and *égalité* has provoked utopian action. Paradoxically and consistently Enlightenment has meant both a quest for absolute knowledge and total/final rationality, as well as utopian restlessness. The motivating force was in both cases the view of the future which was identifiable by dreams of a better world that were characteristic to the modern project.

Bauman on this basis further qualifies the meaning of intent in the case of modern genocide, which goes far beyond merely killing a group. The intention in modern genocide is in fact utopian, to establish a new and better society.

> Truly modern genocide is different. *Modern genocide is genocide with a purpose.* Getting rid of the adversary is not an end in itself. It is a means to an end: a necessity that stems from the ultimate objective, a step that one has to take if one wants to reach the end of the road. *The end itself is a grand vision of a better, and radically different society.* Modern genocide

---

[17] MOSSE, G., 1975.

is an element of social engineering, meant to bring about a social order conforming to the design of the perfect society.[18]

It is here that that genocide is fundamentally linked not only to modernity but also to Enlightenment, the utopian concept of creating an ideal society, and where it is not a practice that has existed for time immemorial.

This is the argument employed by Göran Rosenberg in the concluding chapter of this volume, an epilogue not only of the book but the whole of the 20th century, which in this case begins provocatively in 1789. This long (200 years) century is based on Enlightenment as a messianic and millenarian project and on the idea of the "march of history". But this long century has finally come to an end, the certainty that was constantly re-established and reshaped through new illusions replacing all the disillusions is gone. The insight gained is that human conditions mean constant uncertainty and continuous choice, not necessarily between good and bad, but more often between good and good. The old Western absolutist idea, with a monotheistic origins, of one truth and one true path of all good values, and one false path of all evil, has finally lost its argumentative power. The heritage of the long 20th century is to live without that idea. What is left is a value pluralism and the insight that no coherence of values is possible, which, however, takes us to the problem of nihilism emphasised by Elbe and the problem of impartiality and neutrality emphasised by Vetlesen. The problem is to find a *modus vivendi* in this fluctuating *Spannungsfeld* of risks and opportunities.

Stalin's murderous policies cannot be referred to as genocide in the verbatim sense of this word, as an attempt to exterminate a whole gene pool or race. Robert Thurston's contribution to this volume raises the question of the connections between old traditions of persecution and mass killing of witches, religious groups and political heretics and modern forms of genocide. It is apparent that this heritage of modernity, based, among others, on the separation between Us and the Others (in diverse fashions), warrants much more attention than it has received. In some formulations Thurston comes close to the creation of mass killing as an anthropological category. By placing the Soviet case in a historical context he offers a view quite distinct from that which is mediated in the *Livre noir*. He also discusses the degree of popular

---

[18] BAUMAN, Z., 1989, p. 91. Bauman's italics.

participation in the Stalinist terror and discerns in this respect analogies to the Third Reich.

Elin Frykman, examining compulsory sterilisation in Sweden, confronts the genocide issue in this volume from a standpoint very different from that of Thurston. Implicit in her discussion is the quite contemporary issue of genic manipulation through biotechnology. Eugenics is promoted by scientific language, first biological and then when it fails, the language of social science. Her view exhibits similarities to that of Bauman insofar as, modernity and Enlightenment, in the name of biological, social and economic sciences, were not significant but necessary preconditions for the sterilisation. The vision that motivated the sterilisation was indeed to create a new and better society. If not racially than economically motivated. Frykman is, however, keen to emphasise that the Swedish sterilisation is difficult to label genocide. It had little to do with ethnic racism. The biological logic behind forced mass sterilisation makes it more justified to talk about eugenics. The aim was to prevent the birth of potential burdens to the new welfare society as it was conceptualised in the 1930s and to create the Swedish welfare state. The idea was not to get rid of a certain people but to reinforce one. The strong medicine was not intended for the extinction of a group of people, but to halt the reproduction of certain individuals representing many groups from the lower strata of society. The mechanisms however, were the very same as those Zygmunt Bauman laid bare.

An ideal of scientific research is to provoke, to question dogma and mythologisation without simultaneously producing structures similar to those it attacks. The problem inherent in this approach is that it is based on a belief in absolute knowledge as the utmost goal, and that for just this reason the critical deconstruction of old truths produce or even reproduce similar epistemological structures, which may even appear to be appealingly new, to transcend. An alternative and possibly more pragmatic strategy may be to recognise the contingent and ephemeral characteristics of ones own work. This approach has drawn considerable criticism, particularly when it puts such events as genocide into question. When the "reality" of genocide is at stake, i.e. its relationship to our civilisation, the stakes are high. Precisely because as Zygmunt Bauman maintains the Holocaust is a reductive mirror through which we understand ourselves. When Bauman set out to explore the Holocaust in an attempt to come to conclusions concerning modernity, he pointed to the central role that the Holocaust plays in contemporary society. An ironic transformation has been under way:

The question of the meaning of the Holocaust has yielded way to the Holocaust is meaning. This transformation could – in an admittedly incisive wording – be seen in the context of the quest for absolute knowledge or truth. By ascribing meaning to Holocaust it could be used to motivate actions as diverse as the pursuit of war in Yugoslavia, campaigns against genetic research and petitions to end abuse of women by the Taliban. Today genocide (and the Holocaust) is meaning.

Academics not unlike other writers create drama. Although this is used with varying degrees of proficiency within the profession, the mechanisms they exploit are very similar if not the same. Birth and death, love and sex, beauty and blemish, form the most basic elements or mechanisms of their texts. Perceived or presented extremes, such as the apexes of civilisation or progress, or the abysses of barbarism and regression. This is one way that careers are made. By mythologisation, by translation of the agony and the ecstasy, almost exclusively, of others. An introspective question rarely voiced on one side of the fence is what right, or responsibility do we – in Bauman's text *les enfants manqués*, in another language the *Nachgeborenen* – have to explore and remember, to judge but unavoidably exploit that which is not ours? How can we understand, and what is the significance of understanding at all, if it is not a part of us?

If this volume should claim anything at all we believe that it primarily has to be, introspective, historiographic, in the sense that we examine ourselves. That if we consider ourselves to be children of the Enlightenment, or enlightened then genocide necessarily belongs to us. This self-criticism may also then imply to a certain degree of self-control and the inhibition of hyperbole in our work which may on the one hand detract from the dramatic of genocide or Enlightenment, but are they not dramatic enough on their own?

CHAPTER 1

The Duty to Remember, – But What?

Zygmunt BAUMAN

Ten years ago I sat down to write a study of the *Wahlverwandschaft* between the Holocaust and Modernity, not to explain the Holocaust but to better understand modernity. I thought then that in terms of the ordinary meaning of the idea of explanation – presenting an event as a chain of causes and effects – all that had to be done to explain the Holocaust as an event in history had already been done. Thanks to the gigantic efforts of many formidable, scrupulous and dedicated historians the train of events, decisions and deeds had been recorded and everyone who wished to know could know who the perpetrators, the victims, and the horrified, self-congratulating or just indifferent bystanders were. One could of course go on, perhaps *ad infinitum*, digging into certain untouched archives and diaries, adding a few names to the list of perpetrators, and otherwise enlarging the huge library of monographic studies of the episodes which united became the most purposeful, systematic, targeted and comprehensive mass murder in human history. But such further research could be only of the "more of the same" nature. The volume of facts would grow, but not necessarily the knowledge or the comprehension of the process.

On the other hand, while thanks to the historians our knowledge of the Holocaust's *wie es eigentlich gewesen* had been growing over the years apace, the efforts of sociologists and social thinkers to grasp the meaning of that knowledge for the orthodox and still prevalent image of modern society lagged far behind; more precisely, that effort never started in earnest although solitary writers such as Theodore Adorno or Hannah Arendt called for it to be addressed long ago. It was my intention to pick up where Adorno or Arendt had left a blatantly unfinished task: to exhortate fellow social thinkers to consider the relation between the event of the Holocaust and the structure and logic of modern life, to stop viewing the Holocaust as a bizarre and aberrant episode in modern history and think through it instead as an highly relevant, integral part of that history; "integral" in the sense of being indispensable for the understanding of what that history was truly about and what sort of society we all inhabit.

I realise now that I made a mistake. Not because my appeal was wrongly addressed or bound to fall upon deaf ears; not because there was something in the nature of contemporary social thinkers and their work that made it difficult to accept and to follow through the significance of the Holocaust for the nature of modernity. I was mistaken for exactly the opposite reason. Contrary to my opinion, whenever the Holocaust is mentioned in contemporary social thought, nothing else is at stake but precisely that significance. As a matter of fact, most of the scholars who speak and write about the Holocaust are – overtly or covertly, consciously or subconsciously – concerned with little else but that significance: with the presence or the absence of the link between the Holocaust and the inner essence of modernity, and thus with the right to salvage or the obligation to revise some of the most coveted assumption which modernity has made about the nature of its own enterprise and to which it has to cling if that enterprise is to continue in its historically shaped and extant form.

In other words – what I did not fully realise a decade or so ago, but seems clear to me now, is that the silence spoke in unison with the voice. Whenever the issue of the Holocaust crops up in the social-scientific discourse, the true topic of debate – and certainly the one most likely to arouse strongest emotions and to inspire most pugnacity – is not so much the question of what did happen in history, but the nature of the world we inhabit today. The hidden agenda of all the current Holocaust discourse is the question of what, if anything, the facts of the Holocaust are capable of telling us about the hidden capacities of the present-day life. With the problem of the guilt of the Holocaust perpetrators by and large settled and with the passage of time losing its urgency and practical edge, the one big remaining question is the innocence of all the rest – not the least the innocence of ourselves.

Social Production of Guilt and Innocence

In more ingenuous times, when the tyrant razed cities for his own greater glory, when the slave chained to the conqueror's chariot was dragged through the rejoicing streets, when enemies were thrown to wild animals in front of the assembled people, before such naked crimes consciousness could be steady and judgement unclouded. But slave camps under the flag of freedom, massacres justified by philanthropy or the taste of the superhuman, cripple judgement. On the day when crime puts on the apparel of innocence, through a curious reversal peculiar to our age, it is innocence that is called on to justify itself. [1]

That much Albert Camus, in 1951, before the book *Eichmann in Jerusalem* appeared and before Eichmann, its hero, appeared in Jerusalem. The possibility that crime is logical, that "murder has rational foundations", is "the question put to us by the blood and strife of our century", Camus insisted. "We are being interrogated." We may refuse to listen to the question and to console ourselves with the eternity of evil and perpetuity of murder only at our peril; and first and foremost peril to our humanity, which is, by definition, our non-animality, the *ethicality* of our being.

Camus recalls that Heathcliff of *Wuthering Heights* would kill everybody to win Cathie – but he would never think of saying that murder is reasonable or theoretically defensible. Heathcliff had no makings of a theorist, he did not theorise, nor did he need a theory. He loved Cathie, he wanted Cathie and that was the only reason that he needed in order to kill – that is, if reason he needed. Murder, were Heathcliff to commit it, would have been a *crime of passion,* and acting out of passion means putting reason to sleep; passion is, by definition, the un-reason. When we speak of passion, we also speak of the non-being of reason. Passion and reason are at loggerheads: one wilts and fades in the face of the other.

Modernity passionately declared war on passion and inscribed Reason, in boldest of letters, on its banners: *in hoc signo vinces.* The modern mind shuns passion, denigrates and disdains passion, and in every manifestation of passion sniffs evidence of its own failure. By doing so, it refuses, not unjustly, to bear responsibility for crimes of passion. Whoever kills for love or hatred is out of modern bounds. There is indeed nothing particularly modern about crimes of passion. And it is hardly the fault of modern ambition that some men and women refuse or fail to listen to the voice of reason and remain slaves to their passions. For the crimes of passion, modernity has no need to apologise.

---

[1] CAMUS, A., 1971 [1951], pp. 11-12 (The original published in 1951 under the title *L'Homme Révolté*).

As long as one can ascribe crimes to the passions of their perpetrators, crime may be condemned without awkward questions about the nature of modern life being asked. Reason, after all, leans over backward to argue away hatred together with blind love. Most people – people like us – listen to reason and stop short of letting their aversions and hard feelings guide their actions and dissolving their bad blood in the blood of their neighbours. Not all, though, have been ennobled, "civilised" in such a way. Some go on doing evil things. When it comes to explaining their evil deeds, the modern mind curiously forgets its declaration of its own omnipotence. Why do some people perpetrate evil? Because they are evil people. Why are they cruel? Because they are cruel people. Why do they perpetrate monstrous deeds? Because they are monsters. Why did some of them kill Jews? Because they liked killing people or they hated the Jews, or both – and so killing people who happened to be Jews gave them particular pleasure.

These are all blatantly pleonastic statements, and tautology is a crude error of logic which does not square well with the self-proclaimed self-discipline of reason. Why Hitler's executioners killed Jews? Because they were anti-Semites. How do you know they were anti-Semites? Because they killed Jews (forget the 250,000 Gypsies and 360,000 mentally retarded Germans who followed or preceded the Jews on the road to the gas chambers and crematoria). If sentences like this go on being offered as explanations, something else, more important than the logic of scientific inquiry, must be the motive. This something else is the distribution or redistribution of guilt and innocence. The issue is how to condemn the criminals while making sure that the innocence of modern men and women at large, together with the kind of society which made them what they are, emerge from the trial with their reputation unscathed. Exoneration is the other face of the coin, and it is by that other side that the value of the coin is appreciated and the coin is made attractive and desirable. In the resulting scramble, Camus' noxious questions about slave camps under the flag of freedom and massacres in the name of philanthropy are, conveniently, all but forgotten.

Neither Hitler nor Stalin was yet born, *Arbeit macht frei!* was not yet legible above the gate of Auschwitz, nor were classes murdered wholesale for the love of mankind, but modern life was already in full swing when Nietzsche noted down the baffling – and horrifying – paradox of our civilisation:

The same men who are held so sternly in check *inter paris* by custom, respect, usage, gratitude, and even more by mutual suspicion and jealousy, and who on the other hand in their relations with one another show themselves so resourceful in consideration, self-control, delicacy, loyalty, pride, and friendship – once they go outside, where the strange, the *stranger* is found, [they] emerge from a disgusting procession of murder, arson, rape, and torture, exhilarated and undisturbed of soul, as if it were "no more than a student's prank, convinced that they have provided the poets with a lot more material for song and praise".[2]

The paradox is, let me repeat just as terrifying as it defies all easy explanation. What is the case here? The beasts of prey relishing their escape from the stuffy and stifling cage called civilisation and falling back, with deafening sigh of relief, on their true nature, as Nietzsche seems to suggest? Or, rather, the once resourceful, now hapless humans, thrown out of their element, their ken and wits, cast into the eerie world where their habits can guide them no more and the rules by which they played their games have been officially declared null and void or simply are no longer applicable? Both answers are as plausible as they are unprovable, and there is little point in arguing their substantive (as distinct from instrumental) merits. One conclusion, though, seems to be beyond reasonable doubt. Roberto Toscano has recently spelled it out with exemplary clarity.

> [W]hat is at stake here is not an attempt to explain individual violence that finds it roots in personal passions, desires, hate, greed. On the contrary, it is significant that the mechanisms of the two kinds of violent action (individual and group) are different and manifest themselves differently in the same individuals, who may have a radically different propensity to have recourse to group versus individual violence.

And Toscano spells out what makes the two situations, and so also the deceptively similar acts of violence that occur in their contexts, so radically different and why do they call for altogether different explanations. Unlike individual violence,

> group violence is by definition abstract [...] real individual neighbours are not necessarily loved, but they are loved or hated for concrete, not abstract reasons. On the contrary, in order to apply group violence to the neighbour as belonging to a category, the concrete individual's face has to be erased: the person must become an abstraction. [3]

---

[2]   Nietzsche, F., 1968, p. 476.

[3]   See Toscano, R., 1998, pp. 63-81.

Categorical Murder

Indeed abstraction is one of modernity's principal powers. When applied to humans, that power means effacing the face: whatever remains of the face serves as a badge of membership, the sign of belonging to a category, and the fate meted out to the owner of the face is nothing more yet nothing less either than the treatment reserved for the category of which the owner of the face is but a specimen. The overall effect of abstraction is that rules routinely followed in personal interaction, ethical rules most prominent among them, do not interfere when handling of a category is concerned. Nazi legislation, propaganda and management of social setting went out of their way to separate the "abstract Jew" from "concrete Jews" known to the Germans as neighbours or colleagues and to cast all "concrete Jews", through deportation and confinement, into the position of abstract ones. Genocide differs from other murders in having a *category* for its object. Only the abstract Jews could be subjected to genocide – the kind of murder oblivious to differences of age, sex, personal quality or character. For genocide to be possible personal differences must be first obliterated and faces must be melted in the uniform mass of the abstract category. Julius Strelcher, the infamous editor-in-chief of equally infamous *Der Stürmer,* had hard time trying to stick the exceedingly popular stereotype of the "Jew as such" his paper forged and disseminated to the concrete Jews the readers knew from their daily intercourse. Similarly Himmler found it necessary to reprimand even the selected elite of his SS henchmen:

> "The Jewish people is to be exterminated", says every party member. "That's clear, it's part of our programme, elimination of the Jews, extermination, right, we'll do it." And then they all come along, the eighty million good Germans, and each one has his decent Jew. Of course the others are swine, but this one is a first-class Jew.[4]

Decent Germans were forbidden to have their own decent Jews – decent because they were their own: next-door neighbours, caring doctors or friendly shopkeepers. Up to six million Jews were murdered wholesale not for what they had done but for how they were classified – just like, quite recently, in another hour of ultimate triumph of all-defining, all-classifying modern bureaucracy, the armed gangs of Hutus and Tutsis of Rwanda set off their victims from the others, meant to kill rather than be killed (the others of the same appearance,

---

[4]   See my BAUMAN, Z., 1989, p. 187.

language and religion as their killers), according to the entries in their passports.

Jock Young coined the name of *essentialisation* for the tendency to "categorise" the others – the tendency perhaps extemporal as far as the human species goes, but most certainly aided and abetted, as Georg Simmel already noted, by the modern powers' knack for abstraction, and practised with particular zeal and put to the widest range of uses in modern times. "Essentialism", Jock Young writes,

> is a paramount strategy of exclusionism: it separates out human groups in terms of their culture or their nature. The advantages have always been there throughout human history but there are obvious reasons why the above strategies should appeal as we enter the late modern period.[5]

Among the reasons for essentialisation to become a favourite modern strategy, Young lists the provision of otherwise sorely missing ontological security, legitimation of privilege and deference otherwise jarring with modern promise of universality and equality, proffering facility to shift the blame onto the other and to project onto the other the inner fears and suspicions about one's own ability to match the standards of adequacy and decency one professed. Treating the others as separate beings endowed with personal virtues or vices would fail to serve such purposes: essentialisation is indispensable, and the modern power of abstraction comes in handy.

The abstracting powers simultaneously underlie and top up the other accoutrements of modernity without which the Holocaust, that exquisitely modern form of genocide, would have been inconceivable. Some of those other necessary conditions available solely in the modern setting are well known and have been repeatedly discussed. Technological tools necessary for mass murder as much as they are indispensable for mass industrial production are perhaps most frequently mentioned. Scientific management as embodied in the bureaucratic organisation – the ability to co-ordinate actions of great number of people and make the overall result independent from the personal idiosyncrasies, convictions, beliefs and emotions of individual performers, comes close second. These two traits of modernity supply the possibility for the genocide, if and when it occurs, to be conducted with the ethically indifferent efficiency and on a scale that set the Holocaust apart from all preceding cases of mass murder.

---

[5] See the chapter "Essentialising the Other: Demonisation and the Creation of Monstrosity" in YOUNG, J.

What may lift that possibility to the level of reality is, however, the characteristically modern order-making zeal; the kind of posture which casts the extent human reality as perpetually unfinished project, in need of critical scrutiny, constant revision and improvement. When confronted with that stance, nothing has the right to exist just for happening to be around; to gain the right of survival, every element of reality must justify itself in terms of its utility for the kind of order envisaged in the project. This is, as I suggested elsewhere, an ambition that can be grasped best with the help of the "gardening" metaphor. Medicine and architecture offer equally useful metaphors.

Genocide as Order-Building

This last point needs particularly strong emphasis, when the affinity between modern life and holocaust-type murder is pondered. Indeed, this point is crucial if one wishes to comprehend the true nature of modernity as modality of being rather than any particular, concrete state of affairs already constructed, projected or adumbrated. Modern modality of being is characterised first and foremost by its endemic un-finishedness; by its orientation towards a state of affairs not-yet-in-existence. To speak of modernity as an unfinished project is to commit tautology; what is modern about any project is precisely its being a step, or two, or a hundred steps ahead of reality; what is modern about modernity is its in-built capacity to self-transcend, to push back the finishing line in the course of running and so to bar itself from ever reaching it.

Modernity is an inherently transgressive mode of being-in-the-world. Visions of order are born out of dissatisfaction with the existing state of things, and attempts to make them into flesh give birth to new dissafections and new, revised and thus thought to be improved, visions. Modernity rolls into one the act of drawing a frontier and the resolve to transcend it. All orders constructed under the aegis of modernity are therefore, even if only unintentionally, local, temporal, until further notice – bound to be reshaped before reaching fulfilment. "Modernisation" is not a road leading to the station called "moder-nity". Modernisation, the continuous, unstoppable, obsessive and in many ways self-propelling modernisation, is the very human condition the concept of "modernity" stands for. Were the modernising thrust ever to grind to a halt, this would not augur the completion of modernity, but its demise. Ulrich Beck has captured that state of affairs splendidly in his portrayal of our times as a process of perpetual "modernisation of modernity" or "rationalisation of rationality".[6]

Referring to the endemically precocious and precarious nature of all partial, local and temporary order-making effort, Ulrich Beck introduced another by now household term – that of the *Risikogesellschaft*: ours is a kind of society in which the order-making urge results in generating a new series of disordered being thereby fraught with risks which one can perhaps roughly calculate in probability terms, but never avoid. What is especially relevant to our topic is that living in a *Risikogesellschaft* is, and is bound to remain, a *Risikoleben*. Life full of risks, the incurably risky life without trustworthy knowledge what future may bring and without possibility to control the outcomes of one's own actions (that – *conditio sine qua non* of rational choice), is an unnerving, disturbing, anxiety generating condition. Perhaps modern life started, as Sigmund Freud suggested, from surrendering a large slice of individual freedom in exchange for collectively endorsed security. In its present-day phase, though, the offer and the promise of social guarantees of individual security have been withdrawn or – if not – is no longer trusted. This state of affairs is a foolproof recipe for life of insecurity and anguish. It is also a prescription for the desperate search of genuine or putative, but trustworthy-looking promise of great simplification of the world too complex to walk safely through.

We may say that the modern order-making urge is thereby self-perpetuating and self-propelling: the object of ordering is as a rule the leftover (the waste, the unanticipated and unwanted consequences) of past ordering bustle. Modernity can be defined as compulsive modernisation. And this means that there is no end to tension seeking desperately unloading and an outlet through which to unload. As things stand now, in our post-modern or late-modern times, there is little the political powers, which remain as local as they were in the times of high modernity, can do about the essentially global causes of rising uncertainty and insecurity. Out of three dimensions of that *Unsicherheit* which haunts the privatised individuals of our times only one, that of safety (bodily safety and the safety of the extensions of the body – personal possessions, home, the street, the neighbourhood, the environment) becomes the only one in which the political states can show themselves to be resolute, resourceful, active and useful, and in which electoral support may be sought and gained. The constantly

---

[6]   See, for instance, the chapter "What Comes after Post-modernity? The Conflict of Two Modernities", in BECK, U., 1998, pp. 19-31.

replenished supplies of anxiety and the pent-up aggression it generates are therefore channelled into concerns with "law and order": into fighting crime, control over the suspicious, unreliable and thus feared elements – mostly foreigners, people of different or opaque customs and life-style who are presently filling the place vacated by the "dangerous classes" of yore. In the age when mobility is quickly turning into the major factor of stratification, privilege and discrimination, a growing section of law-and-order concerns focuses on the figures of prowler, stalker, traveller – on which the diffuse fears of increasingly alien, wayward and erratic *Umwelt* converge; and on tough police force, long prison sentences, high security prisons and capital punishment, as well as isolation and deportation of "undesirables" – these and other similar deemed remedies for the novel off-putting and disturbing experience of the fluidity of space.

There is a lot of political capital in the present-day safety obsession. And there is no shortage of political players eager to deploy that capital in the power game. Thanks to the late-modern surfeit of mutually cancelling authorities and irredeemable polyvocality which goes together with political democracy and the weakening grip of state powers, the prospect of such players gaining an upper hand and deploying the absolute powers of the state to set a Holocaust-style "solutions" in motion is remote. Yet to say with any degree of self-assurance that the forces eager for *Endlösung* type of actions and either the necessary or sufficient conditions of their acting in that way are no more present today would be equally premature and imprudent.

Living with the Memory of the Holocaust

Not much more than half a century ago the Holocaust was unimaginable; half a century ago it was still, for most people, unbelievable. Today, one cannot imagine a world in which a holocaust is impossible. And if a vision of such a world were painted, one would not quite – not unreservedly believe the picture. After all, everyone knows now that vexing problems may have their "final solutions", that setting people apart, rounding them up and deporting or physically destroying, "cleansing" whole territories of great masses of people, is one of the options whenever the confused and messy reality clashes with the image of the orderly world, the world "as it should be"; and that – if only one plays his hand right (and better still, if one manages to secure a hand stronger than the next player) – this is quite an attractive option, considering that one can get away with it until the job is done, and even forever after, as long as one stays stronger, avoids defeat and so the trial by the victors. In such a world, we all guess now, there can be someone, somewhere, who contemplates another holocaust at this very moment – and such a world cannot be a safe place to live. In this remarkable turn-around consists, in the nutshell, the profound and durable – social, political, cultural and psychical – significance of the Holocaust.

George Steiner remarked once that Voltaire's or Matthew Arnold's privilege was their ignorance of what we know about the hidden potential and the aftermath of the great modern adventure. After the Holocaust and the Gulag, we can no longer claim ignorance. We cannot hide behind the *naïveté* which is the age of innocence's redeeming grace. But having lost our innocence, we are not certain about the contents of knowledge we have acquired instead. These contents remain a moot and hotly contested matter. But like the Holocaust itself, the way in which it is remembered is the matter of life and death.

By comparison with its *posthumous* life, the *reality* of the Holocaust seems in retrospect simple and straightforward: certain people methodically and systematically murdered certain other people earmarked for extermination, while some other people watched extermination, while some other people watched – in despair, with indifference or with barely concealed joy – but did too little or nothing at all to stop the murder. There were evil murderers, innocent victims, and bystanders of varying degree of evil and innocence. Except for the lunatic fringe of "revisionist historians" and Nazi mourners, a broad consensus has been reached about who was who and who did what in Auschwitz. Today, however, things look much more confused. The most confused of them all is the question what is to be learned from the Holocaust, who is to learn it and to what effect. Today, the lines dividing evil from innocence, guilt from good reason, clear from dirty conscience are anything but straight and uncontentious.

Mind-boggling and spine-chilling as the Holocaust was, one could still measure the scale of its fiendishness counting the corpses and weighing the ashes. But can one measure the damage done by the *memory* of gas chambers and crematoria? Over half a century later that memory pollutes the world of the living, and the inventory of insidious poisons seems anything but complete. We are all to some degree possessed by that memory, though the Jews among us, the prime targets of the Holocaust, are perhaps more than most. Among the Jews in the first place, living in a world contaminated with the possibility of a holocaust rebounds time and again in fear and horror. To many, the world appears suspect to the core; no worldly event is truly neutral. Each event is burdened with sinister undertones, each contains an ominous message aimed especially at the Jews, a message that can be overlooked or played down only to the Jews' own peril. As the late E. M. Cioran put it,

> To be afraid is to think of yourself continually, to be unable to imagine an objective course of events. The sensation of the terrible, the sensation that it is all happening *against you,* supposes a world conceived without *indifferent* dangers. The frightened man – victim of an exaggerated subjectivity – believes himself to be, much more than the rest of his kind, the target of hostile events... [He has attained] the extremity of a self-infatuated consciousness; everything conspires against the one [...].[7]

Self-defence calls the victim to learn the lesson of history, though in order to learn it, the victim needs to decide first what the lesson is. The precept of staying alive as the sole thing that counts, as the supreme value that dwarfs all other values, is among the most tempting, and the most common, interpretations of the lesson. As the direct experience of the victims recedes and fades, the memory of the Holocaust thins down and congeals into a precept of survival: life is about surviving, to succeed in life is to out-live the others... The survivor – wins.

This reading of the Holocaust's lesson has been recently displayed – to a world-wide acclaim and huge box-office success – in Spielberg's, now well-nigh canonical, image of the Holocaust. According to the *Schindler's List* version of the Holocaust experience, the sole stake of the tragedy was to remain alive – while the quality of life, and particularly its *dignity and ethical value* was at best of secondary importance and above all of no consequence; it was never allowed to interfere with the principal goal. The goal of staying alive took care of moral concerns. What counted in the last resort, was to outlive the others – even if the escape from death required being put on a separate, and unique, list of the privileged (offered by the Commandant of Birkenau a replacement for "his Jewesses", Schindler refuses; it was not saving of lives that counted, but saving of specific, selected lives). The value of staying alive was not diminished by the

---

[7]   CIORAN, E. M., 1975, p. 71.

fact that others, less fortunate, travelled to extermination camp; the viewers of *Schindler's List* are invited to rejoice in the sight of Schindler's master of works pulled out in the nick of time – he alone – from the train destined for Treblinka. Through a wilful travestation of Talmud's precepts Spielberg's film translates the issue of the salvation of humanity into the decision who is to live and who to die.[8]

That elevation of survival to the rank of the supreme, perhaps the only value, is not Spielberg's invention and a phenomenon by no means – confined to the artistic representations of the Holocaust's experience. Soon after the end of the war psychiatrists coined the concept of the "survivor's guilt" – a complex psychical ailment which they ascribed to the survivors' asking themselves why did they stay alive when so many of their near and dear perished. According to that interpretation, the joy of escaping death was among the survivors permanently poisoned by the uncertainty about the propriety of sailing safe out of the sea of perdition, with the disastrous consequences for the survivors will to live and to succeed in life after their rescue. Many practising psychiatrists acquired fame and fortune treating so construed "survivor's syndrome". Whether the syndrome was rightly spotted and the psychiatric treatment well aimed, is – to say the least – debatable; what is rather obvious, though, is that in the course of time the "guilt" aspect, looming prominently in the beginning, has been progressively exorcised from the model of the "survival complex", leaving the pure and unalloyed, unambiguous and no more contested approval of self-preservation for self-preservation sake. It was just the haunting pain left by those sufferings that staying alive required which has been blamed for the persistence of the "syndrome".

Such a shift brings us dangerously close to the spine-chilling image of the survivor as painted by Elias Canetti – as the man for whom "the most elementary and obvious form of success is to remain alive"; for Canetti's survivor, the survival – unlike the mere self-preservation – is targeted on other, not on the self: "they want to survive their contemporaries. They know that many die early and they want a

---

[8]   "The Talmud", pointed out the late Gillian Rose, sublime philosopher and Judaic scholar, in her last public lecture "is ironic – the most ironic holy commentary in world literature: for no human being can save the world", Rose spoke of the "ruthlessness of saving one or one thousand" and comments that while the original Thomas Keneally's book, *Schindler's Arc*, "makes clear the pitiless immorality of this in this context", Spielberg's film Schindler's List "depends on it as congratulation", recorded in CHEYETTE, B. and MARCUS, L., 1998.

different fate for themselves". At the far end of the obsession, Canetti's survivor "wants to kill so that he can survive others; he wants to stay alive so as not to have others surviving him". "The survivor's most fantastic triumphs have taken place in our own time, among people who set a great store about the idea of humanity [...]. The survivor is mankind's worst evil, its curse and perhaps its doom."[9]

The wider repercussions of that cult of survival contain dangers of potentially formidable proportions. Time and again the lessons of the Holocaust are reduced for popular consumption to a simple formula: "who strikes first, survives"; or to an even simpler one: "the stronger lives". The awesome two-pronged legacy of the Holocaust is, on one hand, the tendency to treat survival as the sole, or at any rate the utmost value and purpose of life, and on the other the positing of the issue of survival as that of the competition for a scarce resource, and so of the survival itself as a site of conflict between incompatible interests in which the success of some depends on the non-survival of others.

There is something else, though, to the status of a "victim by proxy" one of belonging to a *sui generis* "aristocracy of victimhood" (that is, having a *hereditary* claim to sympathy and ethical indulgence owed to those who suffer). That status can be, and often is, brandished as a signed-in advance and *in blanco* certificate of moral righteousness; whatever the offspring of the victims do, must be ethically proper (or at least ethically correct) as long as it can be shown that it was done in order to stave off the repetition of the lot visited on their ancestors; or as long as it can be shown to be psychologically understandable, nay "normal", in view of the super-susceptibility of the hereditary bearers of victimhood to the threat of a new victimisation.

The ancestors are pitied, but also blamed for letting themselves be led, like sheep, to slaughter; how can one blame their descendants for sniffing out a future slaughterhouse in every offensive looking street or building and – more importantly still – for taking preventive measures to disempower the potential slaughterers? Those which need to be disempowered may have nothing to do with the perpetrators of the Holocaust and in no juridical or ethically sensible way be charged with responsibility for the ancestors' perdition; it is, after all, the heredity of the "hereditary victims", not the continuity of their assumed victimisers, which makes the "connection". And yet in a world haunted by the ghost of the Holocaust they are guilty in advance, guilty of

---

[9]   CANETTI, E., 1973, pp. 290-293, 544.

being seen as prone or able to engage in another genocide. Standing accused or just *being suspect,* true to the message of Kafka's Trial, is already their crime, the only crime needed to cast them as criminals and to justify harsh punitive measures. The ethics of hereditary victimhood reverses the logic of the Law: the accused remain criminals until they have proven their innocence – and since it is the prosecutors who conduct the hearings and decide the validity of the argument, they have slim chance that their arguments might be accepted by the judges and every chance of staying guilty for a long time to come whatever they do.

Self-Reproduction of Victimhood

Thus the status of hereditary victim may take the moral reprobation off the new victimisation – this time perpetrated in the name of erasing the hereditary stigma. Its is a banal truth that violence breeds more violence; but it is true as well that victimisation breeds more victimisation. Victims are not guaranteed to be morally superior to their victimisers, and seldom emerge from the victimisation morally ennobled. Martyrdom – whether lived in a real or a virtual reality – is not a warrant for saintliness. Memory of suffering does not assure the life-long dedication to the fight against inhumanity, cruelty and pain-inflicting as such, wherever they happen and whoever are the sufferers. At least equally probable outcome of martyrdom is the tendency to draw an opposite lesson: that humankind is divided into the victims and the victimisers, and so if you are (or expect to be) a victim, the point is to reverse the tables. We observe that perverse logic time and time again: we watch it today (making little or no effort to cut the vicious circle) in the see-saw of violence in Rwanda, all over the part of Europe known until recently under the name of Yugoslavia, in Sudan, Congo, Somalia, Angola, Sri Lanka, Afghanistan and countless other places. It is this lesson that the spectre of the Holocaust whispers into many ears; Israeli political leaders lifted that lesson to the rank of the official state policy and crowning argument of its diplomacy. And for this reason we cannot be sure whether the lasting legacy of the Holocaust was not a very opposite to the hoped-for by many, and anticipated by some, moral re-awakening or ethical purification of the world as a whole or any of its sections.

The pernicious legacy of the Holocaust is that today's persecutors may inflict new pains and create new generations of victims eagerly awaiting their chance to do the same, while acting under conviction that they avenge yesterday's pain and ward off the pains of tomorrow; while being convinced in other words, that ethics is on their side. This is perhaps the greatest among the Holocaust's curses and Hitler's posthumous victories. The crowds which applauded Goldstein's massacre of the Muslim worshippers, in occupied Hebron, which flocked to his funeral and go on writing his name on their political and religious banners, are the most terminally afflicted, but not the only bearers of that curse.

At the end of his pioneering study of the ardour with which the ordinary folks enlisted to the 101st Police Reserve Battalion fulfilled the order to kill, Christopher R. Browning mused: if the men of the 101st battalion could become murderers, what human group cannot? Unlike his student Daniel Jonah Goldhagen, Browning was puzzled – puzzled by the fact that ordinary people, like the rest of us, could turn into murderers given the right conditions. Browning did not seek consolation in the idea that it is anti-Semites who have the patent for the miraculous avatar of this kind.

Pondering the poisoned after-history of the Holocaust, two Israeli scholars, Ariella Azoulay and Adi Ophir, wondered what the "we" in the language of Israeli politics means these days:

> We are the last place in Europe where the Nazi past is still profitable – because the State has converted the destruction of European Jewry into a national property, symbolic capital... We are a site of experiments for testing the universalizability of evil – the principle of universalizability being a European legacy and the practices for the production of evil imported from a Europe which no longer exists, The hypothesis to be corroborated (one that has not yet been refuted) is: "it can happen to everyone"; the victims of yesterday may always become today's victimisers. Every person can find herself participating in the hatred, humiliation, and oppression of the "Other", in racial discrimination, in ethnic cleansing of neighbourhoods and cities; everyone may end up co-operating with a regime that produces and distributes evil systematically.[10]

"Hereditary victimhood" is the principal socio-psychological device serving such systematic production and distribution of evil. One should beware of confusing the phenomenon of hereditary victimhood with genetic kinship, or with the family tradition preserved through the parental influence over the educational setting. Heredity in this case is mainly imagined, acting through the collective production of memory

---

[10]   AZOULAY, A. and OPHIR, A., "One Hundred Years of Zionism; Fifty Years of Jewish State", in *Tikkun*, 2/1998, pp. 68-71.

and through individual acts of self-enlisting and self-identification. Thus the status of the "Holocaust children", that is of hereditary victim, is open to every Jew, whatever his or her parents (or grandparents) might have been "doing in the war" or whatever had been done to them during that war (in fact, embracing the status of hereditary and categorical victim has turned for many into a main vehicle of Jewish self-definition). Psychiatrists conducted ample studies of the biological descendants (and/or educational objects) of the inmates of concentration camps and the dwellers of ghettos; but the swelling numbers of the "sons and daughters of the Holocaust" who are not children of either, still await a comprehensive study. There are many clues, though, of what such studies might reveal. It may well transpire that the complexes of such "imagined children", children-through-self-assignment (and for the same reason "children *manqués*") are more severe and vicious, and burdened with more sinister consequences, than those which the psychiatrists have described thus far.

One may say: this stands to reason (whatever "reason" may mean in the world of the possessed). For the "children *manqués*", the site they occupy in the world, from which they view the world and in which they want to be viewed by the world, is that of martyrdom, but it so happens that they are not, nor have been, personally, the butt of anybody's wrath and wrongdoing. The world seems reluctant to harm them and make them suffer, and under the circumstances such a world is too good to be true – since the reality of a harmless world means irreality of life which derives its sense from the harm done to it and the harm yet to be done.

Living in a not-hostile and harmless world means the betrayal of the sense-giving pedigree. To reach completeness, to fulfil their destiny, to get rid of their present deficiency and efface their vexing (and in the end humiliating) impairment, to efface the qualification *"manqués"* from the status of offspring and heirs, they would need to reforge their own imagined continuity of victimhood into the real continuity of victimisation in the "world out there". That can be done only through acting *as if* their present site in the world was really and truly a site of the victims; through abiding by a strategy which would be rational only in a victimising world. Children *manqués* cannot be fulfilled unless the world they live in reveals its hostility, conspires against them – and, indeed, contains the possibility of another holocaust.

The awesome truth is that contrary to what they say and think they wish, children *manqués* – the "flawed children" – are unfit to live, and feel out of place in a world free of that possibility. They would feel more comfortable living in a world more like that other world, populated by the Jew-hating murderers who would not stop short of including them among its victims if given a chance and having their blood-soaked hands untied. They draw a sense-giving reassurance from every sign of hostility towards them; and they are eager to interpret every move of those around them as overt or latent expression of such hostility (a recent study reporting disappearance of anti-Semitism in the USA has been reviewed under the telling-it-all title – *Can the Jews take it?*). The macabre paradox of being a hereditary victim is to develop vested interests in the hostility of the world, in fomenting hostility of the world and keeping the world hostile. One can almost hear a sigh of relief exhaled by political leaders of the country and the many thousands of men and women who elected them to lead, whenever their victims pushed to the end of their tether plant a new terrorist bomb.

The flawed children of the martyrs do not live in homes; they live in fortresses. And to make their homes into fortresses, they need them besieged and under fire. Where else can one come closer to their dreams than among the famished and destitute, despaired and desperate, cursing and stone-throwing Palestinians... Here, the comfortable and commodious, all-mod-con houses are unlike the houses the children *manqués* have abandoned those comfortable and commodious, all-mod-houses over there, in the stale and dull, too-safe-for-comfort American cities, where children would be bound to stay as they are, *manqués*. Here, one can tightly wrap the houses with barbed wire, one can build watchtowers in every corner and one can walk from one house to another proudly caressing the gun hanging from one's shoulder. The hostile, Jew-baiting world once forced the Jews into ghettos. By making a home in the likeness of the ghetto (this time round, though, a heavily armed ghetto) one can make the world to look once more hostile and Jew-baiting. In that fully and truly flawed world, the children, at long last, would be no more flawed. Its chosen representatives, who want to be seen as its spokesmen as well, would have repossessed the chance of martyrdom missed by the generation.

Whichever way you look at it, the ghost of the Holocaust appears self-perpetuating and self-reproducing. It made itself indispensable to too many to be easily exorcised. Haunted houses have an added value, and being possessed has turned for many into a valued, meaning-bestowing life formula. In this one can spy the greatest posthumous triumph of the *Endlösung* designers. What the latter failed to accomplish when alive, they may yet hope to achieve after death. They did not manage to turn the world against the Jews, but in their graves they can still dream of turning the Jews against the world, and thus – one way or another – to make the Jewish reconciliation with the world, their peaceful cohabitation with the world, all that more difficult, if not downright impossible. The prophecies of the Holocaust are not quite self-fulfilling, but they do fulfil – render plausible – the prospect of a world in which the Holocaust may never stop being prophesied, with all the deleterious and disastrous psychical, cultural and political consequences which such prophesising is bound to bring forth and propagate.

Living in a One-Dimensional World

Jean-Paul Sartre proposed that the Jew is a person who others define as a Jew. What Sartre must have meant was that the act of such defining is also the act of reductive selectiveness: one of the manifold traits of irretrievably multi-faceted person is hereby given prominence, rendering all other traits secondary, derivative or irrelevant. In the practice of the possessed, the Sartrean procedure is conducted once more, though in the opposite direction. The others, the non-Jews, emerge as one-dimensional as the Jews appeared in the vision of their haters. The others are not benign or cruel *patri familiae,* caring or selfish husbands, benevolent or malicious bosses, good or bad citizens, peaceful or pugnacious neighbours, oppressors or oppressed, objects or culprits of injustice, pained or pain inflicting, privileged or dispossessed, threatening or threatened; more precisely – they may be all that, but the fact that they are all that and more is but of secondary and minor importance and does not count for much. What truly counts – perhaps the only thing that counts – is their attitude towards the Jews. And the stance taken to every person who happens to be *also* a Jew is read out as a manifestation and derivative of the attitude taken towards the Jews as such. Like the hereditary victimhood, so the one-dimensionally of the world-view has a self-perpetuating propensity.

It is tremendously difficult to square with the one-dimensional worldview the fact in the course of Hitler's war against the Jews many declared anti-Semites stoutly refused to co-operate with the perpetrators of the Holocaust; and that, on the other hand, the ranks of the executors were full of law-abiding citizens and disciplined functionaries who happened to be free of any peculiar grudge against the Jews as such and in particular bore no grudge whatsoever against the concrete

Jews they shot or gassed. It is similarly difficult to come to grips with the fact that "the deportation of the Jews" (as the annihilation of European Jewry was officially defined), derived its meaning in the Nazi thinking from the overall, audacious plan of wholesale *Umsiedlung*, the vision of European continent in which well-nigh everyone will be transported from their present, contingent site to the place where reason orders them to be[11] (and that could entail nothingness; as the Holocaust progressed, even Jewish graveyards were proclaimed out of order and replaced with chimney smoke). Or to accept that the extermination of the Jews was conceived in the framework of a total "cleansing of the world" operation (which included also mentally deficient, physically handicapped, ideologically deviant and sexually unorthodox) by a state powerful enough and sufficiently immune to all opposition to afford such total plans and to execute them without fear of effective dissent. Finally, to comprehend that the Nazis behind the Holocaust, whatever creatures they must have been otherwise, were also *"Bürger"*, who like all *Bürgers* then as much as now, here as much as there, had their "problems" which they dearly wished to "resolve".[12]

All this said thus far does not intend to imply that warnings against the possibility of another holocaust are unfounded, that the world we live now in differs from the world of the Holocaust to an extent which makes the present-day world Holocaust-proof. But it does mean that the threat of such holocausts as may yet come is all too often sought and located in the wrong places and the sight is diverted from the grounds in which *genuine threats* are rooted; a sinister trait of one-dimensional world-view is that while concentrating attention in one direction we close the eyes to the manifold nature of dangers.

The acclaim accorded to Daniel Goldhagen's version of the Holocaust as primarily the story of the voluntary and Jew-hating helpers of Hitler adds to such risks. Goldhagen's thesis, as well as the poorly concealed satisfaction with which it has been received in so many circles, can be only fully comprehended in the context sketched above; the context which entails, as its primary ingredients, the phenomenon of hereditary (yet *manqué*) victimhood, intertwined with the one-dimensional world-view.

---

[11] Cf. The penetrating, thoroughly researched study in ALY, G. and HEIM, S., 1991.

[12] As Klaus Dörner convincingly argues in DÖRNER, K., 1988, pp. 12ff.

This view of mine seems to be shared, as a matter of fact, by Goldhagen himself and the most zealous of his eulogists and defenders. When Ruth Bettina Birn and Norman Finkelstein had published a scathing critique[13] of the one-sided uses Goldhagen made of the archives, the criticised author rather than own up to mistakes or defend his version of the facts charged his critics with perfidious political intentions and resorted to *argument ad hominem* dismissing the critics as "crusaders of anti-Zionism"; by the same token, he obliquely admitted that the dispute ostensibly about his rendition of the Holocaust is, in the ultimate account at least, a matter of defending certain quite contemporary political cause. Others who rushed to Goldhagen's rescue were more outspoken yet. And so Abraham Fox, speaking on behalf of the Canadian Branch of Anti-Defamation League, declared that the problem is not to know whether Goldhagen's thesis is justified or not but whether its critique is "legitimate" and did not cross the border of the permissible.[14]

Tom Segev of the Israeli daily *Haaretz* has been right on target, summing up the sense of the on-going debate in the following words:

> The Jewish establishment embraced Goldhagen as if he was Mr. Holocaust in person. This is absurd, since the critiques raised against Goldhagen are well founded...

This is, Segev explains, understandable nevertheless, since what is at stake is the "Zionist character" of Goldhagen's thesis. What truly matters is that, in the end,

> not just the Germans, but all Gentiles hate the Jews. Hence the need of unity and solidarity of the Jews. Hence also the need of ever more numerous books on anti-Jewish hatred, and the more simplistic and superficial they are, the better. [15]

That some of the participants of mass murder did enjoy their part in crime either because of their sadistic inclinations or for their hatred of the Jews or for both reasons simultaneously – is not, of course, Goldhagen's fantasy; though it is not his discovery either. Taking that

---

[13] BIRN, R. B. and FINKELSTEIN, N., 1998. Let us note that the "Nation" in the title of the book is German. In his response, the author of the criticised thesis saw Israel as the nation put on trial.

[14] As quoted in *The New York Times*, 10 January 1998.

[15] In *Haaretz*, 15 May 1998. See VIDAL, D., "Nouvelles polémiques autour d'un livre sur la Shoah: De 'Mein Kampf' à Auschwitz", *Le Monde Diplomatique*, August 1998, p. 8.

fact, however, as the explanation of the Holocaust, as its central point or the deepest meaning – says a lot about the contemporary political uses to which the memory of the Holocaust is being put, while turning the attention away from what is the most sinister truth of that genocide and what is still the most salutary lesson which our haunted world could learn from the recent history which contains the Holocaust as its major event.

Social Production of Killers

The point to remember is that for every villain of Goldhagen's book, for every German and non-German who killed his victims with pleasure and enthusiasm, there were dozens and hundreds of Germans and non-Germans who contributed to the mass murder no less effectively without feeling anything about their victims and about the nature of actions involved. And the point is that while we know quite well that prejudice threatens humanity and we know even how to fight and constrain ill intention of the people tainted and poisoned with prejudice, we hardly know how to stave off the threat of a murder which masquerades as the routine and unemotional function of orderly society. On the contrary – the knowledge of how to deploy people free of any murderous instincts in the service of "legitimate killing", and the skills and technology needed to apply such knowledge in practice, is by now, thanks to the united efforts of psychologists, technologists and the experts in scientific management considerable and continually growing.

Robert Johnson[16] produced a meticulous, scrupulous and imaginative in-depth study of the dull daily routine of the death-row suspended animation and the festive routine of the days of execution in penal systems in the United States, notoriously fond of capital punishment; and also of the thoughts and feelings of the main actors of both. The huge data Johnson elicited and gathered may serve as rich empirical evidence for Nils Christie's insights in his pioneering study of *Crime Control as Industry* (the English version first published by Routledge in 1993). All the major insights of Christie find in Johnson's report ample empirical corroboration: the routinisation of killing procedure, the bureaucratic division of labour and "agentic state" of all individuals involved in the collective accomplishment, the thorough "emotional disenchantment" of the whole process, neutralisation of

---

[16]   See JOHNSON, R., 1998.

ethical considerations and moral scruples, depersonalisation of the victims. Modern civilisation has made us all (or most of us at least) to dislike and shun violence. But civilisation has also invented the means to make this aversion and loathing of violence irrelevant when it comes to the complicity in the commitment of violent acts – particularly when the acts are to be committed in the name of civilised values.

"Complicity is obvious in that the death row officers expressly hold the prisoners for the purpose of execution" Johnson notes. The officers interviewed by Johnson are aware of that and cannot help feeling bad because of it. "The reality of that last family visit really made me feel bad. It was depressing to be there" admits one of them. But then adds, as an afterthought, "It's supposed to be part of the job, like being a doctor or something. You lose a patient and that's just it, but it's not that easy. You never forget this type of thing, but you can put it behind you." And behind he and his mates put it, most of them, most of the time. How this feat gets to be accomplished?

First of all, by pushing aside moral consideration, replacing ethical measures with technical ones which arouse no emotions and do not concern the moral persons beliefs, and repeating what the people in charge keep telling and everyone around keeps repeating after them: "It's not a job I like or dislike, I try to go about every job in the most professional manner. If they would stop the death penalty, it wouldn't bother me. If we had ten executions tomorrow, it wouldn't bother me" says one of the wardens. "It's done professionally; it's not no horseplaying. Everything is done by documentation. On time. By the book" adds another.

Secondly, all those people partake of the act of killing, but no one is (or, rather, needs to feel like) a killer. At no point there is but one trigger to be pulled by one finger. As Johnson puts it, "members of the deathwatch team referred to themselves... as simply 'the team'". Working in "the team" is salutary; it is the team that killed without making any of its members a killer. Johnson quotes one warden's words: "We can honestly say that we did not do it."

Thirdly, no member of the deathwatch team performs his job for the love of killing or even for the enthusiasm for the death penalty. Motives or their absence have nothing to do with what is going on. "Only a few members of the execution team support the death penalty outright and without reservation" Johnson observes. When filling the vacancies, prison governors did not advertise for sadists or "law and order" militants and vigilantes. Strong feelings of whatever kind would, if anything, interfere with the smooth running of the bureaucratic procedure. It is safer, and above all much more efficient, to put the emotions aside. Were emotions not defused, too much would depend on the erratic and bureaucratically uncontrollable shifts of mood. It is so much more effective when everything is done "by the book". In the bureaucratic organisation in the killing industry, personal sympathies and antipathies are better left in the cloakroom before clock-in time.

Some thoughtful people in supervisory positions go a step further: they are positively and firmly *against* employing men who betray a special inclination not for good performance as such, but for performing this particular kind of job because of what that job is like.

> I don't want nobody who would like to do it... And if I suspected or thought anybody on the team really's gettin' a kick out of it, I would take him off the team. I would like to think that every one of them on the team is doing it in the line of duty.

This particular supervisor's idea is faithful to the modern spirit; when recruiting soldiers for the *Einsatzgruppen* ordered to round up and shoot out Bolsheviks and Jews on the conquered Soviet territory, precautions had been reputedly taken to eliminate rabid anti-Semites and people with sadistic inclinations. The power of modern ways and means consists precisely in making the success of the enterprise *independent* of the presence or absence of dedication.

Modernity would not get where it has got were it to rely on things as erratic, whimsical, and thoroughly un-modern as human passions. Instead, it relied on the division of labour, on science, technology, scientific management and power of the rational calculation of costs and effects – all a thoroughly unemotional stuff. Stephen Trombley's remarkable study[17] does for the "execution industry" what the previously quoted eye-opening work of Götz Aly and Susanne Heim had done for the Nazi murderous enterprise: it shows beyond reason-able doubt that the setting which in modern society renders mass or regular killing possible is indistinguishable from that which makes mass production and unstoppable technological progress possible. Aly and Heim documented the crucial role played by the thousands of high-class experts – engineers, architects, builders, doctors, psycholo-gists and countless others in making mass extermination on heretofore unheard-of scale feasible. And we learn from the carefully documented

---

[17]   See TROMBLEY, S., 1993.

history of electric chair written by Trombley that the first electrocution (of William Kemmler, held on 6 August 1890 in New York's Auburn State Prison) "excited a great deal of medical interest, and of the twenty five witnesses who watched Kemmler killed by electricity, fourteen were doctors". We also learn that the invention of the electric chair became an occasion of thorough scientific debate about the respective advantages of alternating and direct currents, and caused a heated public argument between such supreme luminaries of modern technology as Thomas Edison and George Westinghouse. We learn in addition that the distinguished members of the Governor Hill's commission set to find the proper methods of execution fell for the arguments carrying the authority of science and progress: what convinced them was that electricity, "the invisible and imperfectly understood form of energy was quintessentially modern", it was also clean and promised to be cheap – and the members of the commission were duly impressed.

Both, Johnson's and Trombley's, studies are priceless; their value lies in the information they supply and perhaps even more in the understanding of modern human conduct and the way modern society works which they imply. That way renders ethical considerations and moral impulses by and large redundant, and the reviewed studies document that redundancy and show how it is achieved and daily, indeed routinely, reproduced. They also list the gains derived from that redundancy; gains in the straightforward sense of profit and profitable use of resources, but also in the not immediately noticeable sense of making plausible and feasible the endeavours which would be unthinkable were they to depend on human motivations and impulses. Participants of the killing operations and the legions of scientists and engineers who supply them with the killing weapons and work out the procedure for efficient action are not evil people. Evil people did evil things at all times. But they are few and erratic, "crazy" by modern standards of reason. It has been perhaps the unique achievement of modern civilisation to enable ordinary folks, "just good workers", to contribute to the killing – and to make that killing cleaner, morally antiseptic and efficient as never before.

Modernity Contra *Homo Sacer*

As Enzo Traverso put it recently in reference to France, the causes of the Holocaust in general, and that "wall of indifference" which surrounded the mass slaughter of the French Jews, need to be sought not in the "Jewish question", as Jean-Paul Sartre saw fit, not even in the circumstances of the genocide itself, but in French pre-Vichy society.[18] There are unwanted strangers in any society, and in any society there are some people who wish such strangers were not be there, but it is not in any society that a genocide of the unwanted strangers can take place. The presence of a quantity of few-haters is not the only, not even the necessary, and certainly not a sufficient condition which needs to be met to make that genocide a possibility. Hannah Arendt pointed out long time ago that in the phenomenon of the Holocaust anti-Semitism may explain at most the choice of the victims, but not the nature of the crime. Nothing happened since then to invalidate Arendt's verdict, while the monumental memoirs of Primo Levi, monumental historical research of Raoul Hilberg and the monumental documentary of Claude Lanzman, to mention but a few landmarks, did a lot to confirm and reinforce it.

A few months ago another important voice has been added – that of the Italian philosopher Giorgio Agamben[19] – to our attempt to pierce through the mystery of genocide. Agamben recalled the legal concept of the *"homo sacer"*, coined in the archaic Roman Law: the concept of a human being which could be killed without punishment, but at the same time – being absolutely Other, alien, indeed in-human – could not be used in ritualistic religious sacrifices. *"Homo sacer"* was totally "useless" – completely outside human society and exempt from all considerations due to other humans on account of their humanity. *Homo Sacer*'s life was "nude" – that is, stripped of all social quality and political rights, and as such unprotected, made into a sitting target for every frustrated sadist or murderer but also a recommended target for everyone seeking to conform and exercise his civic duty.

"Homo sacer" was a legal construction; and as a legal construct, it appealed to the loyalty and *discipline* of the law-abiding subjects, not to their beliefs and sentiments. Like all legal constructs it cast feelings and personal beliefs, also the moral emotions, into irrelevance. The point about law is that it is expected to be obeyed *whether or not* the law abiding person likes it, dislikes, or has no feelings about it.

---

[18]   Cf. TRAVERSO, E., 1996.

[19]   AGAMBEN, G., *Il potere sovrano et la nuda vita*, here quoted after French translation, AGAMBEN, G., 1997.

That particular legal construct of *homo sacer* was in Roman legal practice an exceptional, marginal and almost empty category. It is different in the modern state, Agamben points out.

True, the concept of *"homo sacer"* is absent from the modern law and largely forgotten. But having appropriated the monopoly over the means of enforcement and violence, over the means and the prerogatives to offer or to refuse the right to live, the entitlement to control the bodies of its subjects including the infliction of pain – the state expanded what used to be an extraordinary category into a subjects' existential status: it has the potentially universal aspect of its thus no need to resort of a special, exceptional category to sustain what has now become a routine prerogative. Concentration camps, also a gruesome invention of the modern world, were a space where what in other parts of the State realm is but a potential had been made into the practically deployed rule.

The invisible presence of the *"homo sacer"* as the potential of the modern state brings into relief once more the most terrifying, and still most topical, aspect of the "Holocaust experience" – that aspect which Goldhagen's thesis thrusts aside and plays down: that in our modern society also people who are neither morally corrupt nor prejudiced may still partake with vigour and dedication in the destruction of targeted categories of human beings; and that their participation does not call for the mobilisation of their moral or any other convictions.

CHAPTER 2

The Enlightenment Project
on the Eve of the Holocaust[1]

Robert WOKLER

When Zygmunt Bauman portrays the Holocaust as providing modernity with its sternest test, he invites our reconsideration of the thesis of Max Horkheimer and Theodor Adorno that it was enlightenment which made genocide possible in that specifically modern form which it took. The Holocaust, we are reminded, was engineered in the most scientifically advanced society of Europe and, in large measure

---

[1] Much of this essay draws upon a number of my other publications, which embrace a fuller annotation of my sources than can be incorporated here. That material includes "The Enlightenment Project and its Critics", *Poznan Studies* 58 (1997), published as LIEDMAN S.-E., 1997, pp. 13-30; "The French Revolutionary Roots of Political Modernity in Hegel's Philosophy, or the Enlightenent at Dusk", *Bulletin of the Hegel Society of Great Britain* 35 (1997), pp. 71-89; "Contextualizing Hegel's Phenomenology of the French Revolution and the Terror", *Political Theory* 26 (1998), pp. 33-55; "The Enlightenment and the French Revolutionary Birth Pangs of Modernity", in HEILBRON, J. *et al.*, 1998, pp. 35-76; "The Enlightenment Project as Betrayed by Modernity", *History of European Ideas* 24 (1998), pp. 301-313; "The Enlightenment, the Nation-State and the Primal Patricide of Modernity" in GERAS, N. and WOKLER, R., 1999, pp. 161-83; "Ethnic Cleansing and Multiculturalism in the Enlightenment", in GRELL, O. P. and PORTER, R., 1999 pp. 69-85; and "Ernst Cassirer's Enlightenment: An Exchange with Bruce Mazlich", *Studies in Eighteenth-Century Culture* 29 (1999), 13-26. In my remarks on Cassirer I owe a substantial debt to two unpublished works, generously supplied to me by each author: on the one hand, the forthcoming intellectual biography of Cassirer by Yehuda Elkana; on the other, "A Bright Clear Mirror: Cassirer's The Philosophy of the Enlightenment" by Johnson Kent Wright, to be published shortly in a collection provisionally entitled *What's Left of the Enlightenment?*, edited by Keith Baker and Hans Peter Reill.

orchestrated by some of its most culturally sophisticated people.[2] It was a phenomenon bred not out of Oriental fanaticism or Balkan ethnic strife, but at the very heart of civilization, and the flame ignited at its Central European core was fanned into a conflagration not only by its perpetrators but also by Western indifference to the fate of its victims. I take Bauman, Adorno and Horkheimer to be agreed that through its enactment of the Holocaust, civilization rendered itself perfectly barbarous, not by abandoning its principles but in fulfilling them, in implementing a strategic plan of moral and social reconstruction that encapsulated the totalitarian character of an Enlightenment faith in the unity of all sciences as well as its instrumental notions of rationality by virtue of which the extermination of the Jewish people could be organised in a wholly methodical manner.

On that reading of the Enlightenment, its philosophy was to culminate in the National Socialist ideology of Dietrich Eckart, Joseph Goebbels and Alfred Rosenberg, and it was to be executed with the clinical precision of Joseph Mengele and Adolf Eichmann. Such positions have a long pedigree, which I cannot begin to rehearse here, except perhaps to remind you that the English language itself is prey to anti-Enlightenment bias. If we cast a glance at the *Oxford English Dictionary* we shall find the *enlightenment* there defined as "superficial intellectualism", marked by "insufficient respect for authority and tradition", while a *philosophe*, the same dictionary tells us, is "one who philosophises erroneously".

In the remarks that follow my objective will be to confront the proposition that the Holocaust is implicit in the Enlightenment by way of putting to you two arguments. I want to show, first, that the modern notion of a nation-state according to which a people partakes of human rights only by virtue of their shared nationality is not an Enlightenment ideal but a French Revolutionary invention which betrayed the fundamentally cosmopolitan strain of Enlightenment thought in its attachment to universal rights and to notions of common humanity. Second, I want to show that the Enlightenment did not just exclude the possibility of the Holocaust but in fact combated ethnic cleansing in all its pre-modern forms and may indeed be centrally defined as an intellectual movement, that is, as an *Enlightenment Project*, by virtue of that crusade against barbarism.

---

[2]   See BAUMAN, Z., 1989, pp. 13 and 17; HORKHEIMER, M. and ADORNO, T. W., 1947 [1944], pp. 5-57 and 100-143; and with respect to the composition of the *Dialektik der Aufklärung*, James Schmidt's contribution to this collection.

With my first point what I have in mind is that the Holocaust was inconceivable without the ideology of the modern nation-state, which was essentially shaped not in the Enlightenment but in the course of the French Revolution. That the Holocaust was also inconceivable without a theology of anti-Semitism and its associated popular prejudice, or a science of eugenics which lends its racism biological credibility, or a central European bureaucracy capable of organising mass extermination and perhaps even remote Eastern European destinations for the principal death camps – all that I take for granted. But a specifically political dimension unheralded anywhere in the world before the French Revolution was required too, and it is that dimension – the establishment of the modern nation-state – which contains those elements of self-corruption, that is, of totalitarian violence stemming from conscientiously liberal principles and of the breeding of terror from pure abstraction, which are to my mind wrongly ascribed to the Enlightenment.

Perhaps no age in our intellectual history was more committed to the establishment of new political modes and orders, and to the reconstitution of society by way of a fresh science of legislation, than the Enlightenment. But unless it is the legal despotism of Le Mercier de la Rivière, there has not been a single major scheme of government conceived by Enlightenment thinkers – not classical republicanism or its modern derivatives meant for large states, not enlightened monarchy, nor democracy, nor the re-establishment of the ancient constitution, nor the mixed constitution, nor even a genuine separation of powers – that has come to prevail anywhere in the modern epoch of the nation-state, first established in the course of the French Revolution. The doctrine of the nation-state, as formulated above all by the abbé Sieyès and his followers in the French National Assembly of 1789 and then by the Jacobins in the course of the Terror of 1793-1794, required a number of ingredients drawn from earlier political thinkers, including above all Bodin's and Hobbes's doctrines of absolute and indivisible sovereignty. In addition to superimposing undivided rule upon its subjects, however, the genuinely modern state has since 1789 further required that those who fall under its authority be united themselves – that they form one people, one nation, morally bound together by a common identity. With some notable exceptions – the United States of America foremost among them, but I also include the United Kingdom – the modern state is of its essence a nation-state, in which nationality is defined politically and political power is held to express the nation's will. Joined together with Hobbes' conception of the unity of the representer, as outlined in the sixteenth chapter of his *Leviathan*, the modern state generally requires that the represented be a moral person as well, national unity going hand in hand with the political unity of the state.[3] While it speaks with only one voice in the manner imputed to absolutist monarchy, the modern nation-state cannot take the form of a monarchical *civitas* along any lines set forth by Bodin or Hobbes. It is instead, as it has been known since the late eighteenth century, a *democratic republic*.

Lack of space here prohibits my rehearsing the several stages by which the modern nation-state came to be born in the period from 1789 to 1793. Suffice it say that the section devoted to "Absolute Freedom and Terror" in Hegel's *Phänemonologie des Geistes*, accurately describes both that birth and its afterbirth, as the nation-state established in the image of freedom descended into a reign of terror. For Hegel, it managed to do so ineluctably, in this way. First came the Estates General's resolution of 17 June 1789, orchestrated by Sieyès, which transformed that body into a single *Assemblée nationale*, with a unicameral political system corresponding to a unitary will, a unified state speaking on behalf of an undifferentiated nation. It next followed that the King of France must be denied any kind of veto over the National Assembly's legislation, since the unity of the nation prohibited the elevation of any particular will above the rest. Then it was agreed that the *people* must be similarly denied any binding mandate over their own delegates, which would have the effect of substituting France's scattered citizens for the collective will of the nation as a whole. Being one and indivisible, the National Assembly must speak with only one voice, as unaccountable to the people at large as to a king.

At the heart of this conception of modernity lay a novel idea of representation which in the eyes of Sieyès and its other advocates was to constitute the most central feature of the French state. That idea

---

[3] In a sense, the establishment of the nation-state, which I here trace to the French Revolution, may be said to superimpose a modern framework of the exercise of sovereign power upon certain ancient and medieval conceptions of national and communal identity in the *rei publicæ* status of citizens joined together by a common purpose. Such control over persons as was exercised by the increasingly monolithic states of early modern Europe did not supersede their control over territories but reinforced it, while the genuinely modern nation-state came apparently to embrace the language of status twice over, in the personification of the body politic as a whole and in the ascription of a corporate personality to all its true members.

required the adoption, in politics, of the same principle of the division of labour as was necessary for a modern economy, thus differentiating *active* from *passive* citizens, with the peoples' *delegates*, the active component, articulating their interests while the people themselves remain passively silent. There could be no confusion in France between representation and democracy such as inspired Paine and others to imagine that the hybrid government of America had nourished a classical principle of self-rule in a large state. Henceforth the populace was to have no political identity apart from that articulated by its representatives.

Of course the Jacobin notion of sovereignty, conceived as residing with the people as a whole, appeared to contradict this logic of modernity, but as Hegel makes plain, the nation which the Jacobins envisaged as comprised of all its people was to prove as monolithic as Sieyès' conception of a nation represented by the state. For when the Jacobins came to power within the Convention in the autumn of 1793, they attempted to root out the people's enemies within the state, just as Sieyès had sought to silence the enemies of the state within the nation. The Terror over which they reigned was to follow directly from their idea of the nation's sublime unity, which required a lofty purity of public spirit that made the vulgar purity of democracy seem an uncouth substitute for virtue. Such persons as happened to resist their ideal merely stood in the way of the agents of the people of the future. As Hegel remarks in his *Phänomenologie*, the sole work of freedom therefore becomes death, the coldest and meanest of deaths, like cleaving a head of a cabbage.[4]

What was it about these phenomena which also came to render the Holocaust possible? The central point at issue is not anti-Semitism but what might at first glance appear to be its opposite, that is, the Revolutionaries' declarations of the rights of man. One of the chief horrors of modernity is that this doctrine of liberation could and did become a warrant for legitimate oppression, emanating not from feudal Germany but from progressive France, as the new dawn of civilization heralded by that nation also launched civilisation's long day's journey into night. It was of the essence of Sieyès' plan that the nation in assembly spoke for all the people and must never be silenced by the people themselves. Over the past two hundred years the nation-state has characteristically achieved that end because it represents the people by way of its assuming their character as the bearer of their collective

---

4   See HEGEL, G. W. F., 1968- [1807], p. 320, lines 9-13.

personality. Much of the world's population now lives in nation-states. All peoples that have genuine identities form nation-states. What Sieyès did not foresee was that in the age of modernity heralded by his political philosophy, a people might not survive unless it constituted a nation-state. In the age of modernity, it has proved possible for the nation-state to become the enemy of the people.

To the Hobbesian theory of representation, the nation-state adds the dimension of the comprehensive unity of the people, the state now identical with the nation, the nation bonded to the state, each understood through the other. As Hannah Arendt rightly noted in her *Origins of Totalitarianism*, it has been a characteristic feature of the nation-state since the French Revolution that the rights of man and the rights of the citizen are the same.[5] By giving real substance and proper sanction to the various declarations of the rights of man within the framework of its own first constitutions, the French revolutionary nation-state joined the rights of man to the sovereignty of the nation.[6] It defined the rights of man in such a way that only the state could enforce them and only members of the nation could enjoy them.

But so far from putting into practice the universal rights of man long advocated by proponents of cosmopolitan enlightenment, the modern nation-state was to ensure that henceforth only persons comprising nations which formed states could have rights, giving rise to the fact that the history of modernity since the French Revolution has characteristically been marked by the abuse of human rights on the part of nation-states which alone have the authority to determine the scope of those rights and their validity. Not only individuals but whole peoples which comprise nations without states have found themselves comprehensively shorn of their rights.

---

[5] See ARENDT, H., 1958 [1951], pp. 230-231. Arendt here comments on what she terms "the secret conflict between state and nation", arising with the very birth of the nation-state on account of its conjunction of the rights of man with the demand for national sovereignty. Her reflections on this subject have occasioned extensive commentary. See, for instance, KRISTEVA, J., 1988, pp. 220-229, and HONT, I., "The Permanent Crisis of a Divided Mankind", *Political Studies*, 1994, special issue on Contemporary Crisis of the Nation-State, DUNN J. (ed.), pp. 206-209.

[6] The phrasing of the third article of the declaration of the rights of man and of the citizen, which begins, *"Le principe de toute souveraineté réside essentiellement dans la Nation"*, is owed principally to Lafayette. For the fullest histories of the sources and drafting of the whole document, and of the deliberations leading to its endorsement by the Assemblée nationale on 26 August 1789, see RIALS, S., 1988 and GAUCHET, M., 1989.

At the heart of what I am content to term *The Enlightenment Project* was the *philosophes'* recognition of the common humanity of all persons. For Kant, who in Königsberg came from practically nowhere and went nowhere else at all, to be enlightened meant to be intolerant of injustice everywhere, to pay indiscriminate respect to each individual, to be morally indifferent to difference, even while obedient to civil authority. But in the age of the nation-state, it is otherwise. Thanks ultimately to Sieyès and the Jacobins, ours is the age of the passport, the permit, the right of entry to each state or right of exit from it which is enjoyed by citizens that bear its nationality alone. For persons who are not accredited as belonging to a nation-state in the world of modernity, there are few passports and still fewer visas. As the Jews learnt too late and the gypsies may perhaps never learn at all, to be without a passport or visa in the modern world is to have no right of exit or entry anywhere, and to be without a right of exit or entry is to risk a rite of passage to the grave. That above all, I believe is the legacy bequeathed to us from the political inception of the modern age in the course of a French Revolution untimely plucked from the age of Enlightenment but not bred by it. It was then that the transfiguration of modernity began, when we started to manufacture Frankenstein's monster from Pygmalion's statue.

I turn now to my second point with regard to the Enlightenment conceived as civilisation's confrontation with barbarism and with the definition of the *Enlightenment Project* as a moral crusade against the malignancy of "ethnic cleansing" and genocide in all their forms, including the Holocaust. Let me begin by reminding readers of this collection that while the notion of an *Enlightenment Project* may lie near the heart of modern social philosophy, most eighteenth-century intellectual historians regard the very idea of such a project as nonsense, unworthy even of the dignity of serious refutation. Whatever might be imagined by communitarian critics of Western liberalism, or by anti-foundationalists, post-modernists or feminist objectors to an allegedly gendered Enlightenment concept of reason, scholars who devote their professional lives to the subject are characteristically exasperated by a term which Alasdair MacIntyre appears to have invented some thirty years after the world had first learnt of the *Manhattan Project* and some eighty years after the first mention of a *Scottish Enlightenment*, similarly unknown in eighteenth century. The expression seems no more than a dreadfully quick fix for the fast-food soundbite culture that requires such nurture. What other period in human history, after all, is endowed with such monumentally crass consistency as to make all its leading philosophers march to the same tune in the direction of the same brick wall? Did Erasmus and Machiavelli plot together to achieve the same humanist project of the Renaissance? Did Luther, flourishing at the same time, join that band as well? What kind of a project is it that has to be invented by later commentators in search of a dead dog they might kick with impunity, so as to blame it for a disease which they believe it had passed down to them?

While such frustration moves me to sympathy, I confess that I am not so unhappy as are some other historians of ideas with the notion of an *Enlightenment Project*. To my mind, the literary salons, journals and academies of the eighteenth century, not forgetting its association of philosophy with kingship which Diderot already then termed *enlightened despotism*, lend warrant to the notion of shared principles, a campaign, an international society of the republic of letters, *a party of humanity* as Hume described it. I have been sufficiently long a student of Rousseau to be convinced that *he* at least believed there was an enlightenment project (by which I do not just mean the international conspiracy to defame him), and I find his perception of the defects of that project – as when he remarks in his first *Discours sur les sciences et les arts* that our arts, our letters, our sciences are but garlands of flowers around the iron chains by which mankind is weighed down – to be illuminating and profound. The connection between *savoir* and *pouvoir* is not just a Marxist, or a Nietzschean or a postmodernist and Foucauldian theme. It forms the kernel of the critique of the Enlightenment Project itself by one of its main protagonists who, if I may here use Hegelian language, was *an sich aber nicht für sich*, that is, who was part of it but in large measure did not subscribe to it. I take Rousseau to have well understood what the project was about, and he recognised his own philosophy as shaped by it, even when in defiance of some of its central aims. His was not a grotesque caricature such as, soon after his death, would embrace his philosophy together with Voltaire's, as if these two fiercest ideological enemies of the whole eighteenth century were some homogeneous Gilbertonsullivan compound, pointing arm in arm to the new dawn of civilization, projecting the Enlightenment together.

Now supposing for a moment that the so-called Enlightenment Project *may* be a suitable subject of historical enquiry, how should we set out to identify its aims? One way which I believe has some merit is to locate it *temporally* before we trouble to establish whether it had sufficient coherence to be termed a *project*. At least with respect to its dates, there seems relatively little dispute as to when the *Enlightenment Project* actually transpired, since almost all commentators agree that this was roughly in the century separating the English Revolution of 1688 from the French Revolution of 1789. To put that point another way, the Enlightenment Project comprises a distinctive period of European intellectual history which may be demarcated by two seminal works on this subject, each of which addresses the epistemic transformation of the age of classicism into the age of modernity, that is, Paul Hazard's *La crise de la conscience européenne*, on the one hand, and Michel Foucault's *Les mots et les choses*, on the other.[7]

How, then, shall we identify the central thrust of the philosophical movements of that period, if there was one? It's not so difficult. In France, the inception of the *Enlightenment Project* as I understand it may be dated from 1685, when the Revocation of the Edict of Nantes by Louis XIV, and subsequently his acceptance of the papal Bull *Unigenitus* of 1713, inaugurated a century-long quarrel between Catholic assenters and dissidents, which was to issue in the remonstrances of the *parlements* and their expulsion by Louis XV, followed by the suppression of the Jesuits and ultimately Louis XVI's convocation of the Assembly of Notables in 1787, succeeded by the Revolution of 1789. That history of the institutionalisation of political and theological intolerance coincides with the history of the French Enlightenment itself, and opposition to it united *philosophes* of all denominations. From Montesquieu's *Lettres persanes* to Diderot's *Supplément au voyage de Bougainville*, sceptics in France railed against theological controversy and the persecution of heretics, often denouncing, like Rousseau in the *Contrat social* or Voltaire in his *Traité sur la tolérance*, the refusal of French Catholic priests to administer the sacraments to Protestants, which thereby disenfranchised them of all their civil rights. Such thinkers deemed the toleration of religious minorities in a nation governed by supersaturated religious faith to be of paramount importance, and if we are to identify the *philosophes* as contributors to just one great Project, I can think of no other principle that might more plausibly describe the commitment they shared than that of *toleration*.

In England in the 1680s, under the reign of a Catholic king, religious dissenters fared little better than did Protestants in France, and it is as much with reference to the same issue – either by way of Locke's *Letter concerning Toleration*, or William and Mary's *Tolera-*

---

[7] HAZARD, P., 1935 and FOUCAULT, M., 1966, respectively.

tion Act, both dating from 1689, that the English Enlightenment may be said to have been launched as well. The idea of toleration lies at the heart of Locke's philosophy in virtually all the domains which engaged his attention, and it was through embracing that idea and the civic culture which gave rise to it that enlightened *philosophes* in France who described themselves as lovers of freedom emulated both Locke's achievement and England's success. At the beginning of the eighteenth century, the English Enlightenment had thus already taken a political form, whereas in France it was to remain more radical, because disenfranchised from the prevalent institutions of both State and Church. By virtue of already established principles of toleration, England's Enlightenment, that is, proceeded as if the requisite rail tracks for high speed travel had been laid on the Dover side of the channel first, giving rise to the claim that if France had been able to enjoy a similar bloodless revolution around the same time, it just might have been possible to change the minds of Frenchmen without first cutting off their heads.

No major eighteenth-century thinker was more convinced of the indispensability of a spirit of religious toleration for the advance of civilization as a whole than Voltaire, and I am inclined to think that, if it had not existed, Voltaire himself would have invented MacIntyre's critique of an *Enlightenment Project* which not only failed but had to fail[8], if only to lend warrant to the most celebrated of all tributes to the principle of toleration produced in the Enlightenment. By that I of course mean Voltaire's treatment of the Presbyterians in his *Letters Concerning the English Nation*, where he remarks upon the peaceable assemblies of the London Stock Exchange, each agent a follower of his church, but jointly professing the same religion, giving the name of *infidel* merely to those who go bankrupt. In such circumstances do Jews, Muslims and Christians trust one another, and then, writes Voltaire, even Presbyterians are at ease with Anabaptists. Only in Scotland, where they are supreme, he concludes, do Presbyterians affect a solemn bearing, behave like pedants and preach through their nose.[9]

With respect to the Revocation of the Edict of Nantes, the most important writings of what I am content here to call *The Enlightenment Project* were those of French Protestants who either fled from France for their safety or, like Pierre Bayle, had been victims of the dis-

---

[8] In MACINTYRE, A., 1981. On MacIntyre's interpretation of the "Enlightenment Project", see especially my WOKLER, R., 1994, pp. 108-26.

[9] See VOLTAIRE, 1733, Letter VI (On the Presbyterians), pp. 42-44.

solution of Huguenot academies already achieved by Louis XIV prior to 1685. It was in Holland, while in exile, that Locke drafted his own account of the need for freedom of conscience and for the silence of civil powers in matters of belief, and it was from Holland that England's new king and queen, committed to religious toleration above all else, would descend. The ethnic cleansing of the French nation after 1685 did not take the form of the St. Bartholomew's Day massacre more than a hundred years earlier, nor was it pursued by way of the terrorist tactics employed in Bosnia three centuries years later. But like all campaigns of ethnic cleansing as distinct from genocide it gave rise to a Diaspora, to a brain drain and an outcast culture which abroad fermented more richly than it had managed under relative tranquillity at home. As much as from any other philosophical, political or economic source, it was from the precipitation of that brain drain, and the depth of the reaction to it among intellectuals in France, that the French Enlightenment of the eighteenth century was formed. Religious intolerance, and the ethnic cleansing of a nation that issued from it, kindled what I take to be the *Enlightenment Project*.

Late seventeenth- and eighteenth-century arguments for toleration were of course developed from many Reformation and humanist sources as well, but in the Enlightenment the case for toleration was advanced by its proponents in fresh idioms, with new weapons and a new vitality. It was put forward in campaigns to reform the criminal law and secure the abolition of torture. It was endorsed by Europe's leading *philosophes* who could suppose, contrary to both Hobbes and Scripture, that human nature was fundamentally good. They could on the other hand be persuaded that it was selfish but sociable, or that it was made of a pliant clay which could be cast in infinitely perfectible ways. What they could not accept, because it was no longer philosophically correct to do so, was the theological doctrine of mankind's original sin, now regarded as a myth invented by clerics to regulate the salvation of gullible souls.

At the heart of their commitment to the progressive education of mankind lay a crusade against all the dark forces of idolatry. *Civilization*, a term which first acquired its current meaning around 1750,[10] came progressively in the eighteenth century to be identified with the abandonment of the trappings of superstition, so that it was in reason's light that philosophers of every denomination now sought to dispel the shadows in which their adversaries lurked. Voltaire, Diderot,

---

[10] See STAROBINSKI, J., 1989

Turgot, d'Alembert and Condorcet joined Helvétius, d'Holbach and other materialists in their perception of the whole of human history as just one great struggle between the friends and enemies of enlightenment – between tyrants, priests and barbarians, on the one hand, and civilised, educated, and thus liberated men of science and letters, on the other. Through the *Encyclopaedia* and the book trade as a whole they sought to build an eighteenth-century Crystal Palace of the human mind, accessible to readers of all vernacular languages, as transparent as the open book of nature. They held Christian theology, by contrast, responsible for fanaticism throughout human history – for wars of religion, for the Inquisition, for barbarism. In promoting schemes of popular instruction, progressive *philosophes* sought to overcome mankind's enthralment to arcane dogmas which stood in the way of each person's attainment of worldly knowledge of the good and a desire to practice it.

All these familiar themes bear repetition only because no trace of them will be found in any of those critiques of eighteenth-century philosophy which portray its ideals as if they comprised the conceptual underpinnings either of the most empty desolation or most dreadful crimes of modernity. Not only MacIntyre and most communitarians, but also Horkheimer and Adorno, and Jacob Talmon[11] and his disciples, together with feminists and postmodernists of all denominations, if they agree about nothing else, and indeed they do not agree about anything else, are convinced at least of this – that in disposing of original sin the Enlightenment unwittingly committed it. Modernity, as they understand it, has been both shaped and scarred by the totalitarian doctrines of the eighteenth-century *philosophes*, who are taken to have embraced the worst features of Christian civilization they deplored while disgorging all that was best. In subscribing to *The Enlightenment Project*, its true believers just sought earthly happiness instead of the unworldly salvation of their souls, thereby recasting a secular world within an ideological mold which merely turned Christianity inside out, in the service of absolutist principles of another sort. That is the central thesis of a book, elegantly written, light-hearted and urbane, but to my mind sinister in its influence, which first appeared in 1932 and has since been published in more editions and in more languages than any other study of eighteenth-century thought I know. The book I mean is Carl Becker's *Heavenly City of the Eighteenth-Century Philosophers.*[12]

---

[11]   In TALMON, J., 1952, see especially pp. 3-11.

[12]   First published in New Haven by the Yale University Press.

According to Becker, the *philosophes* demolished the city of god only to rebuild it upon the terrestrial plain.[13] The Enlightenment thus loved the thing it killed and took on its mantle in the very act of destroying it, by substituting dogmatic reason for dogmatic faith.

In the same year, 1932, there also appeared another work, couched in a wholly different idiom, which ought to have served as a rebuttal of Becker's text around which all the true friends of Enlightenment could have rallied. If there is a single book in any language which might be said to encapsulate the true *Enlightenment Project*, supposing that there was one at all, it is Ernst Cassirer's *Die Philosophie der Aufklärung*.[14] Here is a book before which scholars of eighteenth-century thought profess to stand in awe, on account of the range of its themes and the depth of its arguments. Michel Foucault, in reviewing the first French translation, published in 1966, hailed Cassirer's work as a masterpiece which had excavated the foundational abstractions of modern philosophy in a manner not dissimilar to Foucault's own archaeological investigations of the constitution of modernity itself.[15]

If only such praise from the *Enlightenment Project's* fiercest post-modern critic had genuinely echoed the esteem in which Cassirer's work was held by eighteenth-century scholars, the history of Enlightenment studies over the past forty years would, I believe, have taken a very different course. In fact, that history has by and large been marked by the abandonment of Cassirer's approach and perspectives by eighteenth-century scholars, as we have descended from his great temple of Parnassus to study instead the grub street pamphleteers and *salonnières* in the mundane world below. Alfred Cobban, on reviewing the book soon after it first appeared in English in 1951, condemned what he took to be the excessively German focus, beginning with Leibniz, on the one hand, and concluding with Kant and Herder, on the other, of a book designed to portray the cosmopolitanism of European thought. Here, wrote Cobban, was a work which almost appears to have joined the "Enlightenment to the genealogical tree of the Nazi

---

[13] See, for instance, BECKER, C. L., 1932, pp. 102-103.

[14] Published in Tübingen by J.C.B. Mohr (hereafter CASSIRER, E., 1932). An English edition, *The Philosophy of the Enlightenment*, translated by Fritz Koelln and James Pettegrove, was published in Princeton by the Princeton University Press in 1951 (hereafter CASSIRER, E., 1951).

[15] See FOUCAULT, M., "Une histoire restée muette", *Quinzaine littéraire* 8 (1966), pp. 3-4.

movement".[16] Peter Gay, once seemingly a disciple, embarked on a fresh career as an historian of sexual manners in the nineteenth century, henceforth no longer stirred by the Enlightenment but by its romantic reaction. Robert Darnton, Daniel Roche and Roger Chartier, have built their careers upon studies of the manufacture and circulation of Enlightenment texts with respect to which the philosophical methods of Cassirer seem antediluvian and irrelevant to the real, contextual and subtextual, treatment of eighteenth-century thought. John Pocock, by way of investigating the plurality of eighteenth-century discourses, is adamant that there never was a single Enlightenment Project, hence no systematic philosophy of the Enlightenment, ergo no call for a book such as Cassirer's.

The main consequence of our collective abandonment of Cassirer has, to my mind, been our disengagement from the battle which has raged around us about the true meaning of the Enlightenment, since we who study its doctrines intensively deny that it has any meaning at all. By way of burrowing beneath the great arches of *Die Philosophie der Aufklärung*, we have declared our indifference to its fate and have acquiesced in the demolition of its ideals on the part of its detractors. We may be students of Enlightenment thought, but we refuse to acknowledge the vacuous cosmopolitanism and spurious unity ascribed to the principles of that intellectual movement as framed by Cassirer's images, and because we believe it never had real substance we do not mind its enemies' deconstruction of the so-called *Enlightenment Project*.

In the little space remaining to me here, I aim to develop just two main points about Cassirer's book, which I read as portraying the connection between the Enlightenment and the age of modernity in a manner largely ignored by social philosophers and intellectual historians alike. First, I should like to show that *Die Philosophie der Aufklärung* does indeed encapsulate what may be termed *The Enlightenment Project* with respect to the avowed objectives of the eighteenth-century republic of letters itself. Second, I shall argue that the circumstances of Cassirer's composition of this work, mainly in a period of a few months in 1932, also encapsulate the central lessons to be learnt from *The Enlightenment Project* in our time. I am convinced that much that is at stake with respect to modernist and postmodernist interpretations of the age of Enlightenment in general hinges upon our

---

[16] COBBAN, A., "The Enlightenment and Germany", *The Spectator*, 26 September 1952, pp. 406-408.

understanding of the cultural universe which Cassirer defended, since his life and thought together point to modernity's betrayal of what I here take to be *The Enlightenment Project* and to the persecution of its leading advocate. I categorically deny the claim of Becker and his postmodernist followers that the Enlightenment loved the thing it killed, but I believe that Cassirer's work, more than any other text produced in this benighted century scourged by waves of ethnic cleansing and genocide, bears witness to the fact that modernity has endeavoured to kill the thing it loved.

Exactly in the manner of d'Alembert's *Discours préliminaire* to the *Encyclopédie*, Cassirer's book forms a kind of manifesto of an age of enlightenment, mapping out the whole "Mind of the Enlightenment" as he entitles his first chapter, in imitation of d'Alembert's own chart of the branches of human knowledge which he appended to *his* text.[17] Embracing what he took to be the essential spirit of eighteenth-century philosophy, Cassirer also notes in his own preface how,

> more than ever before [...] the time is ripe for applying [...] self-criticism to the present age, for holding up to it that bright clear mirror fashioned by the Enlightenment.[18]

"The fundamental tendency of the Enlightenment", he claims, had been "to portray [life] in terms of reflective thought", to shape it so as to bring about "that order of things which it conceives as necessary".[19] He accordingly envisaged the Enlightenment as comprising an interconnected set of philosophies which sought not only to interpret the world but to change it.

That notion of reason as an active power Cassirer ascribes to the spirit of the Enlightenment as a whole, whose subtle difference from the spirit of seventeenth-century philosophy he attempts to explain along the same lines that d'Alembert had invoked in the *Discours préliminaire* in his contrast between the seventeenth-century's *esprit de système*, on the one hand, and the eighteenth-century *esprit*

---

[17] See d'Alembert 1760, *Mélanges de littérature, d'histoire et de philosophie, nouvelle édition. Amsterdam: Aux dépens de la compagnie*, vol. I, p. 246. As Thomas L. Hankins remarks in HANKINS T. L., 1970, p. 2, Cassirer "apparently found [the] most characteristic exemplification [of the "mind" of the Enlightenment] in d'Alembert".

[18] See CASSIRER, E., 1932, p. xvi; CASSIRER, E., 1951 [1932], p. xi.

[19] CASSIRER, E., 1932, p. xii; CASSIRER, E., 1951 [1932], p. viii.

systématique, on the other.[20] Cassirer remarks that d'Alembert had made this distinction – in effect embracing the difference between the philosophies of the age of classicism and the age of modernity – "the central point of his argument"[21], and in elaborating that proposition in his own fashion, he was to reinvigorate it as a central theme of his *Philosophie der Aufklärung*.

By way of chapters devoted to "Natural Science", "Psychology", "Religion", "History" and "Law", much of *Die Philosophie der Aufklärung* is designed to provide treatments of the unity of the Enlightenment's conceptual origin.[22] Here, too, Cassirer largely follows d'Alembert in granting pride of place to the scientific method and epistemologies of British luminaries. As distinct from d'Alembert, however, Cassirer adds a predominantly German dimension to the vitalist perspective he ascribes mainly to Frenchmen and the empiricist approach he associates with the scientific method of Englishmen, Irishmen and Scots. To his opening chapter on "The Mind of the Enlightenment", he appends a section devoted largely to the philosophy of Leibniz, while in the final, and by far his longest, chapter – on "Aesthetics" – his most elaborate treatment is reserved for the philosophy of Baumgarten, whose aesthetic ideals of "richness... abundance and nobility" are deemed to have reached their apotheosis in the mind of Lessing.[23] Following Goethe, Cassirer portrays Lessing as possessing a magic power "in the whole realm of eighteenth-century philosophy. It is above all because of [Lessing] that the century of the Enlightenment... did not fall prey to the merely negative critical function", he remarks. Because of Lessing, "it was able to reconvert criticism to creative activity and... the constant renewal of the spirit".[24] With this tribute to the majesty of two German poets at the dusk of the age of Enlightenment, Cassirer's *Philosophie der Aufklärung* comes to its close.

---

[20] See d'Alembert's "Discours préliminaire" in his *Mélanges de littérature*, vol. I, pp. 36 and 156-157. d'Alembert here elaborates a theme of his *Recherches sur la précession des équinoxes* of 1749, which is pursued as well in somewhat different terms in Condillac's *Traité des systèmes* of the same year, an intellectual link noted by Cassirer himself.

[21] CASSIRER, E., 1932, p. 9; CASSIRER, E., 1951 [1932], p. 8.

[22] See CASSIRER, E., 1932, p. viii; CASSIRER, E., 1951 [1932], p. v.

[23] See CASSIRER, E., 1932, pp. 477-478; CASSIRER, E., 1951 [1932], p. 357.

[24] See CASSIRER, E., 1932, p. 482; CASSIRER, E., 1951 [1932], p. 360.

Cobban could not have been further from the truth when he denounced the German dimension of Cassirer's work as providing a kind of genealogy of Nazism. The whole thrust of Cassirer's argument with respect to German thinkers was designed to portray their influence within the European Enlightenment as a whole. "As in all other fields in the eighteenth century", he remarks, "so in aesthetics... it is impossible to draw a sharp line of demarcation along national cultural barriers".[25] By way of a German philosophical tradition through Leibniz, Wolff and Baumgarten, Cassirer identified "a new intellectual orientation" of the mind of man, which heightened its sensibility and added creative vigour to its critical temper.[26] Even Herder's break with the age of Enlightenment, in his insistence upon the unique atmosphere of every age and every nation, is depicted as fundamentally inspired by the metaphysics of Leibniz[27] and made possible "only by following the trails blazed" by other Enlightenment thinkers. According to Cassirer, "the conquest of the Enlightenment by Herder is... a genuine self-conquest".[28] There is no trace in *Die Philosophie der Aufklärung* of a German Counter-Enlightenment in the manner of Isaiah Berlin.

In his chapter devoted to "Law, State and Society", Cassirer addresses seventeenth- and eighteenth-century notions of the apriority of law, universally valid for all persons. On such foundations, he claims, was the doctrine of human and civil rights as we know it built up in the age of Enlightenment.[29] Rousseau's notion of the *general will*, together with Voltaire's notion of the "freedom of the pen", comprise the real "Palladium of the rights of the people", as he termed it.[30] In Rousseau too, on whose philosophy he had just completed a study, *Das Problem Jean-Jacques Rousseau*, Cassirer found a kindred soul who, like Herder, transferred the Enlightenment's centre of gravity to another position.[31] In the mirror of his state of nature as portrayed in the *Discours sur l'inégalité*, Cassirer contends that the present form of the state and society could both behold and pass

---

25 See CASSIRER, E., 1932, p. 444; CASSIRER, E., 1951 [1932], p. 331.

26 CASSIRER, E., 1932, p. 43; CASSIRER, E., 1951 [1932], p. 33.

27 See CASSIRER, E., 1932, pp. 308-309; CASSIRER, E., 1951 [1932], pp. 230-231.

28 CASSIRER, E., 1932, pp. 311-312; CASSIRER, E., 1951 [1932], p. 233.

29 See CASSIRER, E., 1932, pp. 326 and 332-333; CASSIRER, E., 1951 [1932], pp. 243 and 248.

30 CASSIRER, E., 1932, p. 337; CASSIRER, E., 1951 [1932], p. 251.

31 CASSIRER, E., 1932, p. 367; CASSIRER, E., 1951 [1932], p. 274.

judgement on themselves.[32] Rousseau's speculum of the politics of the age of Enlightenment, putting its moral corruption under scrutiny by way of self-reflection, takes up the "bright clear mirror" which Cassirer in his preface holds up to his own time. To put my point another way, *Die Philosophie der Aufklärung* stands to the whole of Cassirer's age of modernity in much the same position as does Rousseau's state of nature with respect to civil society or civilization. As I read it, his book was conceived as the lens of the *Enlightenment Project*.

I turn now, finally, to my second point about the circumstances of the book's composition or what, in Cambridge, would be termed its intellectual context. *Die Philosophie der Aufklärung* was the last work Cassirer produced in Germany before his exile. It was written in great haste, mainly in the winter and spring of 1932, and his turning to it had only been made possible at all by his premature resignation of the Rectorship of the University of Hamburg, which had freed him sufficiently to spend the summer of 1931 at the *Bibliothèque Nationale* in Paris, where in addition to reading the materials he required for his book on the Enlightenment he also launched his study of Rousseau. While Cassirer was drafting his work, the Weimar Republic was itself in its death throes. Hindenburg dissolved the *Reichstag* on 4 June 1932; on 31 July the Nazis won a resounding victory in the national elections, only to find an otherwise fractious collection of opposition parties determined to preserve the Republic against the threat which they posed; on 30 January 1933 Adolf Hitler was made Chancellor of Germany; a few months later the Republic itself was destroyed, and with it, Bertolt Brecht, Albert Einstein, Walter Gropius, Wassily Kandinsky, Thomas Mann, Paul Tillich, Bruno Walter and many other luminaries of twentieth-century science and culture, as well as Cassirer, had gone into exile.[33]

How has it been possible for contemporary social philosophers to abandon these orphans of the *Enlightenment Project* and to nominate Eckart, Goebbels and Rosenberg in their stead? It's enough to drive the Fundamentalist Right of American politics into the arms of Hillary Clinton. If the notion of an "Enlightenment Project" has any plausible validity at all, if just one guiding thread may be identified as marking the passage from *l'âge classique* to *l'âge moderne* delimited by the Revocation of the Edict of Nantes in 1685, on the one hand, and the *Déclaration des droits de l'homme* of 1789, on the other, it can only be

---

[32] CASSIRER, E., 1932, p. 364; CASSIRER, E., 1951 [1932], p. 271.
[33] See GAY, P., 1968, p. xiv.

the principle of religious toleration, which united Spinoza, Bayle, Locke, Montesquieu, Voltaire, Diderot, Rousseau and *philosophes* of almost every persuasion in common cause against religious bigotry. In the year 1932 *Die Philosophie der Aufklärung* stood in much the same relation to the Weimar Republic as had Hegel's *Phänomenologie des Geistes* with respect to the survival of the city of Jena in 1806 when it was bombarded by Napoleon. It formed the expression of a civilization besieged by the armed World Spirit of an alternative culture. In the case of Cassirer's work, it in fact constitutes what might be termed the last will and testament of this civilization, whose principles he held aloft in that bright clear mirror which he understood to form the mind of the Enlightenment.

Once before, in 1916, Cassirer had completed a work ostensibly devoted to the history of philosophy, at a time of great national calamity. His *Freiheit und Form* dealt with many themes of German intellectual history that were to be taken up again in his *Philosophie der Aufklärung*. By way of raising in a fresh idiom Kant's four fundamental questions – *Was kann ich wissen?, Was soll ich tun?, Was darf ich hoffen?* and *Was ist der Mensch?* – he attempted to show in metaphysical terms that the real spirit of Germany was not in fact nationalist and militarist but rather humanist, tolerant, pluralist and cosmopolitan, in the tradition of Leibniz and Goethe.

The political crisis through which Germany passed sixteen years later was itself prefigured philosophically in the celebrated debate between Cassirer and Heidegger which took place in the Hochschule of Davos, in Switzerland, in the spring of 1929, two years after the explosive impact of the publication of Heidegger's *Sein und Zeit*.[34] Although outwardly a courteous exchange with regard to the interpretation of Kant's *Kritik der reinen Vernunft*, the confrontation of Cassirer and Heidegger proved to be a spirited battle over the soul of Kant and, indeed, as Cassirer later came to believe, over the soul of Germany itself. Theirs was a renewed exchange between Erasmus and

---

[34] On the meeting of Cassirer and Heidegger in Davos, see especially *"Davoser Disputation zwischen Ernst Cassirer und Martin Heidegger"*, in HEIDEGGER, M., 1991 [1934], pp. 274-296; AUBENQUE, P., 1972; AUBENQUE, P., 1990, pp. 82-96; KROIS, J. M., "Aufklärung und Metaphysik: Zur Philosophie Cassirers und der Davoser Debatte mit Heidegger", *Internationale Zeitschrift für Philosophie* 2 (1992), pp. 273-289; and WAITE, G., "On Esotericism: Heidegger and/or Cassirer at Davos", *Political Theory* 26 (1998), pp. 603-51.

Luther, and once again, to the great discomfiture of Cassirer, it appeared to be the voice of Luther *cum* Lucifer that triumphed.

Cassirer and Heidegger disagreed fundamentally with respect both to the ethics of Kant and to his conception of language, in each case from a different perspective on Kant's philosophy as a whole, with Cassirer emphasising epistemological problems and Heidegger stressing instead the metaphysical foundations of the finite existence of man. The two philosophers agreed that the notion of circumscribed human capacities formed the kernel of the Kantian approach, but for Cassirer that psychological truth remained compatible with the universality of Kant's notion of the moral law, and while he allowed that the irreducible diversity of languages excluded the transposition of terms from one to another, it still remained the case that speakers of different languages could make themselves intelligible to one another by virtue of their partaking of language in general. The multiplicity of symbolic forms did not exclude their objectivity, he insisted.

For Heidegger, by contrast, Kant's categorical imperative was only a specific form of the moral law appropriate to beings ignorant of any transcendent notion of the good, and to Cassirer's sense of the underlying *logos* of discursive exchange he opposed the idea of the *Unterscheidung* or *differentiation* of points of view, which would later be taken up by postmodernist thinkers, most notably Derrida, in *his* focus upon the intransitivity of difference. Cassirer took offence at Heidegger's own abridgement of their dialogue, in which Heidegger ascribed to Kant the destruction, or *Zerstörung*, of the foundations of Western metaphysics. A fortnight after the Davos encounter, in a talk in Hamburg in celebration of the two hundredth anniversary of the birth of Lessing and Mendelssohn, he elaborated on the meeting of minds which could be achieved by a Protestant and a Jew in the age of Enlightenment, when it had been possible to achieve salvation by way of humane mutual understanding. When later that year, in the midst of wildly anti-Semitic propaganda, he accepted the Rectorship of the University of Hamburg, he began, as never before in his life, to examine the nature of his own Jewish identity and to reassess the profoundly Jewish background of Hermann Cohen, who had at Marburg been his principal teacher of the philosophy of Kant and who, in 1873, a year prior to Cassirer's birth, had become one of the first Jews, and among them the most conspicuous, to hold an academic appointment in Germany.

Cassirer had been greatly disturbed by his confrontation with Heidegger and by the hypnotic power he had seen Heidegger exercise upon his audience, and especially its most youthful members. In *The Myth of the State*, published posthumously in 1946, he offered the following assessment of his adversary in a philosophical encounter which he believed had presaged the violence of Germany's transfiguration over the last sixteen years of his life. "In order to express his thought Heidegger had to coin a new term", he wrote:

> He spoke of the *Geworfenheit* of man (the being-thrown). To be thrown into the stream of time is [an ...] inalterable feature of our human situation. We cannot emerge from this stream [...] I do not mean to say that these philosophical doctrines had a direct bearing on the development of political ideas in Germany [...] But the new philosophy did enfeeble [...] the forces that could have resisted the modern political myths. A philosophy of history that consists in sombre predictions of [...] the inevitable destruction of our civilization and [...] sees in the *Geworfenheit* of man one of his principal characters [...] renounces its own [...] ethical ideals. It can be used [...] as a pliable instrument in the hands of [...] political leaders.[35]

It was in such times, and with such anxieties weighing upon him, that Cassirer launched and completed his *Philosophie der Aufklärung*. Following his exile, he never again set foot in Germany. After settling briefly in England and then moving to Sweden, he embarked in 1941 for the United States of America, where he was to die just before the end of the war, having passed directly from the moral Chernobyl of the Old World into the cultural Disneyland of the New, forever committed to an Enlightenment Project that appeared to have been extinguished with the fall of the Weimar Republic. Perhaps the European Community, and in some respects the European University Institute as well, can be said to have aspired to breathe fresh life into Cassirer's great endeavour, but the recent history of Bosnia and Kosovo suggests that our success in that aim may be doubted. The most fundamental principle on which our community was built – the principle of *Never Again* – seems currently less secure than it has been throughout most of its history, postponing a final verdict on the influence of the *Enlightenment Project* at least beyond the second millennium if not indefinitely. In assessing the political achievements of the twentieth century as a whole, however, it seems to me that, on balance, so far from having triumphed by virtue of embracing the thing it killed, it would be more accurate to describe the *Enlightenment Project* as our god that failed.

---

[35] CASSIRER, E., 1946, p. 293.

CHAPTER 3

Genocide and the Limits of Enlightenment: Horkheimer and Adorno Revisited

James SCHMIDT

In 1941, the exiled Institute for Social Research published the proposal for its "Research Project on Anti-Semitism" in the pages of the *Zeitschrift für Sozialforschung*. It began by noting:

> In spite of the many excellent works written on the subject, anti-Semitism is still regarded too casually and viewed too superficially, even by those whom it immediately affects. For too many people anti-Semitism is nothing more than a pitiable aberration, a relapse into the Dark Ages; and [...] it is on the whole viewed as an element foreign to the spirit of modern society.[1]

Against this view, the proposal advanced the thesis that "anti-Semitism is one of the dangers inherent in all more recent culture".

Over half a century later, debate continues on the question of whether Nazi genocide is best understood as a regression into a barbarism whose explanation lies in the peculiar pathologies of German history or as evidence of a potentiality for mass slaughter that is inherent in modernity itself. Daniel Goldhagen, for example, has recently insisted that no progress can be made in understanding Nazi genocide unless we rid ourselves of the conventional assumption that during the nineteenth and twentieth centuries Germans were:

---

[1] "Research Project on Anti-Semitism", *Zeitschrift für Sozialforschung* IX:1 (1941), p. 124.

more or less like us or, rather, similar to how we represent ourselves to be: rational, sober children of the Enlightenment, who are not governed by "magical thinking", but rooted in "objective reality".[2]

He maintains that,

> The Holocaust [...] was completely at odds with the intellectual foundations of modern western civilization, the Enlightenment, as well as the Christian and secular ethical and behavioural norms that had governed modern western societies.[3]

For Goldhagen, the crimes of the Third Reich represented nothing less than "a radical break with everything known in human history".

Seven years before the publication of *Hitler's Willing Executioners*, Zygmunt Bauman suggested that interpretations that focus on the "Germanness" of Nazi genocide run the risk of ignoring its broader, and more troubling, significance.

> The implication that the perpetrators of the Holocaust were a wound or a malady of our civilization – rather than its horrifying, yet legitimate product – results not only in the moral comfort of self-exculpation, but also in the dire threat of moral and political disarmament. It all happened "out there" – in another time, another country.[4]

For Bauman, we miss the meaning of Nazi genocide if we see it as a break with history or a regression to pre-modern modes of behaviour: it must be understood, instead, "as a rare, yet significant and reliable, test of the hidden possibilities of modern society".[5] While Goldhagen holds the Enlightenment innocent of any responsibility for the Nazi genocide (at one point equating a faithfulness to "Enlightenment principles" with an adherence to "anti-antisemitic principles")[6], Bauman argues that the fatal combination of racism and "social engineering" that was the hallmark of Nazi policy towards the Jews would have been inconceivable without the transformation of western attitudes towards nature and society that the Enlightenment brought about.[7]

---

[2] GOLDHAGEN, D. J., 1996, p. 27.

[3] *Ibid.*, p. 28.

[4] BAUMAN, Z., 1989, p. xii.

[5] *Ibid.*, p. 12.

[6] GOLDHAGEN, D. J., 1996, p. 74.

[7] BAUMAN, Z., 1989, pp. 68-72.

Neither Goldhagen nor Bauman have much to say about the discussion of anti-Semitism offered in Max Horkheimer and Theodor Adorno's *Dialectic of Enlightenment*. This is hardly surprising in the case of Goldhagen: given his emphasis on the "social scientific" character of his research – and his repeated attacks on historians whose work he sees as lacking in this regard – it is easy to see why he might be ill-disposed towards most baffling of books. Yet Bauman's silence is puzzling: in attempting to show how the "self-destructiveness" that they saw as inherent in rationalism manifested itself in Nazi anti-Semitism, Horkheimer and Adorno would appear to lend support to the argument of *Modernity and the Holocaust*. But, while Bauman criticises the approach adopted by Adorno, Frenkel-Brunswik, Levenson, and Sanford in *The Authoritarian Personality* for its neglect of social – as opposed to psychological – factors, *Modernity and the Holocaust* has nothing to say about the more comprehensive (albeit sometimes maddeningly elusive) account of anti-Semitism offered in *Dialectic of Enlightenment*.

My intent here is to reconstruct the argument about anti-Semitism in *Dialectic of Enlightenment* and see how this fits into the book's more general claims about the relationship of mythology and enlightenment. I hope to show that the account is more complex than is sometimes assumed, and that the complexity of the account resides, paradoxically, in two features of its argument that are among the more problematic aspects of the book: its use of a notion of "enlightenment" that is so expansive as to flout all canons of historical interpretation and a treatment of anti-Semitism that is at best contingently related to the book's discussion of Fascism. Without attempting to diminish the problematic character of both of these aspects of the book, I will argue that, in partial compensation, these two aspects of the book may also account for the curious power of its argument today.

Myth and Mimesis

In May 1943, Max Horkheimer – who had now been living in Pacific Palisades, California, for about a year and was at work with Theodor Adorno on the manuscript that would eventually become *Dialectic of Enlightenment* – received a memorandum from his life-long friend Friedrich Pollock summarising a discussion that had taken place in New York between Pollock, Paul Tillich, and Adolph Lowe regarding Julian Benda's *La trahison des clercs*. Horkheimer had reservations about the course of the discussion, and suggested that

Tillich and Lowe's focus on the question of whether "clerks" or the masses they sought to mobilise were worse today than they had been in earlier times missed the essential point. Horkheimer advised

> The process to which they should refer instead is the one which I have been dealing with during the last two years [...]: the process of enlightenment as it was marked out in the first thought a human being conceived, that same process of which Hegel says that if started it is irresistible.[8]

He then quoted a passage from Hegel's *Phenomenology* which likened the spread of enlightenment to the gradual penetration of a disease into an organism:

> [...] the struggle against it betrays the fact that the infection has occurred. The struggle is too late, and every remedy adopted only aggravates the disease, for it has laid hold of the marrow of spiritual life [...]; there is thus no power in it which could overcome the disease.[9]

This passage, which would also be quoted near the start of the *Dialectic of Enlightenment*, appears to have had a particular fascination for Horkheimer. It provided a model, of sorts, for what he and Adorno were attempting to do.

In Hegel's account, enlightenment's victory over the forces of faith and superstition is both easy and empty: easy because all of faith's efforts to resist the spread of enlightenment only aggravate the disease, empty because ultimately faith and enlightenment are only different expressions of the same basic attitude towards the world. Enlightenment defeats faith, but in doing so, undermines itself by revealing that it is nothing more than a faith of a different sort: a faith in reason. Subjecting everything in the world to the cold calculus of utility, enlightenment culminates in the furious destruction that, for Hegel, epitomised the fatal trajectory of the French Revolution as it collapsed into the Terror. Seeking to remake the world in its own image, enlightenment ultimately can produce only:

---

[8] HORKHEIMER, M., 1996 [1941-1948], p. 446. See also Adorno's letter to Löwenthal of June 3, 1945, quoted in WIGGERSHAUS, R., 1994, p. 332.

[9] HEGEL, G. W. F., 1970, vol. III, pp. 402-403; HEGEL, G. W. F., 1977 [1807], pp. 331-332.

death, and indeed a *death* that has no inner depth or fulfilment; [...] the coldest, shallowest of deaths, with no more significance than cleaving a cabbage head or swallowing a gulp of water.[10]

The account of the relationship between enlightenment and mythology that opens *Dialectic of Enlightenment* follows the broad outlines of Hegel's account.[11] Enlightenment battles mythology – but proves ultimately to be fighting only itself. The goal of the Enlightenment, as Horkheimer and Adorno understood it, was "to dissolve myths and to depose imagination though knowledge".[12] Yet, "the myths which fell victim to Enlightenment were its own product".[13] In both the *Phenomenology* and the *Dialectic of Enlightenment*, Enlightenment battles itself and wins; but Horkheimer and Adorno placed an even greater stress on the bitterness of the victory than their predecessor. They argued that the Enlightenment's attack on mythology presses forward until the fundamental normative commitments of the Enlightenment itself have been denounced as mythical. By the time the Enlightenment has run its course, there is no longer a distinction to be made

between the totemic animal, the dreams of a ghost seer, and the absolute Idea. On the path to modern science men renounce any claim to meaning. They substitute formula for concept, rule and probability for cause.[14]

The figures of myth give way to philosophical concepts which are finally abandoned in favour of the formulae of science, which seek to dispense with traditional philosophical categories altogether.[15]

---

[10] HEGEL, G. W. F., 1970, vol. III p. 436; HEGEL, G. W. F., 1977 [1807], p. 360 (translation modified).

[11] For a more detailed discussion (from which the rest of this section draws) of the relationship between myth and enlightenment in the *Dialectic of Enlightenment* see my "Language, Mythology, and Enlightenment: Historical Notes on Horkheimer and Adorno's *Dialectic of Enlightenment*", *Social Research* 65:4 (Winter 1998) pp. 807-838.

[12] HORKHEIMER, M., 1987 [1940-1950], p. 25; HORKHEIMER, M. and ADORNO, T., 1972 [1944], p. 3.

[13] HORKHEIMER, M., 1987 [1940-1950], p. 30; HORKHEIMER, M. and ADORNO, T., 1972 [1944], p. 8.

[14] HORKHEIMER, M., 1987 [1940-1950], p. 27; HORKHEIMER, M. and ADORNO, T., 1972 [1944], p. 5.

[15] HORKHEIMER, M., 1987 [1940-1950], p. 27- HORKHEIMER, M. and ADORNO, T., 1972 [1944], pp. 5-6.

The Enlightenment's victory thus comes at a considerable cost. The Enlightenment winds up dismissing as "myth" the very values that once animated it. As Horkheimer subsequently argued in *Eclipse of Reason*,

> The more ideas have become automatic, instrumentalised, the less does anybody see in them thoughts with a meaning of their own. They are considered things, machines. Language has been reduced to just another tool in the gigantic apparatus of production in modern society. [... J]ustice, equality, happiness, tolerance, all the concepts that [...] were in preceding centuries supposed to be inherent in or sanctioned by reason, have lost their intellectual roots.[16]

Indeed, even the term "reason" itself has come to be viewed as "a ghost that has emerged from linguistic usage", a name used to designate a "meaningless symbol, an allegorical figure without a function [...]". It survives only in the guise of "a pragmatic instrument oriented to expediency [...]".[17] Reason has been reduced to a strategy of self-preservation which, in the end, "boils down to an obstinate compliance as such" which is "indifferent to any political or religious content".[18] All thought that does anything other than make its peace with existing powers stands condemned as "poetry" or as empty "metaphysics".

Were this all that the *Dialectic of Enlightenment* had to say, the book would have long ago found a comfortable resting place among the many critics of the Enlightenment who have argued that the grand project of freeing mankind from illusion ultimately culminates in nihilism. Thinkers from Edmund Burke to Hans-Georg Gadamer have argued that the Enlightenment's attack on prejudices was itself a prejudice, and have called for a greater deference towards tradition. Thinkers from Nietzsche to the postmodernists have basically agreed with their conservative brethren that reason has undermined its own foundations – though, less concerned about the results, they have been inclined to endorse Nietzsche's dictum: "That which is falling [...] Push!" What prevents the *Dialectic of Enlightenment* from fitting in easily with other critiques of the Enlightenment lies in the first part of

---

[16] HORKHEIMER, M., 1947, pp. 22-23.

[17] HORKHEIMER, "End of Reason" in ARATO A. and GEBHART, E., 1978, p. 27-28; "Vernunft und Selbsterhaltung" in HORKHEIMER, M., 1987 [1940-1950], p. 323

[18] HORKHEIMER, "End of Reason" in ARATO A. and GEBHART, E., 1978, p. 34; "Vernunft und Selbsterhaltung", HORKHEIMER, M., 1987 [1940-1950], p. 332.

the *chiasmus* around which its argument is woven: "myth is already enlightenment, and enlightenment reverts to myth."[19] Where other critics of the Enlightenment respond to its alleged failings by seeking to reactivate modes of thinking that had not been corrupted by enlightenment rationality, this path is not available to Horkheimer and Adorno.

Horkheimer's letter to Pollock amply testifies to the audacious use that he and Adorno made of the term *"Aufklärung"*: their goal was to trace "the process of enlightenment as it was marked out in the first thought a human being conceived".[20] Understood in this way, enlightenment stretches back to the very beginning of human history, and there is no form of thinking that is not already implicated in it. *Dialectic of Enlightenment* is thus concerned not with "the Enlightenment" (with a capital "E", and preceded by a definite article) but rather with the fate of the ideal of "enlightenment" (small "e", no article) – an ideal which the Enlightenment of course embraced, but an ideal that, nevertheless, had a career before and after the period we call the Enlightenment.[21] Hence the motley assortment of figures who populate *Dialectic of Enlightenment*: we find a few from the eighteenth century (most famously Kant and the Marquis de Sade) but they tend to be lost among a cast that includes Francis Bacon, Friedrich Nietzsche, Sigmund Freud, Odysseus, Bette Davis, Harpo Marx, and Adolf Hitler.

As a result, it is difficult to reconcile the account offered in *Dialectic of Enlightenment* with conventional treatments of the relationship between enlightenment and modernity. When conceived as a historical period, the Enlightenment can be seen as standing on the threshold of modernity. Typically, it is credited with elevating the natural sciences to the pre-eminent position they enjoy in modern culture and with inaugurating a scepticism towards tradition and authority that decisively influenced modern attitudes towards religion,

---

[19] HORKHEIMER, M., 1987 [1940-1950], p. 22; the chapter on the culture industry in the 1944 mimeograph ended with the words "(to be continued)". HORKHEIMER, M., 1987 [1940-1950], p. 196.

[20] HORKHEIMER, M., 1996 [1941-1948], p. 446.

[21] Horkheimer opened his 1959-1960 course on "The Enlightenment" by distinguishing between two different senses in which the term *"Aufklärung"* is used: one usage refers to a particular philosophical movement in England, France, and Germany, the other to a project which spans the history of philosophy: the battle against mythology, superstition, and error. HORKHEIMER, M., 1989 [1949-1972], p. 571.

morality, and politics. In the optimistic version of this story, the legacy of the Enlightenment is a vision of history that sees mankind, through the unfettered use of reason, at last escaping from that state of "immaturity" to which it had been condemned by the forces of super-stition, prejudice, and dogma. In the pessimistic version, the Enlighten-ment fosters a constricted conception of reason that can offer nothing beyond instrumental efficacy as a criterion of rationality. From within the iron cage of this conception of rationality, even genocide becomes nothing more than a complex technical problem demanding the efficient organization and utilisation of a nation's resources.

While much in *Dialectic of Enlightenment* (and even more in Horkheimer's *Eclipse of Reason*) resembles the latter of these two stories, the argument of the book nevertheless resists both accounts of the relationship between enlightenment and modernity. Horkheimer and Adorno had found in Walter Benjamin's vision of "history as permanent catastrophe" – as articulated in Benjamin's "Theses on the Philosophy of History", which Hannah Arendt delivered to Adorno in New York in June 1941[22] – a powerful expression of the argument they were attempting to make. In Benjamin's account, modernity is defined above all by its inability to produce anything that is new: it is a dream form that ceaselessly repeats the same things.[23] The task Benjamin had set himself in his interpretation of nineteenth-century Paris was that of finding an approach to the study of history that would break through the illusions of progress and decline that were so central to maintaining this illusion.[24] The eighth of his "Theses on the Philosophy of History" was uncompromising on this point:

> One reason why Fascism has a chance is that in the name of progress its opponents treat it as a historical norm. The current amazement that the things we are experiencing are "still" possible in the twentieth century is *not* philosophical. This amazement is not the beginning of knowledge –

---

[22] See Adorno's letter to Horkheimer of June 12, 1941 in HORKHEIMER, M., 1996 [1941-1948], pp. 59-61.

[23] For a discussion of the way in which this theme is developed in Benjamin's *Passagen-Werk* see BUCK-MORSS, S., 1989, pp. 106-109.

[24] See especially notes N2,2 and N2,5 in the methodological introduction to the *Passagen-Werk*, translated by Leigh Hafrey and Richard Sieburth as "Theoretics of Knowledge, Theory of Progress" in *The Philosophical Forum* XV:1-2 (1983-1984), p. 5.

unless it is the knowledge that the view of history which gives rise to it is untenable.[25]

In this spirit, Horkheimer and Adorno called into question the easy connection between enlightenment and progress: enlightenment cannot be viewed simply as the progressive banishing of myth, nor can Fascism be understood as an unexpected "regression" into a mythology that undoes all that enlightenment had achieved. Instead, enlightenment and myth must be seen as locked in a fruitless struggle whose fatal implications have become clearer over time.

They located the crucial break that inaugurates this dialectic with the transition from magical or mimetic relationships with nature to mythical world-views. Drawing on the work of Marcel Mauss they argued that magic presupposed neither a unity of nature nor a unity of the subject: deities are local and specific and the shaman must take up various cultic masks in order to imitate the objects over which mastery is to be gained.[26] Mythology, in contrast, represents an attempt both "to report, to name, to say the origin" and to "present, preserve, and explain".[27] In place of the milieu-bound practices of magic, mythology requires a separation of ideas from reality that was first achieved by the reality adjusted ego.[28] The origin of individuality lies on this side of the line between magic and mythology.

The transition from magical to mythical world-views took place during a period which witnessed a centralisation of power and the development of a division between mental and manual labour. "The lyrics of Homer and hymns of the Rig-Veda", Horkheimer and Adorno note, "date from the time of territorial domination and the secure locations in which a dominant warlike race established themselves over the mass of vanquished natives".[29] Following Durkheim, they proposed that even the categories of subordination and superordination in logic

---

[25] BENJAMIN, W., 1969 [1940], p. 257.

[26] HORKHEIMER, M., 1987 [1940-1950], pp. 31-34; HORKHEIMER, M. and ADORNO, T., 1972 [1944], pp. 9-11.

[27] HORKHEIMER, M., 1987 [1940-1950], p. 31; HORKHEIMER, M. and ADORNO, T., 1972 [1944], p. 8.

[28] HORKHEIMER, M., 1987 [1940-1950], p. 33; HORKHEIMER, M. and ADORNO, T., 1972 [1944], p. 11.

[29] HORKHEIMER, M., 1987 [1940-1950], p. 36; HORKHEIMER, M. and ADORNO, T., 1972 [1944], p. 13.

had their basis in new forms of social domination.[30] Likewise, with a nod to Hegel's account of the dialectic of master and slave, they maintained that the separation between subject and object is grounded on the distance from the thing which the master achieves by means of his power over the mastered.[31] With the move beyond magical/mimetic relations to the world, language has renounced the claim to be like nature and instead limits itself to the tasks of calculation and control.[32]

The "irresistibility of enlightenment" that Hegel had proclaimed must ultimately be credited to that most fundamental of impulses: fear. In Vico's account of the origin of language, the gasp of surprise at the unusual becomes its name.[33] Hence the inability of mythology to provide any comfort for man: the names of the gods are the petrified sound of human fear.[34] Enlightenment is this mythic fear turned radical, pressing onward, distinguishing appearance and essence, activity and force, seeking to produce a world in which everything is repeatable and calculable. In its drive to create a world in which there is nothing to be feared, it spares no remnant of mythological thinking except for the foundation of mythological thinking itself: the abstract fear of the collectivity.[35] The "noontime panic" in the face of nature is replaced with a fear of social forces that can only be assuaged by a relentless effort at self-preservation that ultimately discards the ideals of enlightenment itself as just another bit of mythology.[36]

---

[30] HORKHEIMER, M., 1987 [1940-1950], p. 44; HORKHEIMER, M. and ADORNO, T., 1972 [1944], p. 21.

[31] HORKHEIMER, M., 1987 [1940-1950], p. 36; HORKHEIMER, M. and ADORNO, T., 1972 [1944], p. 14.

[32] HORKHEIMER, M., 1987 [1940-1950], p. 40; HORKHEIMER, M. and ADORNO, T., 1972 [1944], p. 18.

[33] HORKHEIMER, M., 1987 [1940-1950], p. 38; HORKHEIMER, M. and ADORNO, T., 1972 [1944], p. 15.

[34] HORKHEIMER, M., 1987 [1940-1950], p. 40; HORKHEIMER, M. and ADORNO, T., 1972 [1944], pp. 15-16.

[35] HORKHEIMER, M., 1987 [1940-1950], p. 45; HORKHEIMER, M. and ADORNO, T., 1972 [1944], p. 23.

[36] HORKHEIMER, M., 1987 [1940-1950], p. 51; HORKHEIMER, M. and ADORNO, T., 1972 [1944], p. 29.

Projection and Anti-Semitism

As early as the summer of 1941, Horkheimer had suggested to Adorno that the work they were planning to write might focus, in part, on the problem of anti-semitism. Speculating that there might be historical parallels between the killing of the insane and pogroms against Jews, Horkheimer argued that both acts represented attacks on those who were "not held spellbound by the goals and purposes people serve today, in the same way that industrious people are". The notion that Jews were tortured to force them to recant their faith was, Horkheimer suspected, a later rationalisation of a more primitive purpose. Physical pain makes the victims the same as their tormentors, forcing them to experience, "in their own bodies", the supremacy of "practical goals". However different Jews might appear to their tormentors, however much their existence might provide an uneasy reminder of the nomadic life that had been renounced with the subjection of mankind to rationally ordered labour, their physical torture served to demonstrate, time and again, "that freedom is not possible". Following this lead, Horkheimer suggested, "[t]he investigation of anti-Semitism leads us back to mythology and ultimately to physiology".[37]

Horkheimer's desire to incorporate a discussion of anti-Semitism into *Dialectic of Enlightenment* was hardly surprising. Since 1939 the Institute for Social Research had been seeking funding for a research project on the topic.[38] In the late summer of 1940, Adorno had noted in a letter to Horkheimer that "everything that we used to see from the point of view of the proletariat has been concentrated today with frightful force upon the Jews".[39] Yet, it was only late in the writing of *Dialectic of Enlightenment* that Horkheimer and Adorno actually began to wrestle with the issue of anti-Semitism: there was no mention of the topic in Horkheimer's March 1943 summary of the parts of the

---

[37] Horkheimer, letter to Adorno of August 28, 1941, HORKHEIMER, M., 1996 [1941-1948], p. 152. Adorno responded enthusiastically to the idea in a letter cited in WIGGERSHAUS, R., 1994, p. 309, but not reprinted in Horkheimer's *Gesammelte Schriften*. See also Adorno's letter to Horkheimer of September 18, 1940 and the note on the relationship of Judaism and Christianity enclosed with it in HORKHEIMER, M., 1995 [1937-1940], pp. 761-764.

[38] For a discussion of the history of the project, see WIGGERSHAUS, R., 1994, pp. 273-279, 350-380.

[39] Letter to Horkheimer of August 4, 1940 in HORKHEIMER, M., 1995 [1937-1940], p. 764 (footnote 5).

book that had been completed.[40] With the addition of this chapter, *Dialectic of Enlightenment* finally achieved a closure of sorts. Just as Hegel would end his account of the dialectic of enlightenment with an analysis of the collapse of the French Revolution into the Terror, so Horkheimer and Adorno employed an analysis of anti-Semitism to mark the "limits of enlightenment".[41]

Cast in the form of seven theses of markedly different lengths (the last of which was added shortly before the manuscript's 1947 publication) "Elements of Anti-Semitism" begins – as the title advertises – with a survey of the different elements in the constellation of anti-Semitism. Anti-Semitism is considered first as a "nationalist movement" [*Volksbewegung*] driven by an urge to equalise, to eradicate differences, to efface that which is other.[42] It is next considered in the particular form of "bourgeois anti-Semitism": as a reaction to relations of domination that, since they remain concealed in the production process, emerge only in the sphere of circulation, the sphere in which Jews – who have historically been denied access to the means of production and thus to the means of extracting surplus value – have been forced to make their living.[43] Finally, Horkheimer and Adorno consider the extent to which anti-Semitism is driven by Christian resentment at the followers of a religion that refused to embrace the "deceptively positive meaning" that Christianity had given to the process of "self-denial", a religion which thus served as a constant and unwelcome reminder that redemption is by no means guaranteed.[44] The main work of the chapter, however, was reserved for the fifth and sixth theses – dealing, respectively, with mimesis and

---

[40] Letter to Ruth Nanda Anshen of March 3, 1943, in HORKHEIMER, M., 1995 [1937-1940], p. 435

[41] The 1941 proposal for the research program hinted at an even closer parallel between the two accounts when it suggested that "progressive modern thought has an ambivalent attitude toward the concept of human rights" and that "the persecution of aristocrats in the French Revolution bears a resemblance to anti-Semitism in modern Germany", *Zeitschrift für Sozialforschung* IX:1 (1941), p. 124.

[42] HORKHEIMER, M., 1987 [1940-1950], pp. 199-202; HORKHEIMER, M. and ADORNO, T., 1972 [1944], pp. 170-172.

[43] HORKHEIMER, M., 1987 [1940-1950], pp. 202-205; HORKHEIMER, M. and ADORNO, T., 1972 [1944], pp. 173-176.

[44] HORKHEIMER, M., 1987 [1940-1950], p. 208; HORKHEIMER, M. and ADORNO, T., 1972 [1944], p. 178.

projection – which together make up nearly two thirds of the chapter in its original form.

Near the start of the fifth thesis, Horkheimer and Adorno argue that civilization rests on the organised and rationalised control of mimesis – and hence must be ever more resolutely on guard against those who would break ranks and revert to more primitive forms of mimetic behaviour. To this end, religions have prohibited the making of images, societies have banished actors and gypsies, and educators have forbidden children to be childish.[45] For Horkheimer and Adorno modern society is thus defined less by what it achieves – *e.g.* a facility at conceptual abstraction that brings with it an unparalleled domination of nature – than by what it struggles (not entirely successfully) to efface. In the modern world, the mimetic legacy of earlier forms of practical activity has been almost completely eliminated. Those mimetic practices that still survive – in such acts as "touching, snuggling, soothing, coaxing" – strike the civilised individual as "*Unheimlich*": *i.e.* as practices which, as Freud explained, strike us as repellently alien because they represent a return of the repressed.[46] The ambiguous victory of instrumental rationality over mimetic practices culminates in a situation where mimesis is mastered either by being repressed or by being instrumentally exploited: the unmoved countenance with which "practical men, politicians, priests, managing directors, and racketeers" carry out the tasks that assure the smooth functioning of bourgeois society has its mirror image in the bellowing of Fascist orators and concentration camp guards. Their howl, Horkheimer and Adorno write, is "as cold as business": like the noise generator on a flying bomb, it is something that can be switched off or on, as the need requires.[47] For this reason Horkheimer and Adorno regard fascist anti-Semitism less as a regression behind what civilization had achieved than as a further ratcheting up of its attempt to rationalise mimesis: "Fascism is also totalitarian in that it seeks to make the rebellion of suppressed nature against domination directly

---

[45] HORKHEIMER, M., 1987 [1940-1950], p. 210; HORKHEIMER, M. and ADORNO, T., 1972 [1944], pp. 180-181.

[46] HORKHEIMER, M., 1987 [1940-1950], pp. 211-212; HORKHEIMER, M. and ADORNO, T., 1972 [1944], p. 182.

[47] HORKHEIMER, M., 1987 [1940-1950], p. 212; HORKHEIMER, M. and ADORNO, T., 1972 [1944], p. 183.

useful to domination."[48] Fascism, in other words, has discovered the secret of miming mimesis in the interest of domination.

The sixth thesis focuses on the psychological mechanism that Horkheimer and Adorno see as the "counterpart of true mimesis": "false projection".

> If mimesis makes itself like the environment, false projection makes the environment like itself. For mimesis the external world is a model to which the inner world clings, the alien becomes intimate; false projection confuses the inner and outer world and defines the most intimate experiences as hostile. Impulses which the subject will not admit as its own even though they are most assuredly so, are attributed to the object: the prospective sacrifice.[49]

Horkheimer and Adorno locate the potential for this type of projection deep in the animal prehistory of mankind, arguing that "[i]n a certain sense, all perception is projection".[50] Reading Kant "anthropologically" (and employing an anthropology that owes as much to Freud as it does to Durkheim and Mauss) they argue that the "system of things" that science organises and classifies is the unconscious product of animal mechanisms of self-preservation: the sensory impressions that might otherwise overwhelm the subject are projected back out onto the world as objects to be avoided or coveted. The development of organised human society rests on a massive effort at refining and inhibiting projection, at creating a clear demarcation between internal affects and external objects, at separating off an individual identity from a world of objects. The faculty of reflection is responsible for this reciprocal creation of ego-identity and objectivity: "The inner depth of the subject consists in nothing other than the delicacy and wealth of the external world of perceptions. If the links are broken, the ego calcifies."[51] True enlightenment thus takes the form of a "conscious projection" in which a subject manages both to hold the external world in its own consciousness and yet recognizes it as other.

---

[48] HORKHEIMER, M., 1987 [1940-1950], p. 215; HORKHEIMER, M. and ADORNO, T., 1972 [1944], p. 185.

[49] HORKHEIMER, M., 1987 [1940-1950], p. 217; HORKHEIMER, M. and ADORNO, T., 1972 [1944], p. 187.

[50] HORKHEIMER, M., 1987 [1940-1950], p. 217; HORKHEIMER, M. and ADORNO, T., 1972 [1944], p. 187.

[51] HORKHEIMER, M., 1987 [1940-1950], p. 219; HORKHEIMER, M. and ADORNO, T., 1972 [1944], p. 189.

The pathology of anti-Semitism resides not in the fact that it is a form of projective behaviour, but rather in the withering of the capacity for self-reflection.

When the subject is no longer able to return to the object what it has received from it, it becomes poorer rather than richer. It loses reflection in both directions: since it no longer reflects the object, it ceases to reflect upon itself, and loses the ability to differentiate. Instead of the voice of conscience, it hears other voices; instead of going into itself in order to take account of the protocol of its own lust for power, it ascribes the Protocols of the Elders of Zion to others.[52]

In paranoiac projection, the world has meaning only in so far as it is a reflection of the blind purposes of the agent. Just as the paranoid individual smoothly incorporates every new piece of information into the seamless web of his own persecution fantasy, so the anti-Semite concocts an ideology in which everything can be attributed to the incessant conspiracies of the Jew. The seductiveness of such theories can be traced to the fundamental weakness in human cognition that they exploit: "Paranoia takes root in that abyss of uncertainty which every objectifying act must bridge."[53] It is "the shadow of cognition".[54] Every individual is thus disposed towards paranoid projection, just as every society has the potential of breaking off the practices of reflection that balance the claims of identity and otherness and descending into the "eternal sameness" of totalitarian ideology.

This explanation of the origins of anti-Semitism, however, runs the risk of proceeding on too deep a level to account for the historical particularity of Nazi genocide. If pathological projection is the spectre that haunts every act of cognition, and if every society must struggle against the temptations of a return to mimetic forms of behaviour, then what accounts for the historical emergence of Nazi genocide in one country at one particular moment? The burden of bridging the gap between the general account of mimesis and projection and particular historical fate of Jews in Nazi Germany falls on those theses that sketched the political, economic, and religious factors that marked Jews as "different" and thus laid the groundwork for that "appeal to

---

[52] HORKHEIMER, M., 1987 [1940-1950], p. 219-220; HORKHEIMER, M. and ADORNO, T., 1972 [1944], pp. 189-190.

[53] HORKHEIMER, M., 1987 [1940-1950], p. 223; HORKHEIMER, M. and ADORNO, T., 1972 [1944], p. 193.

[54] HORKHEIMER, M., 1987 [1940-1950], p. 225; HORKHEIMER, M. and ADORNO, T., 1972 [1944], p. 195.

idiosyncrasy" that constitutes the "old answer of all anti-Semites".[55] It is by no means obvious that the brief arguments along these lines that Horkheimer and Adorno offer in *Dialectic of Enlightenment* are sufficient to the task at hand. The more ambitious research program outlined in the *Zeitschrift für Sozialforschung* suggests how much more would have to be done to provide a convincing genealogy of Fascist anti-Semitism. The 1941 research proposal called for a study of selected historical events (the First Crusade, the crushing of the Albigensian heresy, "Jew baiting" in twelfth and thirteenth century England, the Reformation, the French Revolution, and the German war of resistance against Napoleon) that would explore the link between attacks on other social groups and attacks on Jews in each of these periods.[56] This part of the study was to be complemented by an examination of anti-Semitism during the last two centuries – "the so-called enlightened era" – with a focus on anti-Semitic elements in the writings of such thinkers as Voltaire, Herder, Kant, Fiche, Hegel, Goethe, and Bola.[57]

While such historical detail is foreign to *Dialectic of Enlightenment*, it is by no means incompatible with the argument advanced in the book. "Elements of Anti-Semitism" represented a first attempt at sketching a general framework for analysis. It cannot be read as a summary of the series of more particular studies of anti-Semitism that engaged the associates of the Institute for Social Research during the last years of their American exile. Indeed, most of these studies were executed after the completion of *Dialectic of Enlightenment*. Yet it is also difficult to view these studies as an elaboration of framework that *Dialectic of Enlightenment* had provided. For a variety of reasons, Horkheimer was unable to bring about the integration of social

---

[55] HORKHEIMER, M., 1987 [1940-1950], p. 209; HORKHEIMER, M. and ADORNO, T., 1972 [1944], p. 179. In a letter to Herbert Marcuse of June 17, 1943, Horkheimer emphasised the need to distinguish between the economic-political factors in anti-Semitism from the anthropological elements in individual who responds to it. HORKHEIMER, M., 1996 [1941-1948], p. 463.

[56] "Research Project on Anti-Semitism", *Zeitschrift für Sozialforschung* IX:1 (1941), pp. 126-129.

[57] "Research Project on Anti-Semitism", *Zeitschrift für Sozialforschung* IX:1 (1941), pp. 130-133.

philosophy and empirical research that he first sketched in his inaugural lecture as director of the Institute for Social Research.[58]

Enlightenment, Modernity, and Genocide

The authors of *Dialectic of Enlightenment* were thus placed in what would seem to be an unenviable position. The conception of enlightenment the book elaborated lacked historical specificity and its account of Nazi genocide ultimately made the choice of victims appear as contingent. The costs incurred by both of these points should not be underestimated.

In the account offered by Horkheimer and Adorno, "enlightenment" has been defined so broadly as to make it virtually identical with the attempt to master nature through instrumental reasoning. As a consequence, any hope of understanding what was historically specific to the eighteenth-century Enlightenment is lost. Efforts at mastering nature through science and technology are hardly unique to the Enlightenment, as is driven home by Horkheimer and Adorno's reliance on Francis Bacon as a spokesman for the "program of enlightenment".[59] Defining the concept of enlightenment so broadly as to include Bacon (let alone Odysseus) runs the risk of blinding us to the cluster of more particular concerns that constituted "the Enlightenment": *e.g.* the dissemination of useful knowledge throughout society, the defiance of the principle of the rule of law, the fostering of religious toleration, the cultivation of a cosmopolitan public sphere of readers and writers, etc. To be sure, efforts on behalf of these concerns may have been thwarted, either by other forces or by inconsistencies or inadequacies in these concerns themselves. But an understanding of how and where the Enlightenment went astray in the pursuit of its particular goals will give us a better sense of the fate of the Enlightenment than the more global arguments about the relation between enlightenment and mythology offered in the *Dialectic of Enlightenment*.

A similar complaint might be voiced with regard to the book's treatment of anti-Semitism: by the end of the discussion, the

---

[58] For a discussion of Horkheimer's concern about the increasingly philosophical direction taken by the work he was doing with Adorno see WIGGERSHAUS, R., 1994, pp. 314-322.

[59] HORKHEIMER, M., 1987 [1940-1950], pp. 25-27; HORKHEIMER, M. and ADORNO, T., 1947 [1944], pp. 3-5.

relationship between Nazism and anti-Semitism has become almost accidental. "Jews were being murdered", Horkheimer and Adorno wrote in 1947, "at a time when the Fascist leaders could just as easily replace the anti-Semitic plank in their platform with some other one, just as workers can be moved from one wholly rationalised production centre to another".[60] They argued that, far from being the product of a long-standing hatred of Jews, Fascist anti-Semitism "must first invent its own object".

> The human beings who were outlawed as Jews must first be located on the basis of complex questionnaires, because – under the levelling pressure of late industrial society – the hostile religions which once constituted the difference have been already converted into mere cultural articles by successful assimilation.[61]

Their colleague Franz Neumann once argued that it was possible to provide an analysis of the Nazi state without once mentioning anti-Semitism – and then noted that he had, in fact, done so in his *Behemoth*. In much the same spirit, *Dialectic of Enlightenment* presents us with an account of German fascism in which anti-Semitism becomes a completely contingent element. If we know anything about Nazism we know that this cannot be true.

While we should not underestimate the shortcomings of the *Dialectic of Enlightenment*, from a distance of a half-century we are also in a better position to appreciate the peculiar strengths that the book nevertheless retains. If it fails to provide the historical specificity that we might desire from an account of Nazi genocide, its discussion of mimesis and projection may nevertheless still offer some insight into the troubling ease with which societies can collapse into genocidal slaughter. And while its discussion of enlightenment may be too historically diffuse to allow us to form a balanced understanding of the role of the Enlightenment in the shaping of the modern world, the book does provide a glimpse of a conception of enlightenment that might still be worth defending. Let me close with a brief consideration of both of these points.

Bauman is perhaps correct in suggesting that an understanding of Nazi genocide which focuses too narrowly on the historical, political,

---

[60] HORKHEIMER, M., 1987 [1940-1950], pp. 237-238; HORKHEIMER, M. and ADORNO, T. W., 1947 [1944], p. 207.

[61] HORKHEIMER, M., 1987 [1940-1950], p. 237; HORKHEIMER, M. and ADORNO, T. W., 1947 [1944], pp. 206-207.

and cultural peculiarities of Germany fosters the comforting sense that these events belong to "another time, another country". In the decade since the publication of *Modernity and the Holocaust*, it has become all too evident that genocide is not a creature of "another time" and that the citizens of any number of countries are quite capable of deciding – with stunning swiftness – to slaughter their fellow citizens. An examination of the particular sequence of factors and circumstances that led to the Nazi genocide may be too finely tuned to confront the troubling prospect that opens before us today. While the Holocaust was historically unique, genocide is not. Horkheimer and Adorno may still have lessons to teach us about the stubborn persistence of genocide. If pathological projection is the "shadow" of cognition, genocide might be viewed as the "shadow" of social solidarity. The renunciation demanded by modern forms of social life may well serve as the breeding ground for explosions of rage against anyone in a society who appears (if only in the delusions of the attacker) to have somehow escaped these demands. To be different is to be at risk.

An explanation of this sort (and surely much more needs to be done to elaborate it) would differ from that offered by Bauman in one crucial respect. Where *Modernity and the Holocaust* emphasises the connection between modernity, abstraction, and bureaucratic rationalisation that reached its deadly perfection at Auschwitz, the account sketched in *Dialectic of Enlightenment* moves in a slightly different direction. While it is easy to overlook this aspect of Horkheimer and Adorno's account, their explanation does not posit a direct link between the triumph of instrumental reason and the mechanised extermination factories of the Third Reich. Their discussion of pathological forms of projection introduces another factor into the account: the psychological costs of the shrinking of cognition to a simple strategy of instrumental manipulation. It is their conjecture that, as the world becomes little more than a series of objects to be manipulated, the ego that carries out this manipulation becomes more and more prone to projecting its own inner conflicts onto the world in the form of threatening forces that must be eradicated. This additional loop in the argument could potentially strengthen Bauman's general argument: while the "gardening metaphor" that he finds operative in Nazi genocide may represent a case of instrumental reasoning run amok, we still need to explain how one of Europe's most assimilated Jewish populations suddenly came to be regarded as "weeds". Horkheimer

99

and Adorno's discussion of pathological forms of projection may offer a means of making sense of this process.

Likewise, Horkheimer and Adorno's emphasis on the furious rage unleashed in pathological projection could provide a different way of understanding a fact that is central to Goldhagen's discussion: while the rationalised killing in the concentration camps may have represented the epitome of the Nazi genocide, it was surround by forms of killing that were sustained by an intensity of emotion that is rather difficult to square with the notion of bureaucratic rationality. Juxtaposing the "rational, planned, scientifically informed, expert, efficiently managed, co-ordinated" killing in the death camps to the "officially encouraged and surreptitiously controlled" mob violence of *Kristallnacht*, Bauman maintains that

> [r]age and fury are pitiably primitive and inefficient as tools of mass annihilation. They normally peter out before the job is done. [...] Ghengis Khan and Peter the Hermit did not need modern technology and modern, scientific methods of management and co-ordination. Stalin or Hitler did.[62]

Yet the police battalions that figure so prominently in the accounts of Christopher Browning and Daniel Goldhagen were hardly exemplars of "modern technology or modern methods of management and co-ordination". While their ruthless killing functioned within a larger bureaucratic structure and while it was surely "planned" and "co-ordinated", it is difficult to characterise it as "rational, scientifically informed, expert, efficiently managed". The slaughter in which these units were involved had little of the scientific rationalisation and bureaucratic distancing that was the hallmark of the death camps. It involved direct, often face to face contact between killer and victim. Those who carried out this slaughter repeated their gruesome assignments with unflagging persistence and were no less effective in their brutal mission than the more rationalised forms of killing represented by the death camps. "Rage and fury" may still be a poor explanation for the forces that sustained these men in carrying out such tasks; but technological rationality and bureaucratic distancing seem equally deficient in explaining their actions. As C. Fred Alford has suggested in a recent critique of Goldhagen's understanding of what it meant to be a "willing" executioner, a re-consideration of the psychological dimension first explored by Horkheimer and Adorno may well be crucial in understanding the ruthless persistence with

---

[62] BAUMAN, Z., 1989, p. 90.

which those who carried out the extermination of the European Jewry went about their task.[63]

Dialectic of Enlightenment may also still have something to teach us about the virtues of enlightenment. The final thesis of the chapter on anti-Semitism in *Dialectic of Enlightenment* ends with the words, "Enlightenment which is in possession of itself and coming to power can break through the limits of enlightenment".[64] Coming at the end of a book that would seem to offer no reason to hope for anything from enlightenment save a further descent into barbarism, these words may well strike many readers as mere whistling in the dark. Yet it bears remembering that Horkheimer and Adorno intended *Dialectic of Enlightenment* to be followed by a sequel. In various notes and letters from the 1940s, Horkheimer spoke of his hope to complement the "negative" account of *Dialectic of Enlightenment* with a "positive" theory of dialectics, tentatively titled, *Saving the Enlightenment*.[65] This work remained unfinished – indeed, the surviving materials in the Horkheimer *Nachlass* suggest that the book could scarcely have been said to have been started. Yet, there is one letter from Horkheimer to Adorno from the early 1940s that offers one possible direction this work might have taken.

In it, Horkheimer reflected on the relationship between reason and language. He drew some rather surprising implications:

> Language intends, completely independent of the psychological intentions of the speaker, that universality which has been ascribed to reason alone. The interpretation of this universality leads necessarily to the idea of the just society. In the service of the status quo, language must therefore find that it constantly contradicts itself, and this is evident from individual

---

[63] ALFORD, C. F., *"Hitler's Willing Executioners:* What does 'willing' mean?", *Theory and Society* 26 (1997) p. 719-738. See also Alford's wide-ranging and provocative study ALFORD, C. F., 1997.

[64] HORKHEIMER, M., 1987 [1940-1950], p. 238; HORKHEIMER, M. and ADORNO, T., 1972 [1944], p. 208.

[65] Some discussion transcripts from October 1946 relating to this work have been published in HORKHEIMER, M., 1985 [1931-1949], pp. 594-605 and, in part, anticipate themes that Adorno would later explore in his *Negative Dialectic*. For discussions of the projected contents of the sequel to *Dialectic of Enlightenment*, see the letter to Paul Tillich of August 29, 1947, HORKHEIMER, M., 1996 [1941-1948], p. 884, Tillich's response of September, 1947 in HORKHEIMER, M., 1996 [1941-1948], pp. 892-893) as well as the editor's note 3 to HORKHEIMER, M., 1996 [1941-1948], p. 873.

linguistic structures themselves. [...] "Critique of language" would thus be a *Genitivus subjectivus*.[66]

Horkheimer's suggestion that the grounds for critique might be found within the very structure of language itself bears, of course, a striking resemblance to the position that Jürgen Habermas would subsequently elaborate, not realising that he was resuming a project Horkheimer had briefly considered several decades before. The reduction of language to an instrument of domination betrays a *telos* that Horkheimer saw as inherent in speech itself.

> To speak to someone is, basically, to recognize them as a possible member of the future association of free human beings. Speech establishes a shared relation to truth, and is therefore the innermost affirmation of another existence, indeed of all that exists, according to its capacities. Insofar as speech denies those capacities, it finds itself in a necessary contradiction with itself. The speech of the concentration camp guard is actually a terrible illogicality, no matter what its content is; unless, of course, it condemns the speaker's own duties.[67]

The last line of resistance to the instrumentalisation of reason lies within language itself. The very attempt to speak to another holds out the image of a society in which individuals are something more than means. If a re-reading of *Dialectic of Enlightenment* suggests the chilling possibility that the demands society places on its members may breed those pathological forms of projection which lay the foundation for genocide, an attempt to work out the implications of the book's unwritten sequel might remind us that language carries within it a force that is strong enough to break through the limits of enlightenment.

---

[66] Letter to Adorno of September 14, 1941 in HORKHEIMER, M., 1996 [1941-1948], p. 171. See the discussions of this letter in WIGGERSHAUS, R., 1994, pp. 504-505 and in my "Language, Mythology, and Enlightenment".

[67] Letter to Adorno of September 14, 1941 in HORKHEIMER, M., 1996 [1941-1948], p. 172.

CHAPTER 4

Modernity Interpreted
through Weber and Foucault[1]

Árpád SZAKOLCZAI

I interpret the theme of this volume, the association of "Modernity, Enlightenment and Genocide", as a puzzle and paradox. We like to connect terms like "modernity" or "Enlightenment" with reason, progress, or civilisation. Yet, the reality is that the 20th century, our "modern" and "enlightened" century, was the location of violence, warfare and even genocide, of an unprecedented scale.

I also take it for granted that the purpose is neither to accuse and denounce, nor to search for the guilty, but to understand. In the sense of the title, however, understanding implies self-understanding. This is why I think that the works of Weber and Foucault, whose entire life-work was a struggle for self-understanding as modern subjects, "products" or "sons" of modernity[2] may be of particular use.

Still, it would seem that there is very little new to say in the framework of a volume on the vision of modernity as seen by Weber and Foucault. It is generally assumed that their views are contained in the classic works *Protestant Ethic* and *Discipline and Punish* which enjoy almost unique estimation in contemporary sociology and social theory. According to accepted wisdom, these contain the main theses of Weber and Foucault on the character of modern society: the Weber "thesis" about the Protestant ethic serving as the foundation of modern capitalism, leading to the "iron cage" of bureaucracy and capitalism, and the "Foucault thesis" about disciplining, surveillance and the

---

[1] For their precious comments on the first draft version of this paper, I would like to thank Bernd Giesen, Gianfranco Poggi, Göran Rosenberg, Bo Stråth and Robert Wokler.

[2] WEBER, M., 1976 [1904-1905], p. 13; WEBER, M., 1988 [1920-1921], vol. I, p. 1.

carceral institutions that provide the hidden but omnipresent foundations of modern society.

Despite the wide and high acclaim these works inspire, they have been and are very fervently contested. These debates, however, not only touch matters of interpretation or vulgarisation, but are frequently founded on a basic misunderstanding of the problem these works were trying to address, their *Fragestellung* or *problématisation*. Furthermore, Weber and Foucault themselves were deeply unsatisfied with and puzzled by their own works, and shortly after completing them, both sought possibilities to go beyond them. Weber completed the *Protestant Ethic* in 1905; Foucault completed *Discipline and Punish* in 1975. Yet, by the following year, each entered a very serious period of crisis.[3]

The reason was not a general doubt concerning their own work, a questioning of its basic direction. They realised however that they had only gone half the distance. They were searching for the proper way to proceed, and eventually both succeeded in gaining a clearer understanding of their own past work and the direction in which it could be successfully continued. However, for various reasons, this work has neither received the attention nor the understanding that remained reserved for their earlier accomplishments.

In this chapter, my aim will be to identify this direction, to resume the central claims of Weber and Foucault concerning modernity, and allude to the work of those thinkers who took up not just the word but also the spirit of Weber, and also Nietzsche, in the past decades, and as such were closest to the spirit of Foucault's research.

The symptoms of the five-year crises of Weber and Foucault were similar: relatively few publications, little satisfaction with the work that was eventually produced, and an intense search for the unity, status and underlying problem of the work. There was also a parallelism in the most important effect of this search: a relatively sudden backward shift of the time horizon of the entire work into the distant past. So far, the relevance and meaning of this shift has not been recognised by social theory. Because of a failure to locate them as answers to the respective crises of Weber and Foucault, these works have generally been considered as idiosyncratic and of relatively little contemporary significance.

---

[3]　For details, see SZAKOLCZAI, A., 1998a.

The main thesis I would like to present is that, quite to the contrary, these works contain the most important ideas Weber and Foucault developed concerning the understanding of the condition of modernity.

As a first step, I will bring in a third thinker whose work shows the exact same dynamics as the works of Weber and Foucault, Friedrich Nietzsche. In the mid-1880s, Nietzsche also intensely reflected upon the underlying problem and the coherence of his own work. He came up with an answer that advances the later formulations of Weber and Foucault: his work consisted of putting question marks behind the thus far taken for granted values of science and morality, and to the evaluation of existence, their "will to truth" implied. Finally, as an effect of these meditative exercises or "techniques of self", Nietzsche was thrown back to a historical investigation of the origins of morality in distant Antiquity.

In all these respects, whether consciously or not, Weber and Foucault have closely followed, if not imitated, Nietzsche. Even more importantly, they took up and further developed in their own work the central concerns Nietzsche identified in his late *Prefaces* and *The Genealogy of Morals*.[4]

The Genealogy of Morals was a diagnosis of the present, an analysis of the distant roots and the long-term processes that led to the contemporary condition for which Nietzsche coined the term "nihilism", and which he set out to analyse in the more systematic theoretical work he was engaged upon at the same time, fragments of which came to be published under the title *Will to Power*.[5] *The Genealogy of Morals* introduced a method and contained a series of substantive ideas. The genealogical method focused attention on the conditions of emergence of a given practice or institution and its lasting effects. In terms of Nietzsche's dual problematic, the question was to study the conditions of emergence of morality (or religion) and science (or philosophy), and the lasting effects of these practices once their taken for granted value has been questioned. The central purpose of this method is to single out for attention the way certain accidental, contingent conditions leave a lasting mark at the level of the taken for granted. This called for an autobiographical angle, an attempt at self-understanding, as opposed to external criticism and judgement.

---

[4]   NIETZSCHE, F., 1996 [1887].

[5]   NIETZSCHE, F., 1968 [1901].

In a substantive sense, the three essays of the Genealogy of Morals focus each around a crucial concept Nietzsche diagnosed at the heart of Christian morality: *ressentiment*, guilt (and bad conscience) and asceticism. However, in his diagnosis, Nietzsche quickly went beyond the caution implied in the genealogical method and simply identified Christian love with *ressentiment*, or the voice of conscience with the inculcation of feelings of guilt. Such claims, however, as Weber was quick to point out, were exaggerated and untenable.[6]

Weber, however, was not satisfied with mere criticism and tried to take up Nietzsche's insights in the spirit of the genealogical method and discern a proper diagnosis. For these purposes he first coined an expression that had a central, if so far curiously unrecognised, place in his work. The term is the "religious rejections of the world", in which he resumed and generalised Nietzsche's concerns with "nihilism", the "hostility to life", and the like. This expression had a central role in Weber's work, as it figures in the title of the single piece of work he considered to be his most important, the *Zwischenbetrachtung*[7], and which by now is recognised as his chief piece of work. The full substantive subtitle, "Theory of the stages and directions of the religious rejections of the world", furthermore contains the two key words "theory" (the only instance in which Weber used this term in this manner) and "direction", indicating the concern with "religious rejections of the world" as a process. In sum, Weber's "genealogy of morals" was diagnostically interested not in the conditions of emergence of "religion" and its effects, not even those of Christian or Judeo-Christian religion, but only in the "religious rejections of the world".

In his genealogy, Weber attempted to analyse the exact conditions under which the major world religions emerged in the past, the way their ethic was "stamped" by religious or "psychological" states and the life-conduct of the most important "carrier" of a particular religion[8], and especially the manner in which certain conditions prevalent during some stage of the development process of these religions stamped into them a world-rejecting mentality. Weber singled out for attention especially two central characteristics of several world religions: prophecy, especially the concern with salvation, and asceticism, especially monasticism.

---

[6] WEBER, M., 1948a [1915], pp. 270-276.

[7] WEBER, M., 1988 [1920-1921].

[8] WEBER, M., 1948a [1915], pp. 268-270.

Weber had a particularly strong interest in prophecy. He rooted the process which led to modern "rationalism" and the disenchantment of the world, in all its ambivalence, to the "great rational prophecies".[9] He also left no doubt that he tied both rational capitalism and political revolutions, these two key features unique to the modern West, to the prophets. Thus, though he was far from identifying prophecy with the "religious rejections of the world", it is where he found the main sources of contemporary nihilism. In singling out the particular aspect of prophetic religions to which this world-rejecting mentality could be traced, however, Weber was not much more successful than Nietzsche. In some of his comments, like in his labelling of the "Sermon of the Mount" as a "religious absolutism", he even repeated Nietzsche's conflation.

Another central concern of Weber was asceticism and monasticism. One of the recurrent criticisms of the *Protestant Ethic* (and, for that matter, of *Discipline and Punish*) was that the processes that Weber rooted in Protestantism started much earlier, in the medieval monasteries. Weber, however, was far from unaware of this factor. Already in the original essay of the *Protestant Ethic*, he made reference to continuities between monasticism and Protestantism. Furthermore, one of the central purposes of his entire project on the "Sociology of Religions" was to situate Puritanism, and Western monasticism, in a comparative perspective. This led him to develop the concept "inner-worldly asceticism". Still, as Weber never got to complete the work on early Christianity he envisaged in his October 1919 announcement of his book project on the "Sociology of Religions"[10], he did not give us an analysis of the conditions of emergence of Western monasticism.

Concerning prophecy and monasticism, subsequent research along the lines laid down by Weber has done much to clarify the issue. However, arguably, the most important of them was Michel Foucault who only recognised the fundamentally Weberian character of his work in his last years.[11]

Foucault started from the other thread indicated by Nietzsche, the history of science or the will to knowledge. In *The Archaeology of*

---

[9]   WEBER, M., 1981 [1920], p. 362.

[10] SCHLUCHTER, W., 1989.

[11] SZAKOLCZAI, A., 1998a, pp. 1-2.

Knowledge[12] he has shown how the modern human sciences took for granted and analysed scientifically the way human beings behaved themselves and manifested signs of mental and physical illness within the context of "closed institutions". In his later works Foucault moved from the knowledge-axis to the ethics-axis, but was preoccupied with the same concern of how individual human beings produce, or are forced to produce, certain kinds of behaviour which then are taken by others, or by themselves, as the truth of their selves.

The parallels between Weber and Foucault are not restricted to similar interests concerning "rationalisation" and "disciplining" of society. But extend to the internal dynamics of their entire life-work. Thus, just as Weber entered a severe crisis shortly after the publication of *Protestant Ethic*, the same thing happened to Foucault. Despite the huge critical and commercial success of *Discipline and Punish*, already in September 1975 he told his friend Claude Mauriac that he felt the book was so bad that he had to start all over again.[13]

Foucault's search for the reorientation of his project eventual led him to a long-term historical study of sexual ethics, going back to Antiquity. The formal and substantive correlates of this search closely mirror those of Nietzsche and Weber. I will only focus on the issues that were singled out in the analysis of Weber's quest: the concern with the "religious rejections of the world" and the technical apparatus that went with it, and that eventually became closely connected to the modern state. As Foucault centred on the history of philosophy and not religion, his project could be interpreted as a study of the "philosophical rejections of the world", its techniques and its direction.

One central direction of Foucault's work in his last period was oriented to conceptual clarification. The central target of this effort, the problem that kept Foucault busy was not that different from the central aim of *Discipline and Punish*. It was oriented to the reconstruction of the shaping of the modern individual. But after 1975, Foucault developed a series of new concepts to better pin down this process. This includes the distinction between "technologies" and "programmes" of power, the crucial innovation of "governmentality", and the later concern with "governmental rationality", "political rationality", "techniques" and "technologies of the self" and the "political technologies of individuals". His last two courses at the Collège de France were

---

[12] FOUCAULT, M., 1969.

[13] SZAKOLCZAI, A., 1998a, p. 236.

delivered under the general title "Government of Self and of Others", and he clearly intended this as a definite statement.

His actual research in the late 1970s and the 1980s was concerned with the history of the techniques of self, or ascetic exercises. In this research, he not only rediscovered, through the work of Pierre Hadot, the ancient concept of philosophy as a way of life as opposed to systematic doctrine, but also the role of monasticism in the development of the Western self. But in his reflections on his work, and his entire trajectory, he placed a large emphasis on the question of "directionality", the "programme" or the "rationality" behind the spread of "techniques of self" and the internal transformation of this application. These reflections focused around the questions of Enlightenment, revolution and criticism.

Foucault's essay *What is Enlightenment?* is so well known today that some of its sentences have become commonplace. However, as this piece has been inserted into the banal "Enlightenment project vs. post-modernity" debate, the central trust of Foucault's argument has not been used to its full potential. Once the argument is restored within the internal dynamics of Foucault's work, the novelty of the argument, and its close links to Weber's similarly still un-pursued project, becomes visible.

The first step is the realisation that Foucault's essay on Kant has a twin, Foucault wrote two pieces on Kant.[14] The themes of both pieces, Kant's reflection on Enlightenment and on Revolution, were closely connected for Foucault. In fact, the joint reading of these two essays by Kant was a main reading experience for Foucault in the late 1970s.[15] The first published reference to this reading experience is in an important 1977 interview that was immediately translated into English. There for the first time Foucault defined his work as a work of philosophy, being concerned with the present moment and the "question as to what we ourselves are", the point that would be elaborated in more detail in the 1984 essay. But immediately after this, Foucault turns, without mentioning explicitly, to the other essay by Kant, the reflection on the revolution, and pins down as the central problem of our age the question of Revolution, in the Kantian sense of revolutionary enthusiasm": "[t]he return of the revolution – that is

---

[14] GORDON, C., 1985.

[15] This reading led Foucault to a partial reinterpretation of the image of Kant he gave in *The Order of Things*, though in a sense it was also a return to the Kant of his "minor thesis", the Introduction to his translation of Kant's "Anthropology".

surely what our problem is. [...] the very desirability of the revolution is the problem today [...]".[16]

One could argue that this was only the voice of the disillusioned revolutionary, talking in the late 1970s. But Foucault stayed with the theme. It took him six years to present fully, in public, his reflections on Kant and Enlightenment – the same six years in which he continuously reflected on his project and finally came up with a formulation and a focus he was happy with. This public presentation came in the first lecture of his 1983 Collège de France course. The first hour of the course was devoted to a first version of the Kant section of the essay "What is Enlightenment?", while the second hour was transcribed verbatim, translated into English as "Kant on Enlightenment and Revolution"[17] But the context of this lecture is of particular importance. This was the first course delivered under the title "Government of Self and of Others". At the start of the lecture, Foucault claimed that his research of twelve years (referring to the years he had spent at the Collège) finally found its point of equilibrium, and then presented, for the first time, the analysis of his own work along the three axes that would become his trademark. Finally, the lecture was the introduction to a course on *parrhesia*, or the practice of truth-telling, that became the central interest of his research in the last years.

At the end of his 1983 Berkeley seminars "The Problematization of *Parrhesia*", Foucault found an even better formulation for the way in which the problem of Enlightenment and revolution had been central to his work. After repeating the distinction between the two traditions in modern philosophy that he traced back to Kant, the "analytics of truth" and the "critical tradition", Foucault stated that his aim in this seminar was "to construct a genealogy of the critical attitude in Western philosophy".[18] A genealogy is not a ceremonial undertaking, neither is it a mere criticism. Foucault's interest, as he came to realise in his last years, was to analyse the conditions of emergence and the lasting effects of a certain kind of "critical tradition" in the West. That tradition goes way back before Kant or the Enlightenment[19], but both the spirit of the "Enlightenment project" and of revolutionary enthusiasm is not restricted to the field of politics, or totalitarian movements,

---

[16] FOUCAULT, M., 1977 p. 160.

[17] FOUCAULT, M., 1985 [1984].

[18] FOUCAULT, M., 1988c, p. 16.

[19] FOUCAULT, M., 1988b, pp. 58-60.

but includes all sorts of religious and ideological fundamentalism, and the belief in scientific, technological and economic utopias.

Thus, at the centre of Foucault's interest was not a defence or a criticism of the "Enlightenment project", the "revolutionary" or "leftist" tradition, but the question of how and why a certain kind of "philosophical rejection of the world" has become part and parcel of the critical tradition, and through this led to the current, revolutionary transformation of the world. Because the concern of Foucault was not the Marxian worry about the failure of the revolution, but the actual incorporation of a certain kind of "revolutionary spirit" into our very governmental rationality; a spirit that in its "secularised" form has become self-perpetuating, producing a self-sustained growth.

With popularity Foucault's work was increasingly misunderstood. For this reason, if one is to look for those works that are closest to the spirit of Foucault, one should not look to most of the Foucaldian genealogies of the 1980s and the 1990s but to those historically oriented sociologists, or sociologically oriented historians, who took up – directly or indirectly – Weber's project in its true spirit and not in the spirit of "Weberian sociology".[20]

These works have three main formal characteristics. First, instead of rooting Weber's work in neo-Kantian philosophy, they recognised the affinity between Weber and Nietzsche. Second, instead of arguing about the validity of the "idealist" thesis about the origins of capitalism, they went ahead and took up, with the necessary critical distance, the project Weber defined at the end of the Protestant Ethic, but especially at the end of the "Anticritical Last Word". Finally, most of them realised the centrality in Weber's work of his essays in the sociology of religion.

The thinkers belonging to this category include Philippe Ariès, Lewis Mumford, Gerhard Oestreich, Franz Borkenau, Norbert Elias, Reinhart Koselleck, Eric Voegelin and Norman Cohn.[21]

Only a few ideas will be listed below that have a central relevance in addressing the theme of this volume, the paradoxical relationship between Enlightenment, modernity and violence leading to genocide.

Elias is not usually considered a sociologist working along Weberian lines. However, the misunderstanding, and indeed self-mis-understanding, is due to the very hostile reaction Elias had to the

---

[20] SCAFF, L., 1984.

[21] For more details, see SZAKOLCZAI, A., 1998b.

"Parsonised" Weber prevalent in the 1950s and 1960s. His original project in the 1930s, however, was clearly inspired by Weber, even in details of terminology.

Though Elias certainly shared a certain Enlightenment prejudice in progress, not as a matter of complacency but as a manner to fortify himself in adverse conditions, his thesis was not simply about the advancement of the "civilising process" but rather the rooting of this process in the pacification of violence, and therefore the constant possibility of its breakdown and the reversal into a process of de-civilization. This problem, and the reason why this process has broken down just where it seemed to have made the greatest strides, in Germany, was a central preoccupation of his work up till the last minute. In his final years, he developed an interest in tracing this process back to the collapse of the Roman Empire, but this was never followed up in print. Had he done so, he may have come up with the conclusion that can be gained by putting together the titles of his two main works in this regard: *The Civilising Process* was indeed the civilisation of *The Germans*, of the Goths and other barbaric tribes that invaded the Roman Empire and thus were the effective cause of its collapse. The European civilising process centred on the taming of the barbaric Germanic tribes – whether they were the Angles and the Saxons of Great Britain, the Frisians of the Low Countries, the Franks of contemporary France, or the various tribes that remained in the current territory of Germany.

Elias may have been prevented in this recognition by his steadfast refusal to grant religious factors any role in the civilising process. Such a position was understandable and correct in so far as matters of doctrine were concerned. Christianity was originally, and for a long time, a matter of urban, therefore already civilised, population. The question was the conversion of the "pagan", and not the civilisation of the "barbarian". However, this latter question gained central importance at the moment when the – by then "Christianised" – Roman Empire collapsed. However, these questions were studied not by Elias but by his old friend, Franz Borkenau, in a work that was done during the 1940s and 1950s, but published only, with little resonance, posthumously in 1981[22].

Underlying Borkenau's work there is the recognition that the Christian church, in its entire legal and institutional structure, was

---

[22] See BORKENAU, F., 1981. On the links between Elias and Borkenau, see SZAKOLCZAI, A., 1997.

thoroughly unprepared to handle the "civilisation" of the "Barbaric" Germanic tribes. They could secure a formal conversion from the chieftains, but that meant very little at the level of the actual conduct of life. The crucial change, and the starting point of the European civilising process, came about with the rise of Western monasticism, especially the arrival of the Irish missionary monks.

Ireland was outside the Roman Empire, therefore the conversion to Christianity took there a very strange turn: the entire Church became based not on bishoprics (that were organised everywhere in the Roman cities), but in monasteries. Due to this structural characteristic, Irish monks had a situational advantage in spreading Christianity among the barbaric pagans, and in doing so, they developed a method combining conversion with civilisation. The central part of this method was the practice of monasticism as a device for education and the methodical regulation of the conduct of life.

The civilising process therefore started in monasteries. This thesis is not contradictory to the emphasis Elias placed on courts, because not only both are examples of "total institutions" in the sense of Goffman, but because the development of the medieval court, since the times of the Carolingians, was closely tied to monks and monasteries. But the next crucial development in the civilising process came about with the dissolution of the monasteries.

Weber much liked to refer to Sebastian Franck, a Lutheran minister living in the 16th century, according to whom "the significance of Reformation" lay "in the fact that now every Christian had to be a monk all his life".[23] However, he never analysed this process. This can be rectified through the work of Gerhard Oestreich.

The focus of Oestreich's work, which began in the shadow of Hintze and Weber, and also strongly relied on Borkenau, Elias and Dilthey, concerned the rediscovery of the importance played by Neostoicism in the emergence of the modern state. According to Oestreich, Neostoicism emerged as a response to the religious and civil wars of the 16th century and the "almost unbearable conditions"[24] they created, "the interminable road of suffering that threatened the structure of the state and the existence of every individual".[25] The task

---

[23] WEBER, M., 1976 [1904-1905], p. 121 see also WEBER, M., 1978b [1910], p. 1112; WEBER, M., 1981 [1920], p. 366.

[24] OESTREICH, G., 1982, p. 13.

[25] *Ibid.*, p. 39.

of the Neostoics was to fortify the individual from the inside to endure and resist these conditions. In this struggle, they put a central emphasis on education.

In the works of the 16-17th century reformers, education had a very specific sense. It was not meant in the classical, theoretical sense of erudition – the scholastics were the great opponents – but was oriented towards practical concerns, the everyday conduct of life.[26] Moral philosophy was conceived by them not in terms of abstract principles and norms but as techniques of conduct.[27] The central task of university education was not simply the transmission of information and knowledge but "the training of men for active life".[28] Thus, in the language of Foucault, the Neostoics returned to the classical philosophical exercises or techniques of self, and the practice of philosophy as a way of life. In this manner, they managed to raise themselves above the confessional divides and were, in fact, endorsed by Calvinists, Lutherans and Jesuits alike.

However, in their concern with education, the Neostoics went beyond the stoics of Antiquity not only in their attempt at the integration of Christianity and Stoicism, but also by putting military education at its centre. By the 16th century, the Netherlands had become "the educational centre of Europe".[29] This was shown both by its universities and great publishing houses. The novelty of Lipsius and Neostoicism was to transpose this advance into the military field.[30]

This resulted in the transformation of Netherlands into the premier military, and also economic, power of the continent. But it also transformed the military from within. The new emphasis on military discipline had an ethical, moralising discursive background.[31] The soldiers, especially the officers, were supposed to perform ethical

---

[26] *Ibid.*, p. 40.

[27] *Ibid.*, p. 163.

[28] *Ibid.*, p. 162.

[29] *Ibid.*, p. 66.

[30] The novelty was not complete, as several of the main founding figures of monasticism, like Pachomius or St. Martin, were former soldiers (see BORKENAU, F., 1981. Furthermore, monastic orders whose main task was the waging of war against the pagans played a major role in the Crusades (see BARBER, M., 1994, and SEWARD, D., 1995). The major difference lay in the new and explicit emphasis on the role of military discipline in a secular setting.

[31] OESTREICH, G., 1982, pp. 77ff.

duties while carrying out their tasks. The army, education and moral improvement became closely interrelated concerns.

Behind the military reforms proposed by Lipsius and his followers, there was "[t]he general idea of educating the men", an entire philosophy of man and society based on "military ethics"[32], a belief that "the subjects" education in the army involved a struggle for the moral improvement of the people as a whole".[33]

Though the explicit aim of Lipsius was to go above the religious divisions of the age, the reforms proposed not only met the approval of the different religious camps, but also had strong religious roots themselves as well. The type of disciplinary ethics Lipsius proposed is strikingly similar to the central concerns of the early writers of monastic asceticism. If Lipsius can be conceived of as a militarised version of Erasmus, he is also a secularised Cassian.

Only two aspects will be singled out for attention here, obedience and idleness. According to Foucault, the single most important concern of early monasticism was obedience. This obedience implied a personal submission to the abbot[34], and it was complete, extending to all activities, even to meaningless ones, thus amounting to an obedience for its own sake[35]. Oestreich also emphasises that obedience became, in the writings of the military reformers, the first in the list of virtues.[36] They considered obedience beneficial and fruitful on its own. The big difference from monasticism was that eventually, through the centuries, in the military context all the restrictions on obedience whether referring to "God, honour, virtue and conscience" have all disappeared.

Another major concern in the monastic setting was idleness. Since the first eremitic writings, monks of all ages were warned against the evils of idleness and were advised to perform both spiritual exercises and manual work in order to fight this evil. Just as obedience was of such importance that it justified in the monastic setting the performance of completely pointless commands, Cassian also mentions approvingly the case of the Abbot Paul who burnt at the end of each

---

[32] *Ibid.*, p. 79.

[33] *Ibid.*, p. 84.

[34] FOUCAULT, M., 1988b, pp. 68-69.

[35] See the 11th Collège de France lecture of 1980, 19 March 1980, tape C 62 (11) A, Foucault Archives.

[36] OESTREICH, G., 1982, pp. 81-82.

year the products of his labour. Idleness was similarly singled out for special attention by the military reforms. "Daily weapon-practice, marching and the digging of fortifications keep the soldiers from idleness, which is the beginning of all vices."[37]

As Oestreich keeps emphasising, these ideas did not remain on paper, but were transformed into reality by generations of military writers in the entire continent.[38] Furthermore, far from a simple, once-for-all effect, there was a long-term dialectic process between the ossification of military life, "dominated by mathematical calculation and soulless discipline", and the call for the renewal of the true spirit of military ethic. A particularly effective resurrection of neo-Stoic ideals provided the "spiritual background" of Prussian military reforms, first in the 17th and then the 19th century.[39]

The works of Borkenau and Oestreich are highly compatible. In fact, Borkenau was one of the most important sources of inspiration for Oestreich. However, as opposed to Borkenau, Oestreich – who remained all his life a professional historian – never went beyond the horizon of the 16th century, and made no effort to connect the concerns of Neostoicism with monastic roots. This can be done, however, through the work of the Dutch historians Johan Huizinga and Albert Hyma, which at the same time sheds light on the reasons for the crucial importance of the Netherlands at this historical breakpoint.

The Northern part of the Netherlands, just like Ireland a millennia before, was a marginal region within Europe, where life was rendered even more difficult by climatic and geographic conditions that transformed existence into a constant struggle with the elements[40]. However, just as in the 5th and 6th centuries Ireland became a refuge for the learned men of Antiquity escaping the chaos of the continent, thus combining marginality with liminality, the Low Countries were the place "where from the days of Charlemagne until the end of the

---

[37] OESTREICH, G., 1982, p. 53; see also the expression "pernicious idleness" on p. 85.

[38] *Ibid.*, pp.79-83.

[39] *Ibid.*, p. 87.

[40] According to Huizinga, "[f]rom the perspective of the wealthy towns of Flanders and Brabant, now the heart of the Burgundian possessions, Holland and Zealand formed a wretched little country of boatmen and peasants [...]. Foreigners visiting these regions North of the Scheldt and the Meuse laughed at the rude manners and the deep drinking of the inhabitants, but they also mentioned their sincere piety.", HUIZINGA, J., 1957 [1924], pp. 2-4. To point out the parallels, such a characterisation could well be applied to the Irish.

fifteenth century the currents of Western thought met and intermingled. Through this middle region French monastic reforms, epics, and chivalry passed into Germany; and whatever ideas came from Germany to France travelled mostly by way of the Low Countries".[41] The Netherlands gained special importance around the end of the 14th century, the starting point of the collapse of the medieval world[42], when it became the scene of an unprecedented cultural and spiritual renewal. Within a few decades, Deventer and Zwolle became the centres of "Northern" or "Christian renaissance".

The central concern of the Christian renaissance in the Netherlands, called – significantly – "Devotio Moderna", a movement which lasted from around 1380 to 1520 and thus just preceding the next "Netherlands' movement", Neostoicism, with the most important Dutch intellectual of the period, Erasmus, serving as the bridge between them, was education. Their aim was to regenerate their world, especially the church, through educational reform. In this context, they gave a new meaning to the term education. As opposed to the scholastics, they emphasised the practical relevance and role of education. They called for the study of the Bible as opposed to the commentaries written on the text, as their central concern was to conceive of Christianity as a way of life. The central treatise of the movement was the book *Imitation of Christ*, compiled by Thomas Kempis that became one of the most influential works in the entire history of Christianity. The movement also produced a series of books with titles like *Rosary of Spiritual Exercises* or *Treatise on Spiritual Exercises*; books which intended to orient the faithful not towards mere contemplation but an active involvement in life. For this reason, the members of the movement were called "practical mystics"[43], and their books were used as guides to "live religion", to "extend the monkish way of life" in the entire society, through a fight against passions.[44] This was a return, within Christianity, to the philosophical way of life – which was not surprising because, as Foucault has argued in his 1980 and 1984 Collège de France lectures, monasticism was the way through which ascetic exercises and related concerns of tech-

---

[41] HYMA, A., 1965 [1924], p. 6, referring to the work of Henri Pirenne; see also HUIZINGA, J., 1968 [1941], p. 142.

[42] HUIZINGA, J., 1990 [1924].

[43] *Ibid.*, p. 114.

[44] *Ibid.*, p. 161.

niques of self and the philosophical way of life were integrated into Christianity.

Though being close to monastic circles, the main figures of the Christian renaissance explicitly tried to avoid closing themselves into monasteries and being just another movement of monastic reform. They founded secular houses like the "Brethren of Common Life". But their most central concern was the founding and management of schools. Their reforms included the introduction of eight classes[45], of shorter hours and more attention to the children's needs[46], attention to the securing of dormitories and private lodging for the students, but most of all a strong emphasis on discipline.

The impact of the movement was vast, especially in the Netherlands and Germany. According to Hyma, the schools of Deventer and Münster invigorated education in the whole Germany.[47] But the educational and spiritual reforms of "Devotio Moderna" had far more distant and important effects, as they were endorsed and continued simultaneously by the warring factions of the 16th century, Jesuits, Calvinists and Lutherans alike.[48] Through these channels, they became the foundations of modern schooling; and through the stamp of the follow-up Neostoic movement, school and army disciplining became closely interwoven, establishing tight and lasting connections between humanist and Enlightenment moralisation and reform, social disciplining, and the formation of the modern state.

Elements of this process were analysed by Philippe Ariès in his histories concerning the emergence of modern attitudes and mentalities regarding childhood, schooling and the family, by Michel Foucault in his histories concerning the disciplinary closed institutions like asylums, hospitals, clinics and prisons, which were reflexively summarised in the central concerns of Foucault's 1978 Collège de France lectures, "reason of state" and "police" – the first being concerned with the governmental rationality providing built-in direction to the rise of the modern state, while the latter taking up a central place in political technologies. However, in the remaining part of this chapter I would like to devote a few words to the work of three thinkers who explicitly tried to capture the "driving spirit" behind the critical-revolutionary

---

[45] *Ibid.*, p. 92.

[46] *Ibid.*, p. 292.

[47] HYMA, A., 1965 [1924], p. 130.

[48] *Ibid.*, pp. 268, 274-275, 284-285.

movements, pointing out the religious and philosophical bases of this world-rejecting, world-changing govern-mentality.

If the works of the Dutch historians provide the crucial link between Borkenau and Oestreich, Koselleck's book *Critique and Crisis* moves from Oestreich to the direction of Foucault's concern with Enlightenment, criticism and revolution[49]. It is also an undertaking parallel and complementary to the works of Cohn and Voegelin, to be analysed shortly.

The work of Koselleck has a double starting point. As a historian, just as Oestreich, he starts with the 16th century, when "the traditional order has disintegrated", giving rise to corruption, violence and murder, a general anarchy that was a problem in need of a solution, and explicitly refuses to go beyond this time horizon.[50] However, as a social and political theorist, his interest was the present, the historical roots of the totalitarian movements of the 20th century and the Cold War, the superpower conflict that "allowed the whole world to drift into a state of permanent crisis".[51] Thus, Koselleck started by recognising a parallel between his own times and those of the 16th centuries, and attributed it to the prevalence of a utopian form of thought or mentality. This recognition gave rise to a genealogical design: the study set out to analyse the conditions under which this utopian mentality emerged and evolved, and then to point to some of its lasting effects[52].

Koselleck starts by arguing that the emergence of the absolutist state was the answer to the chaotic, liminal conditions of the 16th century. The absolutist state responded to a state of emergency, but did so by developing the idea of the ruler and his repressive apparatus lying outside any legal control. This situation, especially once the state managed to control the overall conditions of confusion, disorder and uncertainty, led to the emergence of an internal intellectual opposition that soon experienced life under the absolutist state as alienating. Due to the powers of the state, these intellectuals

---

[49] In fact, in his Preface to the English edition, Victor Gourevitch characterised Koselleck's work as a "critical history of criticism" (KOSELLECK, R., 1988 [1959], p. ix), exactly the term used by Foucault for his own works in his last year.

[50] KOSELLECK, R., 1988 [1959] pp. 7, 17.

[51] *Ibid.*, p. 5.

[52] The omnipresence of Nietzsche in Koselleck's work is probably due to the impact of Heidegger, Gadamer and Carl Schmitt in his formative years.

had to have recourse to secrecy, camouflage and mystification.[53] It is in these reactive and resentment-driven intellectual movements that Koselleck locates the origins of the Enlightenment.

These conditions gave rise to a dualistic mentality dominating the 18th century and the Enlightenment, and frustrated efforts to elaborate utopian plans for the transformation of the social and political order. Koselleck talks about a "series of concepts and counter-concepts that mark the literature of the Enlightenment", the "dualistic world-view" of the era that "turned the world into a stage of opposing forces".[54] One of the most important of these conceptual oppositions was the contrast set up between "state" and "society".

The positive ideas of the Enlightenment utopians were developed on the basis of a universalisation of their experience of alienation and the misrecognition of their own existential condition. They forgot both the fact that the absolutist state was a successful response to a genuine problem, and that their own exclusion from politics was the reason for their general opposition to politics and the state. Sulking on their real or imagined deprivations, they self-divinised themselves in their imagination, as "the critic [...] believed that, like God on Judgement Day, he had the right to subject the universe to his verdict".[55] In subsequent generations, the forgetfulness and self-misunderstanding became even more pronounced, the irony of Voltaire was lost, "[c]riticism gave birth to hypocrisy", mendacity and humourlessness.[56] With this, we enter the world of utilitarian moralists and prison-reformers led by Bentham and analysed extensively by Foucault.

The stage was thus set, according to Koselleck just as for Foucault or Voegelin, "for the Terror and for dictatorship".[57]

The arguably most significant and insightful genealogies of the "spirit of revolution" are contained in the parallel life-works of Eric Voegelin and Norman Cohn. Voegelin and Cohn both developed their projects in order to get an understanding of the reasons for the nightmares of the century, which they personally experienced. They knew of each other's work of which they had a great mutual respect. Each life-work has shown a similar backward shift of the time horizon,

---

[53]   KOSELLECK, R., 1988 [1959], pp. 54, 74-77.

[54]   *Ibid.*, pp. 100, 102.

[55]   *Ibid.*, p. 118.

[56]   *Ibid.*, p. 117.

[57]   *Ibid.*, p. 2.

first moving back to the early Middle Ages[58], and then to Antiquity[59], the period of the "axial age".[60] The parallels include not only the formal characteristics of the trajectory but extend to matters of content, as they analysed the two perhaps most important forms of the "religious rejection of the world", the gnostic and apocalyptic tendencies and movements. Cohn singled out for interest the former, while Voegelin the latter.

The works of Cohn and Voegelin start from the concern that was put at the centre stage in the sociology of religion by Weber, but that has been identified as a major concern already by Marx and Nietzsche: the relevance of the experience of suffering for the emergence and spread of the great world religions. For Marx and Nietzsche, this was the full story, and thus declared religion the "spirit in a world without spirit" and "the opiate of people" (Marx), and Christianity the revaluation of values and the religion of *ressentiment* (Nietzsche). This was unacceptable for Weber. He structured his first summary essay on the sociology of religions around a critical elaboration of the theses of Marx and Nietzsche; his second, "intermediate" reflections had the expression "religious rejections of the world" in its substantive title; and finally, in his last year, was confident enough to add to it the word "theory". In his essays, he attempted to theorise the links between prophecy and the promise of salvation, innerworldly and otherworldly asceticism, and the problem of teodicy, the intellectual urge to rationalise fortune and merit, but he did not, and probably could not, come up with a proper discernment between the religious experiences and the "religious rejections of the world". He did not have enough time; he also had to work in a highly isolated environment; but perhaps even more importantly, he did not yet have access to the documents that are vital for the identification and analysis of the apocalyptic and Gnostic tendencies within the great world religions.

Cohn and Voegelin had access to a broader literature and were also able to recognise the links across the centuries that escaped the experts. They recognised that the insertion of these tendencies into the world religions occurred during very particular times of lasting distress and oppression that led to a widespread feeling of meaninglessness and alienation. Under such conditions, particularly alienated and desperate

---

[58] COHN, N., 1970 [1957]; VOEGELIN, E., 1952; VOEGELIN, E., 1994.

[59] COHN, N., 1993, VOEGELIN, E., 1956; VOEGELIN, E., 1957a; VOEGELIN, E., 1957b; VOEGELIN, E., 1974.

[60] EISENSTADT, S. N., 1986.

intellectual strata developed radical ideas. Some of these, the gnostic variants, declared the cosmos the creation of evil forces, the world an alien place for the "spirit", and came up with the opposite but still closely related ideas concerning the need for the most severe asceticism on the one hand and complete licence and normlessness on the other. Given that the world for them was an alien place, not just due to the confusion of the times but due to the very manner in which the world was created, the only available source of orientation for the individual spirit "thrown" into this alien world was knowledge, as the experience of participation, sociability or love, or the sense of "humankind" so important for Hume, James or Weber in this context, made no sense. Salvation therefore was only attainable through knowledge.

In related apocalyptic currents, the imbalance based on the absolutisation of the experience of suffering and alienation was expressed in the opposite excesses of the complete condemnation of the world as it is, a desperate wish for its complete destruction, and the hope of the imminent coming of a new, faultless, perfect world of millennial peace and order.

The gnostic sects of the perfect elects and the utopian and millenarian social movements led by apocalyptic prophets were the main opponents of the world religions from the moment they have appeared in the turbulent times of the "ecumenic empires"[61], Persia, Macedonia and Rome. Though driven underground and losing appeal in periods of relative stability and order, they returned to the surface in periods of unrest during the Middle Ages, and especially at the dissolution of the medieval world order. According to Cohn and Voegelin, with the collapse of the unity of the medieval world, these tendencies escaped their prison and limits, and became, first through the sects and the absolutist states of the 16th and 17th centuries, and then through the various sorts of moralising, enlightening, reforming and revolutionary ideologies of the left and the right, of politics and science, of the positivists and the technocrats, led to the contemporary condition of "gnostic modernity".[62] It is enough to glance back to the analyses of Koselleck on the dualistic and Utopian nature of the Enlightenment to realise that Voegelin is not isolated in his diagnosis.

---

[61]   VOEGELIN, E., 1974.

[62]   VOEGELIN, E., 1952.

Through the work of these thinkers, it is possible to give further substantive content to the concepts Foucault distilled in the last years of his work, "political technologies" and "governmental rationalities", by the different directions and modes of the religious and philosophical rejections of the world. In the history of the Western civilising process, these techniques first received a monastic stamp and then a deflection into an education oriented towards discipline, redirecting the complete obedience and devotion developed within the monasteries towards the divine into a secular, and in particular military, direction, while maintaining a moralising tone. In this way, the potentials liberated by the methodically regulated, rational and efficient conduct of life not only became subject to abuse, but confusion was inserted at the very heart of personality formation and conscience that was central to the axial religions and philosophies.

This situation was all the more explosive as the secularised techniques did not simply gain a dynamics on their own, like the ideas concerning the domination of "instrumental reason" would let us believe, but became mobilised on a massive scale by similarly secularised versions of the main directions of the "religious rejections of the world", the apocalyptic, utopian and gnostic movements and their at once childish and terrifying attempts to eliminate the gap between Heaven and Earth by realising, through the deployment of modern governmental technologies and rationalities, Paradise on Earth.

The dismal experience of those movements that, fortunately, have come to their full cycle will hopefully help us to better understand in our midst those tendencies and movements that are rooted in the same acute and pathological sense of world-hostility.

CHAPTER 5

Of Seismographs and Earthquakes: Nietzsche, Nihilism and Genocide

Stefan ELBE

Can one be a saint without God?
Albert Camus[1]

Can Nietzsche illuminate our understanding of the relationship between modernity and genocide? Traditionally, this question would, in all likelihood, have been answered by implicating Nietzsche in the very processes which contributed to the rise of Nazi Germany and ultimately to the genocide it committed. Indeed, as recently as 1994, a Nietzsche scholar still has to note that, "[i]n spite of all that has been written about Nietzsche since the Second World War it remains the case that anyone who approaches his work for the first time [...] does so with these Nazi connotations."[2] As the title suggests, however, this article wishes to argue that such a position would, metaphorically at least, be akin to making culpable a seismograph for the occurrence of an earthquake. What follows below, therefore, is a reading of Nietzsche's corpus that seeks to show how his writings can be seen as an insightful and penetrating articulation of the experience of European modernity, an awareness of which can further illuminate our understanding of several key aspects of the Nazi genocide.

As a pioneering sociologist analysing the relationship between modernity and the Nazi genocide, Zygmunt Bauman has justifiably reminded his readers that despite the increase in the number of historical studies on the Holocaust, there exist relatively few attempts

---

[1] CAMUS, A., 1948, p. 208.
[2] ANSELL-PEARSON, K., 1994, p. 28.

to probe the deeper meaning of this knowledge, especially its implications for our understanding of modern existence. In his celebrated book, *Modernity and the Holocaust*, Bauman turned to precisely this task and demonstrated how the implementation of the Holocaust was facilitated by the organisation of modern societies, especially their reliance on instrumental rationality and their increased bureaucratisation. In Bauman's view, therefore, modern civilisation was a *necessary* precondition for the Holocaust and consequently he argued "in favour of assimilating the lessons of the Holocaust in the mainstream of our theory of modernity and the civilising process [...]".[3] This article, in turn, wishes to continue in Bauman's general quest of emphasising the nexus between modernity and the Holocaust, albeit by probing whether this relationship can also be established along non-sociological lines. After all, if Arne Johan Vetlesen is correct to point out, as he does in his contribution to this volume, that modernity can be understood and analysed in multiple ways, then it seems to follow that its relationship to the Holocaust might similarly exist on multiple levels. It is for this reason, then, that this article wishes to probe whether there might be an *additional* relationship between modernity and genocide committed by the Nazis.

In doing so, James Schmidt's analysis of the *Dialectic of Enlightenment* offers a convenient point of departure. Schmidt points, in passing, to the "many critics of the Enlightenment who have argued that the grand project of freeing mankind from illusion ultimately culminates in nihilism".[4] Nietzsche would undoubtedly fall into this category when he claims that nihilism is the "really tragic problem of our modern world [...]".[5] This article focuses in greater detail on precisely this concept of nihilism, especially as articulated by Friedrich Nietzsche at the end of the 19th century, in order to probe how it might further illuminate our understanding of the nexus between modernity and the Holocaust. The article commences by briefly drawing attention to the general importance of nihilism for our understanding of the violent nature of the 20th century. Subsequently, Nietzsche's discussion of nihilism is reviewed in greater detail in order to argue that this discussion can illuminate our understanding of the Holocaust in at least four important ways. It will be concluded that Nietzsche's reflections

---

[3]   BAUMAN, Z., 1989, pp. xiv, 13.
[4]   James SCHMIDT in this volume.
[5]   NIETZSCHE, F., 1967- [1885-1887], p. 291.

on European nihilism should be included in a comprehensive account of the relationship between modernity and genocide.

Nietzsche, Nihilism and the 20th Century

Long before Nietzsche was thought of as a post-modern thinker, he was internationally recognised for his profound insight into the cultural pathology of the West and the onset of what he called the "afterglow of European civilisation".[6] For the present purpose, this "earlier" Nietzsche, with his analysis of European culture is of the most interest. His discussion of the concept of nihilism, which he used mainly to denote the widespread experience of meaninglessness that arose in modern European culture, promises to be particularly pertinent for two reasons. Firstly, Nietzsche himself clearly intended his analysis of European nihilism to pertain to the 20th century (and perhaps even the twenty-first). He claimed that "[w]hat I relate is the history of the next two centuries. I describe what is coming, what can no longer come differently: *the advent of nihilism*."[7] Nietzsche identified the signs of emerging nihilism in European culture at the end of the 19th century and anticipated that the phenomenon would reach its zenith in the course of the 20th century. Incidentally, this also accounts for why Nietzsche thought that he would be born "posthumously", *i.e.* that the significance of his work would not be recognised until well into the 20th century when European nihilism would have begun to embark on its destructive course.

A second reason for paying particular attention to Nietzsche's discussion of nihilism derives from his prediction that the spread of European nihilism would eventually manifest itself in violent catastrophes. Indeed, Nietzsche identified a "tortured tension" within European culture that was growing "from decade to decade" as if towards a catastrophe: "restlessly, violently, headlong, like a river that wants to reach the end, that no longer reflects, that is afraid to reflect."[8] In another passage he remarked that "internally" there would be an "ever greater weakness of man" while "externally [there would be] tremendous wars, upheavals and explosions".[9] In yet a third passage, he concluded that:

---

6   PIPPIN, R. B., 1996, p. 255.
7   NIETZSCHE, F., 1968 [1901], p. 3.
8   *Ibid.*, Preface, p. 3.
9   *Ibid.*, 130, pp. 79-80.

For when truth enters into a fight with the lies of millennia, we shall have upheavals, a convulsion of earthquakes, a moving of valleys and mountains, the like of which has never been dreamed of. The concept of politics will have entirely been merged with war of and for minds; all power structures of the old society will have been exploded – all of them are based on lies: there will be wars, the like of which have never been yet on earth.[10]

Writing in 1944 against the background of the Second World War, Eric Voegelin urged his readers to interpret Nietzsche's predictions on the level of empirical description. According to Voegelin, the wars Nietzsche predicted were immense because the experience of nihilism was eroding the political framework which determined the purpose, and therefore also the limits, of war. In Voegelin's interpretation, therefore, the "impeding wars" conformed to Nietzsche's description of "[n]ihilism as a pathological interlude"; they were, moreover, "the expression of a pneumato-pathological situation" marked by "the struggle of instincts between the extirpation of an old and the birth of a new spiritual order".[11]

Yet even if we do not heed Voegelin's advice, and discard Nietzsche's predictions as mere hyperbole, or as referring only to wars of knowledge, this does not alter the remarkable circumstance that many of the violent excesses of the 20th century, including genocide, seem to be compatible with his analysis of European nihilism and its consequences. So much is this the case, that it is possible for the philosopher Erich Heller to argue that at the end of the 20th century, with all its human disappointments, Nietzsche is one of the few who would not be "too amazed by the amazing scene upon which we now move in sad, pathetic, heroic, stoic, or ludicrous bewilderment".[12] It comes as no surprise, then, that Nietzsche is, even today, still considered the most influential philosopher of the 19th century.[13] Irrespective of the status we assign to Nietzsche's predictions, his works promise to be a fruitful source to investigate in pursuit of a deeper understanding of the violent nature of the 20th century in general, and the Holocaust in particular.

---

[10]   NIETZSCHE, F., 1967 [1887], p. 327.

[11]   VOEGELIN, E., "Nietzsche, the Crisis and the War", *The Journal of Politics*, Vol. 6, No. 2, May, 1944, pp. 180-181.

[12]   HELLER, E., 1988, p. 1.

[13]   ROSEN, S., 1989, "Friedrich Nietzsche is today the most influential philosopher in the Western non-Marxist world", p. 189.

In fact, the fruitfulness of such an approach has long been recognised by a wide array of scholars who have related Nietzsche's notion of nihilism to many of the great European catastrophes of the 20th century. Writing about the First World War, the German philosopher Karl Löwith, for example, argued that "[n]ihilism as the disavowal of existing civilisation was the only real belief of all truly educated people at the beginning of the 20th century" and, consequently, that "[n]ihilism is not a result of the Great War but, on the contrary, its cause".[14] The concept of nihilism has also been specifically related, by Hermann Rauschning and Albert Camus, to the rise of the Nazi movement and, by Aron Gurwitsch, to totalitarian movements in general.[15] Gurwitsch argued that the totalitarian movement is "the culmination of nihilism: all its elements and all the tendencies originating therein may be found again in the totalitarian ideology". In his view, therefore, "totalitarianism must be seen as the most representative phenomenon of nihilism which has found here its full expansion and the realisation of all its potentialities".[16]

In 1949 the Munich Professor of Theology Heinrich Fries, in turn, concluded that after the Great War it was evident that Nietzsche's thoughts on nihilism were no longer the distant voice of a past pessimist, but, alas, bitter reality. The Second World War confirmed Nietzsche's vision yet again, and Fries, at the time of his writing, was unwilling to speculate whether it would be the last manifestation of European nihilism.[17] More recently, and despite taking issue with Nietzsche's explanation of the origins of nihilism, Michael Allen Gillespie has both reiterated and aptly summarised the perceived importance of the relationship between nihilism and the violent nature of the 20th-century when he claimed that "[t]he great wars and totalitarian experiments of our century have borne an all too faithful witness to Nietzsche's prescience and we have consequently come to accept his explanation of the origin and meaning of nihilism as

---

[14]   LÖWITH, K., "The Historical Background of European Nihilism", *Nature, History and Existentialism*, p. 10. Löwith's view has been supported more recently by STROMBERG, R., 1982.

[15]   RAUSCHNING, H., 1939 [1938], first published in German in 1938 under the title *Die Revolution des Nihilismus*, by Europa Verlag; CAMUS, A., 1971 [1951].

[16]   GURWITSCH, A., "On Contemporary Nihilism", *The Review of Politics*, Vol. 7, No. 2, April 1945, p. 187.

[17]   FRIES, H., *Nihilismus, Die Gefahr unserer Zeit*, 1949, pp. 17, 19. Quoted in KOPF, A., 1988, p. 23.

correct".[18] What all these writers have quite plausibly argued, is that the crucial political events of the 20th century, would not have been thinkable without the prior collapse of the spiritual and ethical ground of western civilisation, *i.e.* the advent of what Nietzsche called European nihilism.[19] There already exists, then, a considerable amount of scholarship arguing in favour of a relationship between the experience of European nihilism and the violent episodes of twentieth-century European history. The present article seeks to complement these studies by relating nihilism to one 20th-century catastrophe to which it has not yet been explicitly related – genocide. In doing so, the first step is to understand in greater detail what Nietzsche meant when he proclaimed that "Nihilism stands at the door". It is to this task that the next section turns.

Nietzsche and European Nihilism

Like most modern philosophy, Nietzsche's reflections on European nihilism result from a dissatisfaction with modernity. Diagnosing his times, Nietzsche observed that the modern European revealed an "unspeakable poverty and exhaustion" in whose inner self "gray impotence, gnawing dissatisfaction, busiest boredom, and dishonest misery" prevailed.[20] Underlying many of these problems, Nietzsche thought, was the inability of modern man to experience a meaningful existence; the question "Why?" found no answer.[21] This inability was bound to provoke disappointment, Nietzsche argued throughout his corpus, because the Christian-Platonic heritage of European man had accustomed him to thinking that an answer to the question "Why?" was necessary to his well-being. Nietzsche traced this development genealogically over the past two thousand years and demonstrated how "[g]radually, man has become a fantastic animal that has to fulfil one more condition of existence than any other animal: man *has* to believe, to know, from time to time *why* he exists".[22] It was, in his account, this desire to live a meaningful existence which eventually separated human beings from the animal kingdom and turned man into what Nietzsche called an "interesting" animal. What has come to distinguish

---

[18]   GILLESPIE, M. A., 1995, p. xii.

[19]   RAUSCHNING, H., 1954, p. 24.

[20]   JASPERS K., 1997 [1936], p. 240.

[21]   NIETZSCHE, F., 1968 [1901], p. 9.

[22]   NIETZSCHE, F., 1974 [1882], p. 75.

man over the past two thousand years, then, is that he needs a goal, and he would rather will nothingness than not will at all.[23]

From this understanding of the impact of the Christian-Platonic legacy on the evolution of European culture, the notion of nihilism emerges in a fairly straightforward manner. Nihilism denotes that state in which it is no longer possible for a man, or a culture, to experience a meaningful existence. As Simon Critchley has pointed out, nihilism refers to the "breakdown of the order of meaning, where all that was posited as a transcendent source of value becomes null and void, where there are no skyhooks upon which to hang a meaning for life".[24] Man, then, seeks to endow his life with meaning but throughout certain epochs of human history, due to factors that will be gone into below, he no longer finds this possible. The latter condition Nietzsche calls nihilism and, as pointed out in the introduction, he understands it be the "really tragic problem of our modern world".[25] Nietzsche, however, would not rest content with merely diagnosing the problem of nihilism; he also sought to identify its origins and to understand the process by which it had arrived in modern European culture. In short, he inquired "[w]hence comes this uncanniest of all guests?"[26] and found that the answer to this question could not be divorced from what has subsequently become the most famous phrase he ever coined – the "death of God".

The Death of God

For Nietzsche, the death of God was the decisive, even defining, event of modern history. In *The Gay Science* he provided the reader with his famous tale of the "Madman" which is worth quoting at some length not only because of its central importance but also because it draws attention to the kind of unsettling questions that arise after "God" loses his grip on the European imagination:

> The madman jumped into their midst and pierced them with his eyes. "Whither is God?" he cried; "I will tell you. *We have killed him* – you and I. All of us are his murderers. But how did we do this? How could we drink up the sea? Who gave us the sponge to wipe away the entire horizon? What were we doing when we unchained this earth from its sun?

---

23 NIETZSCHE, F., 1996 [1887], p. 136.

24 CRITCHLEY, S., 1997, p. 7.

25 NIETZSCHE, F., 1967- [1885-1887], pp. 7[8], 291.

26 NIETZSCHE, F., 1968 [1901], p. 7.

Whither is it moving now? Whither are we moving? Away from all suns? Are we plunging continuously? Backward, sideward, forward, in all directions? Is there still any up or down? Are we not straying as through an infinite nothing? Do we not feel the breath of empty space? Has it not become colder? Is not night continuously closing in on us? Do we not need to light lanterns in the morning? Do we hear nothing as yet of the noise of the gravediggers who are burying God? Do we smell nothing as yet of the divine decomposition? Gods, too, decompose. God remains dead. And we have killed him.[27]

The atheists standing around the marketplace and whom the "madman" was addressing, had not yet realised the implications of living in a godless universe. Yet, as the passage anticipates, once these questions would be genuinely confronted, a pervasive disenchantment might befall European culture. Moreover, Nietzsche thought, such a fundamental confrontation was not easily avoidable.

Why would a confrontation with the consequences of the "death of God" be unavoidable? The reason, Nietzsche argues, and this aspect simultaneously makes his treatment of the "death of God" unique, is that he claimed that the collapse of the Christian worldview is due to its own moral structure; the highest values, Nietzsche maintains, devalued *themselves*. Specifically, Nietzsche identified within virtually all post-Platonic Western philosophy, as well as Christianity, a profound cultivation of the pursuit of "truth". Yet this unconditional pursuit of the truth, Nietzsche further explains, ultimately worked to undermine the very metaphysical framework which had made it initially intelligible. The latter state of affairs was accomplished mainly through the discoveries of modern science. As he explains:

> But among the forces cultivated by morality was *truthfulness*: this eventually turned against morality, discovered its interested perspective – and now the recognition of this inveterate mendaciousness that one despairs of shedding becomes a stimulant. To nihilism. Now we discover in ourselves needs implanted by centuries of moral interpretation – needs that now appear to us as needs for untruth; on the other hand, the value for which we endure life seems to hinge upon these needs. This antagonism – not to esteem what we know, not to be allowed any longer to esteem the lies we should like to tell ourselves – results in a process of dissolution.[28]

Ironically, then, it was Christianity's own moral hierarchy which ultimately brought it to the verge of collapse; it was Christianity's

---

[27] NIETZSCHE, F., 1974 [1882], pp. 181-182.

[28] NIETZSCHE, F., 1968 [1901], p. 10.

emphasis on the pursuit of truth which ultimately brought Europeans to the conclusion that their concept of God "proved to be [their] most enduring lie".[29] "We outgrew Christianity", Nietzsche argued, "not because we lived too far from it, rather because we lived too close, even more because we grew out of it. It is our strict and over-indulged piety itself that today forbids us still to be Christians."[30] It is for this reason, then, that Nietzsche sees the advent of European nihilism is the course of the twentieth century as being endowed with a certain inevitability, that nihilism is the *necessary* consequence of our valuations so far.

The Meaninglessness of Science

The "death of God" might not have been such a profound problem for European culture if modern science had successfully accommodated the needs formerly addressed by Christianity. Nietzsche, despite his prominent criticism of Christianity, was aware of its ability, for some time, to avert the onset of nihilism. Christian morality, he argued, "was the great antidote against practical and theoretical nihilism" in that it "protected life against despair and the leap into nothing".[31] Christianity provided human existence with meaning and dignity, even in the face of grave suffering and death.[32] Modern science, however, had trouble fulfilling these needs and was unable to avert a crisis of meaning. Nietzsche realised, quite rightly, that science ultimately has no responsibility and no goal.[33] One of his notes, for example, reads that: "*All* science (and not only astronomy, on the subject of whose humiliating and humbling effect Kant made the remarkable confession: 'it annihilates my importance'[...]), all science [...] today aims to talk man out of his previous self-respect [...]."[34] Nietzsche further pointed towards the "nihilistic consequences of contemporary science [...].

---

29 NIETZSCHE, F., 1974 [1882], p. 283.
30 NIETZSCHE, F., 1967- [1885-1887], p. 165. Translated by Carr, K. L., 1992, p. 40. Moreover, in NIETZSCHE, F., 1974 [1882], *The Gay Science* he added: "You see what really triumphed over the Christian God: Christian morality itself, the concept of truthfulness that was understood ever more rigorously, the father confessor's refinement of the Christian conscience, translated and sublimated into a scientific conscience, into intellectual cleanliness at any price." p. 307.
31 NIETZSCHE, F., 1968 [1901], pp. 36 ,4, 9-10.
32 NIETZSCHE, F., 1967 [1887], pp. 162-163.
33 KOPF, A., 1988, p. 22.
34 NIETZSCHE, F., 1996 [1887], p. 130.

Since Copernicus man has been rolling from the centre toward X."[35] Copernicus, in Nietzsche's view, inaugurated an intellectual trajectory whereby man would become increasingly de-centred – both physically and spiritually – from his privileged position in the universe[36]. The consequence of modern science, is that "the faith in his worth, unique-ness, irreplaceability in the chain of being, is a thing of the past" – he has become an animal, an animal in the literal sense, without qualification or reservation, who previously believed himself almost a god ("child of God", "demigod").[37] In Nietzsche's view, then, science cannot create or determine its own meaning or values.

The problem of nihilism is exacerbated by the compelling nature of the insights provided by modern science. The British philosopher Bertrand Russell spoke for many when, in 1929, he insisted that any future interpretation or explanation of existence must incorporate the findings of modern science:

> That Man is the product of causes which had no prevision of the end they were achieving: that his origin, his growth, his hopes and fears, his loves and beliefs, are but the outcome of accidental collocations of atoms: that no fire, no heroism, no intensity of thought and feeling, can preserve an individual beyond the grave: that all the labours of the ages, all the devotion, all the inspiration, all the noonday brightness of human genius, are destined to extinction in the vast death of the solar system, and that the whole temple of Man's achievement must inevitably be buried beneath the debris of a universe in ruins – all these things, if not quite beyond dispute, are yet so nearly certain, that no philosophy which rejects them can hope to stand. Only within the scaffolding of these truths, only on the firm foundation of unyielding despair, can the soul's habitation be built.[38]

The compelling nature of the insights of modern science makes a simple "return" to Christian faith increasingly untenable and unlikely, leaving man with the possibility of appreciating past ways of endowing existence with meaning, but not being able to take part in them. The psychological, or spiritual, impact of such an understanding of exis-tence is portrayed well by Sartre's character Antoine Roquentin in his novel *Nausea*. Roquentin laments that "I hadn't the right to exist. I had

---

[35] NIETZSCHE, F., 1968 [1901], p. 8.

[36] See MARTIN, G., 1989, p. 12.

[37] NIETZSCHE, F., 1996 [1887], p. 130.

[38] RUSSELL, B., *Mysticism and Logic*, New York, W. W. Norton & Company, 1929, pp. 47-8, quoted in GLICKSBERG, C., 1975, pp. 316-317.

appeared by chance. I existed like a stone, a plant or a microbe".[39] At a minimum science does reveal certain limitations for those seeking in it guidance for the conduct of a meaningful life.

To conclude this section, then, nihilism may be seen as the spiritual disappointment that set in amongst many Europeans when they realised, either consciously or unconsciously, that science cannot easily address the needs formerly addressed by Christianity and yet, due to the compelling nature of the discoveries, a reversion to traditional Christian faith was no longer a viable option. In Nietzsche's view, a nihilist is a man who judges, of the world as it is, that it ought *not* to be, and of the world as it ought to be, that it does not exist.[40] For Nietzsche this is indeed the pathos of modernity:

> But the tragic thing is that we can longer *believe* those dogmas of religion and metaphysics, once we have the rigorous method of truth in our hearts and heads, and yet, on the other hand the development of mankind has made us so delicate, sensitive and ailing that we need the most potent kinds of cures and comforts – hence arises the need that man might bleed to death from the truth he has recognised.[41]

After having sought a "meaning" in all events, and after having come to believe that some goal is to be achieved through the process, modern man loses faith in the existence of such a meaning and suspects that becoming aims at nothing and achieves nothing. Consequently, "the most universal sign of the modern age" is that "man has *lost* dignity in his own eyes to an incredible extent".[42] Through his discussion of European nihilism, Nietzsche thus draws attention to the important "inner", or religious, disappointment which, like the sociological aspects already highlighted by Bauman, is similarly characteristic of modernity. As will be argued in the next section, this religious disappointment which Nietzsche describes can similarly illuminate our understanding of the genocide committed against the Jews during the Holocaust.

---

[39] SARTRE, J.-P., 1964 [1938], p. 84. This connection is drawn by CROSBY, D., 1988, p. 39.

[40] NIETZSCHE, F., 1968 [1901], pp. 316-317.

[41] NIETZSCHE F., *Human, All too Human,* III, 109, p. 78, cited in CARR, K. L., 1992.

[42] NIETZSCHE, F., 1968 [1901], p. 16.

Nihilism and Genocide

With Nietzsche's discussion of European nihilism in mind, it is now possible to inquire how it might illuminate our understanding of the Nazi genocide. In doing so, it should be clear from the outset that, as a philosopher, Nietzsche's corpus does not aim to provide, nor does it articulate, a general theory of genocide. What is possible, however, and as will be argued, is the identification of at least four different ways in which the onset of European nihilism, which he diagnosed so perceptively, may have facilitated the genocide committed against the Jews. Due to the central importance of the Holocaust in the history of the 20th century many of these aspects will already be familiar to the reader. All too often, however, it is overlooked that these phenomena share, at least in part, a common origin. Emphatically, the motivation behind highlighting this common origin is not the desire to propagate a crude reductionism by arguing that nihilism is the only or even the most important of factors in accounting for the Holocaust. Rather, the aspiration is to draw attention to the fact that nihilism (in addition to the many historical, economical and social factors already documented by historians) did play an important role in the advent of the Holocaust and that, consequently, an additional relationship between modernity and the Holocaust can be established along non-sociological lines.

The Elusive Quest for Meaning

The first way in which the onset of European nihilism can be related to the genocide committed against the Jews is by bearing in mind the unsettling nature of the experience of nihilism. Nihilism refers, Nietzsche reminds his readers, to a condition of tension, and, in Karen Carr's words, "a disproportion between what we want to value (or need) and how the world appears to operate".[43] The psychological impact of nihilism entails, in Nietzsche's view:

> the recognition of the long waste of strength, the agony of the "in vain", insecurity, the lack of any opportunity to recover and regain composure – being ashamed in front of oneself, as if one had deceived oneself all too long. This meaning could have been the "fulfilment" of some highest ethical canon in all events, the moral world order; or the growth of love and harmony in the intercourse of beings; or the gradual approximation of a state of universal happiness; or even the development toward a state of universal annihilation – any goal at least constitutes some meaning. What

---

[43]   CARR, K., 1992, p. 25.

136

all these notions have in common is that something is to be achieved through the process – and now one realises that becoming aims at nothing and achieves nothing.[44]

As Nietzsche describes it, the experience of nihilism involves a loss of virtually everything Europeans had previously lived for. It is a condition, he writes, that one cannot endure though one does not wish to deny it.[45]

The crucial question, of course, is how man would deal with such a profound crisis. One option would be simply to side-step the crisis by relinquishing his claim to live a meaningful life. This, however, was extremely unlikely in Nietzsche's view. In light of the long and formative influence of the Christian-Platonic legacy on European culture, it was more likely that the absence of meaning in their lives would produce only the opposite; it would lead them to demand such meaning with even greater intensity than before.[46] European man was thus left in the peculiar circumstance where the religious instinct was growing powerfully at exactly the same time that he refused theistic satisfaction with deep suspicion.[47] What, then, Nietzsche asked, was left to fulfil this need in light of the "death of God"? How would Europeans comfort themselves in future? Nietzsche feared that only intoxication was left, intoxication with music, with cruelty, with hero-worship, or with hatred. Some sort of mysticism, art for art's sake, truth for truth's sake, as a narcotic against self-disgust; some kind of routine, indeed, any silly little fanaticism.[48] Whole portions of the earth, he added elsewhere, might be used for conscious experiments. From a Nietzschean perspective, the Nazi movement might thus be seen as a perverse experiment which combined intoxication with hero-worship, hatred, mysticism and fanaticism.

Indeed, if Nietzsche is correct about the psychological effects of nihilism, then it is possible to better understand how a people suffering from it might turn to a powerful and charismatic leader like Hitler for deliverance from this condition. Nietzsche himself had already observed about his own times that:

---

[44] NIETZSCHE, F., 1968 [1901], p. 12.

[45] NIETZSCHE, F., 1968 [1901], p. 13.

[46] NIETZSCHE, F., 1998 [1889], p. 119.

[47] NIETZSCHE, F., 1989 [1886], p. 66.

[48] NIETZSCHE, F., 1968 [1901], p. 20.

Whoever has preserved, and bred in himself, a strong will, together with an ample spirit, has more favourable opportunities than ever. For the trainability of men has become very great in this democratic Europe; men who learn easily and adapt themselves easily are the rule: the herd animal, even highly intelligent, has been prepared. Whoever can command finds those who *must* obey: I am thinking, *e.g.* of Napoleon and Bismarck.[49]

From today's perspective it is not difficult to see that Napoleon and Bismarck were not the last to find those who "must" obey. Klaus Mehnert, Christopher Coker has noted, saw the inter-war period as "a journey from dialectic to magic", from Lenin to Stalin in the Soviet Union, and, more decisively for the Holocaust, from Liebknecht to Hitler in Germany.[50] Magicians they were, casting a spell on their populations and endowing their lives with a sense of meaning in a world otherwise characterised by hardship and meaninglessness, in a world where, in Nietzsche's words, the "*redeeming* class and human being" were otherwise lacking.[51] In the 20th century, and after the "death of God" men would, as Nietzsche anticipated, choose to worship human gods, even "the very serpents that dwell amongst His [God's] ruins".[52]

Martin Heidegger, for one, fatefully invited his readers to see Hitler and the Nazi party as precisely such a counter-movement to the painful experience of European nihilism.[53] That such a relationship between the onset of nihilism and the popularity of the Nazi movement is not all too fantastical can be seen, for example, in the work of the historian Fritz Stern. Stern rightly argues that Hitler was the cataclysmic event of our time and that "we need seismographers of the spirit to understand the faults that made possible the earthquake in comparison to preceding, lesser ones".[54] On more than one occasion, Stern turned to Nietzsche as precisely such a seismographer. Writing about the phenomenon of National Socialism, he remarks that "the zeal of the millions who joined the [Nazi] movement even before 1933 calls to mind Nietzsche's dictum: 'Weariness that wants to reach the ultimate

---

[49] NIETZSCHE, F., 1968 [1901], p. 79.

[50] COKER, C., "Post-modernity and the End of the Cold War: Has War been Disinvented?", *Review of International Studies*, Vol. 18, 1992, p. 194.

[51] NIETZSCHE, F., 1968 [1901], p. 8.

[52] COCKER, C., 1994, p. 41.

[53] See GOLOMB, J., 1997, p. 17.

[54] STERN, F., 1987, p. 119.

with *one* leap, with one fatal leap, a poor, ignorant weariness that does not want to want anymore: This created all gods and other worlds."[55]

Stern also cites Theodor Heuss (later to become the first president of West Germany) who had already been aware of such a relationship as early as 1931. Lecturing in Tübingen, Heuss inquired "Is National Socialism Germany's Salvation?" thereby drawing attention to the fact that salvation was precisely the promise that Hitler and the Nazi movement held out for Germany; the Nazis would deliver salvation and the "Führer" was to be their saviour.[56] Heuss concluded, much to his credit, that National Socialism was not Germany's salvation. Not surprisingly, though, his books would later be burned by the Nazis for their "un-Germanness". Two years after Heuss' lecture, in April of 1933, Thomas Mann too would make this connection between the "death of God" and Hitler, concluding that Hitler "this ludicrous tin god [...] has become a religion for millions"[57]. Finally, it is also worth recalling the words of Carl Friedrich von Weizsäcker written in 1982. Speaking about his own relationship to Nazism he wrote:

> It is true that I could not develop any interest in the Nazis' ideology either before or after their assumption of power. Nonetheless, I was very much tempted after 1933 to join the movement in some way or another. But that had nothing to do with the ideas these people had but solely with an elemental reaction to what Wilhelm Kuetemeyer has called a pseudo-outpouring of the Holy Spirit in 1933.[58]

In the end, of course, National Socialism was not Germany's salvation, but its destruction. Nevertheless, Stern rightly insists that there was a strong religious-mythical element in Nazism which appealed to many Germans. The spiritual disappointment entailed in the experience of nihilism, in addition to the many political, economic and historical factors already documented by historians, can illuminate our understanding of the origins of this appeal. Indeed, to the extent that the experience of nihilism is provoked by the death of God, it can even help to explain why people would turn to secular leaders for redemption from their suffering rather than mediating their hardship within the traditional Christian framework. If nihilism contributed to the success and appeal of the Nazi movement, and the Nazis, in turn, bear the

---

[55] STERN, F., 1987, p. 149.
[56] STERN, F., 1987, p. 147.
[57] STERN, F., 1987, p. 174.
[58] Quoted in STERN, F., 1987, p. 174.

responsibility for the Holocaust, then the advent of European nihilism, too, is important for our understanding of the Holocaust.

Racial Fanaticism

In Nietzsche's view, intoxication with hero-worship was not the only way that men might seek to overcome their experience of nihilism; they might similarly turn to any "silly fanaticism" that would intoxicate them with hatred and cruelty. The racist ideology employed by the Nazis against the Jews can be seen as such a "fanaticism", a secular ideology and a false religion to relieve oneself of the experience of nihilism. Eric Voegelin has already drawn attention to the important role performed by ideologies in the modern age, even equating the latter with the existence of the former. In Voegelin's view, Ted McAllister reminds his readers, ideologies such as racism are closed systems of human knowledge which serve "as means of achieving earthly felicity"; they attempt, moreover, to "re-divinise" the world and seek to "replace the uncertainty of faith with the certainty of ideology".[59] The recent work of the semiotician and psychoanalyst Julia Kristeva similarly sheds light on how a racist ideology might be drawn upon in order to endow life with new meaning. In particular, Kristeva argues that the dissolution of traditional structures may provoke temporary defensive reactions consisting of "community bonding whose only identity comes from efforts to sustain *hatred for the other*".[60] Nietzsche argued that the experience of nihilism entailed precisely such a dissolution of traditional structures. As he wrote:

> Disintegration characterises our time, and thus uncertainty: nothing stands firmly on its feet or on hard faith in itself; one lives for tomorrow, as the day after tomorrow is dubious. Everything on our way is slippery and dangerous, and the ice that still supports us has become thin: all of us feel the warm, uncanny breath of the thawing wind, where we still walk, soon no one will be able to walk.[61]

In the lack of any clear way of binding the community together and providing for a meaningful existence, there existed the danger of simply binding a community through the hatred of an "Other". Part of the attraction of Hitler's racial policy, then, can be seen to lie in its

---

[59] MCALLISTER, T. V., 1996, pp. 17, 22.

[60] KRISTEVA, J., "Comment on the Hutchinson Paper: Which Individual for the Twenty-First Century?", in KIKIN, K. K. and SENTA, N.-B., 1995, p. 268.

[61] NIETZSCHE, F., 1968 [1901], p. 40.

ability to deliver an illusion of order and meaning in a world otherwise characterised by meaninglessness.

Martin Heidegger shared a similar interpretation of modern ideology, seeing, as Michael Allen Gillespie argues, Nazism's distinction according to race as being so "utterly arbitrary" that it was possible only in an age where nihilism had "overturn[ed] all standards of truth, morality, and right..."[62] Hitler and his racial ideology gained popularity, at least in part, because together they solved the problem of meaning and values insofar as such determinations "eschew[ed] Reason altogether and rested upon his unthinking and unknowable instincts".[63] Where Reason was paralysed by nihilism, Hitler's bold instinct and deeds took over. As he himself is known to have remarked: "I decide who is a Jew."[64] It seems that the demand for meaning and order was so strong that it did not even matter that the supremacy of the Aryan race should be propagated by the likes of Hitler, with his dark hair and small eyes, Goebbels with his club foot, or Rosenberg, whom even his colleagues mocked because of his "Jewish" looks.[65] By the virtue of their ability to act decisively alone, they could, however briefly, create an illusion so appealing that the obvious ridiculousness of the situation hardly mattered. If, then, we want to understand what drove men in the 20th century to put themselves in the service of such destructive, predatory and racist an ideology as Nazism, and even die and kill for it, we cannot ignore Nietzsche's discussion of nihilism and its impact on modern, European culture.

Such an interpretation of the racial ideology also sheds additional light on Bauman's sociological observations about modernity. In his contribution to this volume, for example, Bauman points to the modern urge of "essentialisation" and "order building". Previously, in his *Modernity and the Holocaust*, he argued that: "The Holocaust is a by-product of the modern drive to a fully designed, fully controlled world, once the drive is getting out of control and running wild"[66] – claims he further elaborated upon in his book *Modernity and Ambivalence*. If, however, we wish to understand *why* modernity exemplified such

---

[62] GILLESPIE, M. A., 1984, p. 133.

[63] GILLESPIE, M. A., 1984, p. 133.

[64] EKSTEINS, M., 1990, p. 319.

[65] EKSTEINS, M., 1990, pp. 317-318.

[66] BAUMAN, Z., 1989, p. 93

characteristics, Nietzsche's discussion of nihilism, which draws attention to the uncertainty and meaninglessness of modern existence, can be seen as providing part of the answer. And, when Bauman claims that the Jews "were seen as deserving death [...] because they stood between this one imperfect and tension-ridden reality and the hoped-for world of tranquil happiness", Nietzsche's notion of nihilism can similarly point us towards some of the origins of the tension that facilitated the genocide.[67]

That the Jews would be designated as the "Other" might not have come as such a surprise to Nietzsche. He himself had already remarked quite ominously that "[a]mong the spectacles to which the coming [20th] century invites us is the decision as to the destiny of the Jews of Europe. That their die is cast, that they have crossed their Rubicon, is now palpably obvious: all that is left for them is either to become the masters of Europe or to lose Europe."[68] Yet Nietzsche himself was no advocate of anti-Semitism. If anything, he attempted to define Germany's identity in cultural terms and not political ones like the race or the nation.[69] As he argued: "Every philosophy which believes that the problem of existence is touched on, not to say solved, by a political event is a joke [...]".[70] Nietzsche himself even suggested to "expel the anti-Semitic squallers out of the country".[71] Elsewhere, he observed, "It is a matter of honour to me to be absolutely clean and unequivocal regarding anti-Semitism, namely *opposed*, as I am in my writings."[72] Although Nietzsche's thought may be anti-liberal, it never justifies itself along nationalist or racist lines.[73] After all, it was Nietzsche who recognised that "Attempts to escape nihilism without revaluating our values so far: they produce the opposite, make the problem more acute."[74]

---

[67] BAUMAN, Z., 1989, p. 76.

[68] NIETZSCHE, F., 1997 [1887], p. 205.

[69] ANSELL-PEARSON, K., 1993, p. 82.

[70] ANSELL-PEARSON, K., 1993, p. 85.

[71] KAUFMANN, W., 1974, p. 45.

[72] KAUFMANN, W., 1974, p. 45.

[73] ANSELL-PEARSON, K., 1994, p. 28.

[74] NIETZSCHE, F., 1968 [1901], p. 19.

The Biology of Hate

To the extent that nihilism describes the process by which modern science comes to challenge the traditional interpretation of the world, it is also important to our understanding of the nature of the genocide committed against the Jews. Irrespective of whether we follow the "intentionalist" school and see the extermination of the Jewish race as being envisaged by Hitler and his close followers from early onwards, or adhere to the "functionalist" school which sees the Holocaust as the outcome of unplanned and unanticipated twists of events, the fact nevertheless remains that what was attempted was the annihilation of a *"race"*. And while it is similarly true that one cannot ignore the long-established distrust of Jews cultivated by religious differences, this cannot overshadow the fact that in the 20th-century, accusations against the Jews were based not only on religious differences but also on perceived "scientific", or medico-biological, differences. As Hannah Arendt pointed out, Judaism was replaced with Jewishness. "Jews had been able to escape from Judaism into conversion; from Jewishness there was no escape."[75] The very attempt to annihilate an entire gene-pool hinges on the existence of a "scientific" understanding of the world, especially its concept of a biologically defined race.

That a scientific understanding of existence had been an important component of the genocide committed by the Nazis had also been evident to the Polish jurist, Raphael Lemkin, who first coined the term "genocide" in 1944. As Lemkin pointed out:

> Hitler's conception of genocide is based not upon cultural but only biological patterns […]. Some groups – such as the Jews – are to be destroyed completely. A distinction is made between peoples considered to be related by blood to the German people (such as Dutchmen, Norwegians, Flemings, Luxembourgers), and peoples not thus related by blood (such as the Poles, Slovenes, Serbs.) The populations of the first groups are deemed worthy of being Germanised. With respect to the Poles particularly, Hitler expressed the view that it is their soil alone which *can and should be profitably Germanized.*[76]

This biological understanding of race also assists in explaining why, as Bauman reminds his readers, the Nazis also killed 250,000 Gypsies and 360,000 mentally retarded Germans in addition to the Jews. While Robert Thurston is surely right to draw attention to the

---

[75] ARENDT, H., 1972 [1951], p. 87.
[76] LEMKIN, R., 1944, pp. 81-82. Quoted in FEIN, H., 1993, p. 9.

existence of large-scale acts of violence throughout previous centuries, this should not gloss over the fundamental difference that the Holocaust was committed in the name of a biological formulation and understanding of race and existence absent in earlier times. It would have been nonsensical indeed to insists on racial purity defined along biological lines prior to the advent of modern science.

In historical perspective this biological understanding of human existence is quite novel. An early and extreme example of such an understanding of human existence can be found in the French race theorist Arthur de Gobineau who's *Essay on the Inequality of the Human Races* (1853-1855) became influential after 1870. Gobineau claimed that historical degeneration was the result of miscegenation. Indeed, the extremity of his position is difficult to surpass as he claims "that the racial question overshadows all other problems of history, that it holds the key to them all, and that the inequality of the races from whose fusion a people is formed is enough to explain the whole course of its destiny".[77] The Holocaust can be seen as an all too overwhelming testament to the potentially disastrous phenomena that such thinking can lead, as the outcome of a scientific understanding of existence which is unable to critically determine its own values.

It is, perhaps, unfortunate that scientists were not more sceptical about the uses to which their theories might be put.[78] They might well have inquired, with Nietzsche, whether the kind of knowledge they pursued was conducive to life and, if not, whether it was worth pursuing at all. Nietzsche challenged scholars to investigate in greater detail the value of truth to which so many scientists aspired. After all, Nietzsche argued, the scientific pursuit is still based on a kind of faith, the faith in truth. But, Nietzsche asked, how is this faith in truth now grounded after the "death of God" and how do scientists justify sacrificing everything for the attainment of truth? As he argued:

> At this point it is necessary to pause and take careful stock. Science itself henceforth requires justification (which is not to say that there is any such justification). Consider on this question both the earliest and most recent philosophers: they are all oblivious of how much the will to truth itself

---

[77] Cited in HANNAFORD, I., 1996, p. 265.

[78] Shortly after the First World War, Albert Einstein did recognise this problem when he lamented the uses to which science was being put: "In the hands of our generation these hard-won instruments are like a razor wielded by a child of three. The possession of marvellous means of production has brought misery and hunger instead of freedom." Cited in LANDAU, R. S., 1998, p. 7.

first requires justification; here the ascetic ideal has hitherto dominated all philosophy, because truth was posited as being, as God, as the highest court of appeal – because truth was not permitted to be a problem at all. Is this "permitted" understood? – From the moment faith in the God of the ascetic ideal is denied a new problem arises: that of the value of truth.[79]

According to Nietzsche, then, scientists often fail to realise that the pursuit of truth for which they labour, is itself in need of evaluation, "the value of truth must for once be experimentally called into question".[80] European man, including the scientist, was thus living on borrowed time, perpetuating practices without realising that, at the core, they have become hollow and would eventually be called into question with catastrophic consequences.

The Collapse of Traditional Morality

Fourthly and finally, nihilism may be related to the genocide committed against the Jews by acknowledging the extent to which it was necessary for traditional ethical and moral precepts to become sufficiently eroded amongst those who assisted in implementing the various stages of the Holocaust. In his *Modernity and the Holocaust* Bauman rightly draws attention to the sociological factors which facilitated such moral collapse. He cites, for example, Herbert C. Kelman who argued that moral inhibitions against violent atrocities tend to be eroded when violence is authorised as well as routinised and the victims are dehumanised. Bauman adds, following Weber[81], the impact of instrumental rationality, the division of labour and bureaucratic forms of organisation which similarly contributed to the decrease of moral inhibitions. In the last chapter of his book Bauman then seeks to investigate in greater detail the "the social production of immoral behaviour". Nietzsche's discussion of European nihilism, however, points to an additional, non-sociological source of moral and ethical collapse. This source recalls the close relationship between "meaning" and "values" which has been emphasised, amongst others, by the Czech philosopher Jan Patocka. Patocka argued that: "Basically [...] values mean nothing other than that being is meaningful, and they

---

[79] NIETZSCHE, F., 1967 [1887], pp. 152-153.

[80] NIETZSCHE, F., 1967 [1887], p. 153.

[81] It is worth bearing in mind that Max Weber's work, which Bauman draws on, is itself greatly influenced by Nietzsche's thought. See, for example, Chapter 3 of STAUTH, G. and TURNER, B. S., 1988. Also SCAFF, L., 1989.

indicate what "gives" it meaning [...]."[82] The experience of nihilism as Nietzsche described it would thus also entail the collapse of traditional values. To the extent, then, that nihilism denotes the spiritual collapse following the "death of God", it also refers to a world in which, as Nietzsche agrees with Dostoevsky, "everything is permitted". As Nietzsche noted:

> [...] how much must collapse now that this faith has been undermined because it was built upon this faith, propped up by it, grown into it; for example the whole of our European morality. This long plenitude and sequence of breakdown, destruction, ruin, and cataclysm that is now impending – who could guess enough of it today to be compelled to play the teacher and advance proclaimer of this monstrous logic of terror, the prophet of a gloom and an eclipse of the sun whose like has probably never yet occurred on earth.[83]

As God and Christianity are called into question, so are the ethical precepts that were derived from it. The problem thus posed by the advent of European nihilism is that of creating meaning and value without recourse to the traditional, metaphysical sources. Until a compelling solution is found to this question, Europe would be faced with the problem of nihilism and its consequences; the hammer with which Nietzsche philosophised would reveal only hollow sounds. In this interim, Nietzsche observed,

> The waters of religion recede and leave behind swamps and ponds; the nations again draw apart in the most hostile manner. [...] Surely there are forces present, immense forces, but they are wild, primitive, and wholly merciless. [...] Now everything on earth is determined only by the coarsest and most evil forces, by the egoism of those engaged in acquisitive pursuits and by the military despots.[84]

Yet it was not only the intellectuals or the political activists who struggled with the problem of nihilism. Eric Voegelin observed that the ethical collapse signified by nihilism was also evident amongst the German population. Indeed, he argued, "[t]he phenomenon of Hitler is not exhausted by his person. His success must be understood in the context of an intellectually or morally ruined society in which personalities who otherwise would be grotesque, marginal figures can come to public power because they superbly represent the people who

---

[82] PATOCKA, J., 1996, p. 55.

[83] NIETZSCHE, F., 1974 [1882], p. 279.

[84] Quoted in LÖWITH, K., 1995, pp. 191-192.

146

admire them."[85] The elevation of Hitler to the status of a representative of the German people was only possible after the cultural and moral framework of German society had vastly decayed. The collapse of moral and ethical certainty did not only manifest itself within Hitler and his entourage, but similarly operated amongst many members of the public. In a nihilistic world, where morality and reason became increasingly untenable and where life contained no special dignity, not everyone could readily argue with great conviction that the annihilation of the Jewish race was entirely wrong?[86] While, then, the ethical collapse evident in the commission of the Holocaust must surely, as Bauman insists, draw on the insights of modern sociology, it may not neglect the extent to which the ethical collapse also occurred "within" the people, not only between them. Thus, if, as Bauman argues, "Phrases like 'the sanctity of human life' or 'moral duty' sound as alien in a sociology seminar as they do in the smoke-free, sanitised rooms of a bureaucratic office", they also sound alien in a world characterised by nihilism. These two phenomena seem far from contradictory; rather they appear to be two sides of the same coin.

To conclude this section, then, it appears that there exists a case for including nihilism in our attempts to understand the Holocaust. While it has not been argued that nihilism leads inevitably to genocide, it has been argued that nihilism facilitated the commission of the Holocaust in four important ways. Nietzsche's discussion of nihilism should, therefore, not be ignored in our attempts to probe the deeper meaning of genocide and its implications for our stance towards modern existence. In particular, Nietzsche's reflections on nihilism introduce the reader to a different, but equally important, side of modernity which Bauman, in his sociological investigation, does not explicitly

---

[85] VOEGELIN, E., *Autobiographical Reflections*, Baton Rouge, Louisiana State University Press, 1989, p. 18.

[86] What is worse, in a world characterised by nihilism, might may even *make* right. If there are no reliable standards on which to base and evaluate actions, success might become its own justification. This relationship has been highlighted by Christopher Coker in his illuminating study on the relationship between modernity and war. As he argues: "modernity was intrinsically aggressive because it was self-referential and therefore self-validating. [...] Since man had no vantage point which could provide a frame of reference from which to perceive his own actions in time, success became its own justification. A nation that won a struggle, or prevailed in a battle, validated its own beliefs. 'You say it is the good cause that hallows every war', wrote Nietzsche, 'I tell you it is the good war that hallows every cause.'" See COCKER, C., 1992.

draw upon. Bauman's valuable, sociological study on the relationship between modernity and the Holocaust may thus be complemented by further analysis which takes into consideration the "inner" experience of meaninglessness which is similarly characteristic of modernity. An additional and welcome consequence, moreover, would be the recognition that it is more fruitful to use Nietzsche corpus for gaining additional insights about the nature of modern existence, than it is holding him accountable for the very disappointments of modernity which he sought to address.

Nihilism, the Enlightenment and Modernity

In light of the persistent experience of nihilism evident in European modernity, one must question, with Alexander Nehamas, the adequacy of the commonplace characterisation of modernity as "an overcoming of tradition as the result of radical progress in scientific, technological, economic, social, and perhaps even moral practices". As Nehamas rightly argues, it is possible to identify an equally commonplace attitude in modernity which contrasts with the "social, progressive, optimistic understanding of modernity", namely a questioning of rationality and "a sense that pre-modern civilisation involved a wholeness and unity that have now been irredeemably fragmented".[87] Does this pessimistic, or disappointing, side to modernity imply, however, that we should simply reject the Enlightenment and modernity for failing to address important human needs which can be ignored only at great peril? Based on Nietzsche's discussion of European nihilism there are two reasons why this is *not* necessarily so. Firstly, it is worth remembering that Nietzsche's discussion of the Enlightenment and of modernity are not of central importance for his understanding of nihilism because he locates this problem in a much greater historical tradition. While the problem of nihilism surfaces in modernity, Nietzsche argues that the origins of this nihilism are already to be found in Athens and Jerusalem. We must return, therefore, to the two crucial figures in the history of Western civilisation, Socrates and Christ, if we want to discover the origins of modern nihilism. Much like Heidegger, then, Nietzsche sees the problem of nihilism as emerging from a much longer historical legacy than that of the

---

[87]   NEHAMAS, A., 1996, pp. 223-224.

Enlightenment or modernity alone.[88] To simply rally against the Enlightenment and modernity would, in Nietzsche's view, be to miss the point that what is needed is a reconsidering of our entire tradition, not just the past couple centuries.

Nietzsche's second reason for not simply turning our backs on the modern legacy is akin to Bauman's argument that it does not follow from the fact that the Holocaust is modern, that modernity is a Holocaust.[89] The nihilism evident in modernity, Nietzsche argues, is ambiguous. On the one hand, nihilism is a "pathological" stage in the history of Europe for the reasons outlined in the previous section. On the other hand, modernity also opens the possibility of determining new goals and meaning. In this sense, Nietzsche also sees nihilism as a sign of "increased power of the spirit".[90] While he fully understood that "the untenability of one interpretation [...] awakens the suspicion that all interpretations of the world are false", he nevertheless found "the inference that there is no meaning at all" to be a "tremendous generalisation".[91] Indeed, while the world may not be worth what we believed, Nietzsche also suggested that, far from having no meaning, the world could be worth much more than we believed.[92] To Nietzsche, then, modernity quite laudably reopens the possibility, for the first time in several centuries of European history, of asking the question "What may yet be made of man?" The onus is now on contemporary Europeans to ensure that in the new century they attempt to answer this question without recourse to undue violence. Perhaps, much will have been achieved if, in the mean time, we agree with Zarathustra when he claims that "blood is the worst witness of truth".[93]

---

[88] For a synopsis of Nietzsche's understanding of this history PANGLE, T. L., "The Roots of Contemporary Nihilism and Its Political Consequences According to Nietzsche", in *The Review of Politics*, Vol. 45 No. 1, January 1983, pp. 45-70.

[89] BAUMAN, Z., 1989, p. 93.

[90] NIETZSCHE, F., 1968 [1901], p. 17.

[91] *Ibid.*, 55, p. 35 and 13, p. 14.

[92] *Ibid.*, 32, p. 22.

[93] NIETZSCHE, F., 1969 [1883-85], p. 116.

CHAPTER 6

Yugoslavia, Genocide and Modernity

Arne Johan VETLESEN

The horror of "Ethnic Cleansing" in former Yugoslavia is the return of a nightmare to Europe. The return, that is, of what happened on the same soil some fifty years ago, of what this continent pleaded should never happen again: genocide.

How does this recent, or rather current, catastrophe reflect on modernity? The answer depends on what we understand by modernity. If we take modernity to denote an historical epoch, and if we take this epoch to be the present one, it follows that everything that takes place now is part of modernity and thus reflects on it. According to this simple logic, the ethnic cleansing of recent years is in some sense a product of modernity and thus a problem for it.

One could, however, take a very different approach. Yugoslavia, it could be argued, is the soil of a "Balkan" mentality characterised by primitive and deep-seated hatreds, being the psychological product as it were of many centuries of antagonism among numerous groups, defined by national, religious or ethnic criteria. The aggression unleashed in ethnic cleansing, then, has a long prehistory that is characteristically part of the *Balkans'* history, not Europe's history. And as for the role of modernity, the historical fact is that we are here talking about a region where the political ideals of which modernity prides itself – democracy, pluralism, tolerance – have never really become integrated in the population's mentality. Hence, when genocide emerges in this particular part of Europe today, this genocide cannot be taken to be a product of modernity; instead it is to be viewed as a misdeed fed by a pre-modern, or perhaps even anti-modern, mentality in a region that has simply never been modernised – in the political sense of the Enlightenment – the way the rest of Europe has. The effect of this approach, then, is that it absolves modernity of any responsibility as far as the Balkan genocide is concerned.

151

Before proceeding, let us note that "modernity" doesn't designate the same thing in the two different approaches; and this of course makes it difficult to draw a direct comparison between them. Whereas the first approach employs "modernity" in an epochal sense, the second employs it in a political and cultural one. Taken epochally, modernity can be said to label the period of European history inaugurated intellectually by the writings of Kant in the late 17th century; alternatively, modernity is the name of the period whose beginning was marked by "spinning Jenny" and the industrial revolution in England, only gradually to spread to other parts of Europe. By contrast, when taken politically and culturally, modernity can be said to refer to a set of specific ideas concerning the proper organisation of economic, social, and political life in society; these ideas are normative ideas equipping the society in question with ideals about how best to go about organising itself as a moral, legal, and political community, in a word, as a self-conscious political project.

As we know, a large number of Western commentators on events in former Yugoslavia have stressed the role played by the Balkan mentality. In this way, what happened there is explained by causes allegedly distinct to that region, its history and its people. The reasons for ethnic cleansing are Balkan reasons, not reasons pointing to features of modernity. I take it that this view holds the epochal sense of modernity to be too general, too global to be able to explain why this genocide happened at this particular time in this particular part of Europe. Furthermore, and more explicitly, this view holds that Yugoslavia is a nation where democracy historically has never taken hold, meaning that what happens there cannot be seen to reflect on modernity in its second sense as political modernity.

Rejecting both senses of modernity as suitable to explain genocide in former Yugoslavia, the view I have described resembles the *Sonderweg* theory about the Nazi genocide against the Jews. According to this theory, the causes explaining the latter will be specifically German causes; it will suffice, that is, to inquire into the particularities of German history in order to identify the factors that, in sum, produced genocide German style. Indeed, the better the grasp one succeeds in getting on these particular German factors, the more one will come to recognise how specifically German this genocide was. It is the difference between Germany and the rest of Europe which explains why the genocide took place in Germany and not elsewhere. As Helmuth Plessner sought to demonstrate in his book *Die verspätete Nation*, written in the mid-thirties, it is precisely Germany's deviation from the evolutionary path of countries such as England and France that makes the rise of a totalitarian regime with genocidal goals an historical fact in Germany at this time. Since the values of liberal democracy, hence of political modernity in the sense given, are so much more entrenched in England and France, these countries continue to stick to a democratic path even in times of global economic crisis where Germany responds with the popular election of a self-proclaimed dictator. In seizing power by means of mass-support, Hitler unfailingly and systematically appealed to the history and values of *das deutsche Volk* which he claimed were threatened by exterior as well as interior enemies. As for the Holocaust, its rationale was specifically German in that the genocide sought to wipe out what was deemed anti- or un-German so as to ensure the integrity and future of the German.

The logical implication of this version of the *Sonderweg* theory is unequivocal: if Germany's deviation from the evolutionary path of modernity of the rest of Europe helped facilitate genocide German style, one may suppose that if Germany – *ex hypothesi* – had been more thoroughly penetrated by the ideals of political modernity, it would have had a political culture resistant to a totalitarian regime and its proclaimed genocidal objectives. To sum up, if one wants to speak of a connection between the Holocaust and political modernity, the connection is a purely negative one.

It is tempting to apply the same approach to genocide Yugoslavian (or rather Serbian) style. Indeed, the material at hand confirming the *Sonderweg* thesis with respect to Yugoslavia seems overwhelming. For example, when one reads the *Memorandum* authored by sixteen prominent (mostly Belgrade-based) intellectuals in June 1985, one is struck by the obsession with the hostile and powerful anti-Serbian environment that Serbs are alleged to be threatened everywhere they live. The word used to describe the gravity of this ubiquitous threat is no less than "genocide"; the repetitive talk about "the physical, legal and cultural genocide of the Serbian population in Kosovo"[1] is only a case in point. The impression evoked in the reader is that what is contended here about the historical fate of the Serbs is similar in kind to what the Nazis used to contend about the Germans. The propaganda utilised in constructing the *Feindbild* is structurally similar in the two cases. When pursuing a genocidal aim, it appears to make only minor difference whether the ideology underpinning the genocidal project is of a racist, nationalist or ethnicist nature. Though admittedly prema-

---

[1] COVIC, B., 1993, p. 324.

ture, the conclusion offering itself is that the portrait painted of self and Other, agent and target group, is structurally the same in all cases of genocide in the 20th century: the action taken by one's own group invariably has the character of self-defence. To the extent that aggression is exhibited, it is presented in the propaganda as but a mirror of the aggression once displayed – or now about to be unleashed – by the chosen target group. The will to genocide is accompanied by a sense of historical and moral entitlement to what is secured for one's own group; if there is a mindset or mentality characteristic of genocidal perpetrators, it is that of self-righteousness.

Let us pause to ask the following question: if the form and content of the ideologies preparing for genocide are so similar, what follows for the *Sonderweg* perspective I have stuck to this far in order to get a grasp on the ideologies in question? The difficulty is this: starting out from premises advocated by the *Sonderweg* approach, what we find when comparing the propaganda material produced by, say, German Nazis in the thirties and extremist nationalist Serbs in the late eighties and early nineties is that the two pieces of ideological material are essentially similar. In both cases, we encounter an obsession with external and internal enemies (or one prime enemy, be it the Jews or the Muslims), with defeats suffered in the remote or recent past (World War I or the battle at Kosovo Polje in 1389, respectively), with imminent threats in the present (Jews about to take over German financial interests, or about to contaminate the purity of Aryan blood; Muslims about to take Serbian girls and women captive into harems), with the strength, solidarity and moral determination required of the entire population in the historic confrontation with its arch-enemy that is now to take place and to decide its destiny. What we find is the same all or nothing, us or them scenario, the same Manicheism fostered by fanatic ideologues and carried over into practice in the form of genocide against the selected enemy.

In the case of ethnic cleansing in Bosnia, the charge of genocide became a signal to begin genocide. In 1992, notes Michael Sells in his book *The Bridge Betrayed*, witnesses began to notice a pattern in the atrocities by Serb forces: "A massacre would take place in a village immediately after the local news announced that the Croats and Muslims were about to exterminate Serbs".[2] The logic according to which the present aggressor portrays himself as the original victim, and

---

[2] SELLS, M., 1996, p. 66.

so the present victim as the original aggressor, is brought out in the following passage in Sells' book:

In justifying the atrocities in Bosnia, Serb nationalists would point to atrocities by Croatian army forces in World War II or in the 1991 Serb-Croat war. When it was pointed out that the largely Muslim population selected for extermination had nothing to do with the Croat army and indeed had been attacked by the Croat army in 1993, Serb nationalists would shift to blaming all Muslims for the acts of those who fought with the Ustashe in World War II. When it was pointed out that many of the families who suffered worst in the Serb army onslaught in Bosnia were families of World War II Partisans who fought against the Ustashe, Serb nationalists would shift to claims of Ottoman depravity and treat the Muslims as Turks. When it was pointed out that the Slavic Muslims were just as indigenous to the religion as Orthodox Christians or Catholics, the discussion would then shift to allegations that the Bosnian Muslims were fundamentalists and that Serbia was defending the West against the fundamentalist threat of radical Islam. When it was pointed out that most Bosnian Muslims were antifundamentalist by tradition and character, the Serb nationalist would move to the final fallback position: that this was a civil war in which all sides were guilty, there were no angels, and the world should allow the people involved to solve their own problems.[3]

Above I noted that Western diplomats and commentators typically would refer to the atrocities taking place in Bosnia as the discharge of mutual "ancient hatreds" between the three groups in question. This perspective may be termed "Balkanism" in that it portrays the people of Bosnia as Balkan tribal haters outside the realm of reason and civilisation. The impression conveyed is that the people affected by Ethnic Cleansing are not our concern because they are "other", "foreign", "different". Balkanism relies upon the domestic audience's prejudices against non-Christians in general and Muslims in particular; it expresses and helps reinforce both anti-Balkan and anti-Islamic sentiments in a Western population shockingly ignorant about the history of Yugoslavia and its different ethnic and religious groups; ignorant, that is to say, not least of Bosnia's history as a multi-ethnic and multi-religious society. In effect, Balkanism is

the distorted depiction of the people of south-eastern Europe as barbaric with the implication that violence, even genocide, is inevitable there and part of the local culture.[4]

---

[3] *Ibid.*, pp. 66-67.
[4] *Ibid.*, p. 125.

The psychological and moral message of the Balkanism paid lip-service to by Western Presidents and top diplomatic envoys is simple: as Westerners and people of the civilised world, we can only feel alienation when confronted with the blood-letting in the Balkans; because of the peculiar history of this part of Europe, the conflict now escalating is inevitable, it was only artificially contained as long as Tito held power; there is little or nothing one can do as outsiders as long as the groups involved are driven by centuries old antagonisms now set fire to by extremists in control on all sides. "Until these folks get tired of killing each other", President Clinton said in a statement representative of Western politicians, "bad things will continue to happen".[5]

Within the perspective I have referred to as Balkanism, one can distinguish between the component of Orientalism and that of Europeanisation. Orientalism represents the Muslim as an alien "other". Extremist Bosnian Serbs charged that Bosnians were Islamists plotting to re-create the Ottoman rule over Bosnia. Bosnian Muslims were accused of desiring a state based on Islamic religious law *(sharia)*. To concretise the threat thereby created to the Serb population of Bosnia-Herzegovina, the extremist Serb propaganda accused Bosnian Muslims of plotting to steal Serb women for their harems (in fact Bosnian Muslims do not take more than one wife) and of drawing up lists of viziers (ministers in the Ottoman Sultanate) to rule the country. Not that such fact-contradicting accusations were a prerogative of extremist Serbs alone. The claim that 110,000 Bosnians were in Egypt studying to become fundamentalists was put forward by Croatian Defence Minister Gojko Susak (in fact the number he gives would represent 5% of the entire Bosnian Muslim population).[6]

But the full impact of this crude Orientalism can only be appreciated when we observe the way it was connected to Europeanisation. A quote from Sells helps explain:

> As Croatian President Franjo Tudjman noted, he had taken his mission to Europeanize Bosnian Muslims from the expressed desires of Western European leaders. Serb President Slobodan Milosevic was equally desperate to play up to Western leaders and be accepted by them. In his 1989 Kosovo speech Milosevic stated that Prince Lazar's battle six hundred years before had been a battle to defend Europe from Islam, that Serbia was the bastion of European culture and religion, and that Serbia's

---

5   *Ibid.*, p. 127.
6   *Ibid.*, p. 119.

future actions would demonstrate that now as in the past, Serbia was always a part of Europe. Tudjman and Milosevic felt a duty as Europeans to destroy the Bosnian Muslims and felt that doing so would facilitate their acceptance by Europe.[7]

The appeal by Tudjman and Milosevic to the values of Europe, meaning to Christianity, to modernity, to Civilisation, exploits Orientalist stereotypes and helps to amplify the Balkanism widespread in Western governments. Much in the manner of Samuel Huntington, a guru among foreign policy experts in the U.S., the common strategy of Tudjman and Milosevic in this case is to partly construct, partly radicalise, a polarisation between "the West" and "Europe" on the one hand and Islam on the other; or, put differently, between modernity and fundamentalism. It must have come as a piece of powerful evidence of the success of the two Presidents' strategy when no less a Western authority than Henry Kissinger, in the fall of 1995, proclaimed that "there is no Bosnian culture". As Sells points out the context for Kissinger's claim was his proposal that Bosnia should be partitioned between Serbia and Croatia (which happens to be precisely the goal Tudjman and Milosevic had had in common for years) and that the Muslims (and presumably anyone else who did not want to be part of ethnically pure Greater Croatia and Greater Serbia) should be placed in what Kissinger referred to as a "Muslim state".[8] The statement "There is no Bosnian culture" is true only to the extent, yet precisely to the extent, that the campaign of ethnic cleansing has succeeded in making it into an empirical truth about the Bosnia that emerged out of four years of genocide, as opposed to the multi-ethnic and multi-religious Bosnia that was a historical fact right up till the onset of Ethnic Cleansing – a historical fact significantly omitted in Kissinger's statement, just as it was invariably denied by the Serb and Croat extremists who saw to it that what was once a fact about this country is so no longer.

Even by its own standards, the indifference, nay betrayal by Western powers of Bosnian Muslims into the hands of genocide for four full years is utterly negative and dangerous. It goes without saying that this betrayal, in action and in words, is likely to strengthen the argument of Islamic militants that the West is "by nature inimical to Islam, thus further polarising elements of Muslim and Christian

---

[7] *Ibid.*, p. 122.
[8] *Ibid.*, p. 149.

populations".[9] The position of Muslims who seek peaceful relations with the Western world will be weakened, and such a development hardly serves the interest of the latter.

Let me continue by making, first, a logical observation regarding the *Sonderweg* perspective outlined above. If the different *Sonderwege* in form and content as far as the practice of genocide is concerned can be seen to exhibit more similarities than differences, the specialness this approach started out by claiming for each case under consideration begins to evaporate. True, there may still be particularly German reasons why the Nazis exterminated Jews, as there may be particularly Serb reasons why extremist Serbs exterminated Muslims. Be this as it may, the accumulated effect is that so many *Sonderwege* can be seen to have led to one and the same thing: genocide. At the end of the day, then, what strikes us is the commonness of the instances of genocide on European soil in this century.

But this logical point is only of minor importance when compared with the effect of the *Sonderweg* approach in terms of alienation. I briefly anticipated this effect above when talking about Balkanism. Balkanism, we may say, is true to the *Sonderweg* approach in its penchant for listing the many particularities, if not idiosyncrasies, of the groups and group leaders involved in the so-called "civil war" at the Balkans. I do not deny that there may be sound historical reasons for focusing upon such particularities. Still I want to warn against focusing too one-sidedly upon what makes "them" "out there" so special – so special as to place them beyond the reach of comprehension, compassion, and concerted intervention. For the fact is that focusing upon specialness is apt to foster alienation: instead of coming to see ourselves as sharing a common humanity and common human aspirations with people affected by genocide, we come to see them not as unique individuals at all but as so many representatives of a collective defined by purely impersonal extrinsic criteria. By accepting, if only on the level of description, such extrinsic criteria, we, as bystanders to the atrocities unfolding, accept a vital element of genocidal logic: namely that collective identity counts for everything and individual identity for nothing. Just as the Nazis attached generic blame to entire races, Serb extremists attached generic blame to entire peoples (Albanians, Croats, Slavic Muslims) for the acts of some individuals during World War II; more centrally, they attached generic blame to Bosnian Muslims for the lost battle at Kosovo Polje in 1389

---

[9]   *Ibid.*, p. 124.

and for the six hundred years of depravity, repression, and cultural genocide that the Serbs allegedly have suffered in the wake of that historic battle against the Ottomans.

Genocide *is* this generic attribution made into an ideology and then turned into a practice. According to the formulation worked out by jurist Rafael Lemkin, adopted in the Geneva Conventions of 1948, genocide is acts committed to "destroy, in whole or in part, a national, ethnic, racial or religious group, as such". Such acts include killing, torture, and efforts to prevent the procreation and regeneration of the targeted people. Genocide in the sense intended here does not necessarily mean the immediate destruction of an entire nation. Rather, it entails "a co-ordinated plan of different actions aiming at the destruction of essential foundations of the life of national groups".[10] Lemkin held the key criterion of genocide to be that violence against individuals is directed against them "not in their individual capacity, but as members of the national group".[11]

Let us now begin to see more clearly the danger entailed in accepting, or in simply failing to question, the logic of generic attribution. What generic attribution does is to *collectivise agency* and its various properties and dimensions – be they moral, legal or spatio-temporal. When the murder of a five year-old Muslim child is legitimised by reference to crimes Muslims allegedly committed against Serbs some six hundred years ago, the logic employed is one according to which an individual's destiny is predetermined: it makes no difference what a particular individual (and be it a child) says, feels or means; what makes a difference – in terms of categories such as friend or enemy, us or them, innocent or guilty, fit for life or not so – is purely collective, extra-individual factors wholly extrinsic to the individual in question. When human agency is thoroughly collectivised, in-group differences evaporate and inter-group differences are polarised in the extreme. Once collectivised, human agency is conceived in such a way that the individual is compelled to answer for everything "his" group does, has done or is said to be about to do; conversely, the group is made to answer for everything a single individual member of it has done, does or is said to contemplate doing. The consequence of collectivising agency is that the distinction between individual and group is blurred to the point of being obliterated. The guilt of one group and the victimhood of the other are

---

[10] quoted in SELLS, M., 1996, p. 24.

[11] *Ibid.*

both eternalised; they are placed beyond the reach of individuals who choose freely and in their capacity as individuals acting on their own behalf as distinct from that of "their" particular group, be it defined by national, religious or ethnic criteria. Such externalisation of victimhood goes hand in hand with the *essentialisation* of identity that is a salient feature of genocidal ideologies.[12]

The alienation caused by collectivising agency can be seen to be at work among different parties and in different contexts. The fact that such collectivising serves to alienate members of groups in conflict – or outright war – with each other is one thing, and only the most obvious one. What is also deserving attention, however, is the way in which collectivising has an impact among non-parties to, say, a case of genocide. Consider Daniel Goldhagen's *Hitler's Willing Executioners*. Whatever the merits of his much-discussed study, Goldhagen's thesis that the Holocaust was the logical, perhaps even inevitable, outcome of what he calls "eliminatory anti-Semitism" in ordinary Germans, runs the danger of implying (to lots of his readers) that these individuals did what they did because of their "Germanness". Two things happen here. First, Goldhagen's approach risks deindividualising the German individuals he is studying and drawing sweeping conclusions about. These individuals are what they are, think what they think, do what they do, because of the uniquely poisonous anti-Semitism they, socialised as they are in Germany in this particular period, have come to be infested by. Take the following statement by Goldhagen as a representative example:

> Jewish survivors report with virtual unanimity German cruelties and killings until the very end. They leave no doubt that the Germans were seething with hatred for their victims; the Germans were not emotionally neutral executors of superior orders, or cognitively and emotionally neutral bureaucrats indifferent to the nature of their deeds.[13]

The way Goldhagen uses the plural here, attributing hatred and the like to "the Germans" *per se*, perpetuates along academic lines the sort of collectivising of agency on behalf of entire groups (or even nations) that is a trademark of genocidal ideology – the very ideology Goldhagen sets out to counter. The second thing that is effected, however unintentionally, by Goldhagen's use of the plural is an alienating separation between Germans and non-Germans. If the Nazi

---

[12] VETLESEN, A. J., 1999.
[13] GOLDHAGEN, D. J., 1996, p. 369.

Holocaust is a German affair *sui generis*, reflecting as it were on what it means to be German and on that alone, it becomes unclear what the world's majority of non-Germans are to make of the story he tells. The German Nazis are faulted for constructing the radical "otherness" of the Jews; Goldhagen follows suit in constructing, and maintaining in more and more obsessional and dogmatic manner, the otherness of Germans.

However, this harsh criticism should not lead us to overlook something of crucial importance that Goldhagen is indeed right about. This is that genocide is a collective action. Genocide modern style is contemplated, thought-out, planned, administered, and carried out by a specific organised collective, by a group. Genocide is the interaction taking place between a perpetrator group and a target group. It follows that genocide is not spontaneous; it is reactive, though it must be said that the moment of reactivity – of responding to, of retaliating against, of pre-empting – is typically grotesquely overstated and overplayed by the perpetrator group so as to create the impression that the action that follows is one of morally justified self-defence, as observed earlier on.

This being so, the task before us consists in breaking the vicious, indeed lethal circle of generic attribution. A human individual "is" not his or her collective. The sort of group identity an individual is born into – be it, again, a national, religious, ethnic or sexual one – in no way determines the worth, the moral, legal or political standing, the sets of rights, obligations, and entitlements, of that individual. The worth of a human individual is not derived from the particular collective it is born as a member of. This is not to say that worth is a matter of merit, of individual achievement, so that some individuals attain greater moral worth than others. For the point is that the category of moral worth as applied to human individuals does not allow of hierarchy – be it construed collectively (as in nationalist or ethnicist ideologies) or individually (as in libertarian meritocracy). The idea rejected here is that of a *Rangordnung* making a moral difference between human individuals *as* group-members and into which they are born; a *Rangordnung* exerting a moral impact prior to the deeds of concrete individuals and evading any sort of human endeavour to alter or altogether neutralise it.

How does this bear on the issue at hand, the connection between modernity and genocide? It is a commonplace that a major difference between pre-modern and modern (or post-modern) society is that of identity as derived and given and identity as chosen. In a word, the identity of the modern individual has become an object of choice, identity has become optional. While some authors have made a career out of lamenting this shift and seeing it as a great loss (MacIntyre immediately springs to mind), others rejoice in it and celebrate it as a major gain of personal freedom (Habermas), while others still choose to focus on the uncertainties and ambivalences it has given rise to among post-modern individuals (Beck, Giddens, Bauman). Let me refer to the shift depicted here as a salient product of the Enlightenment and hence of political modernity.

The two instances of genocide on European soil in this century under discussion here – the Holocaust and Ethnic Cleansing – can be regarded as protests against and negations of the development of political modernity in which identity is rendered optional for each individual. Optionalisation of identity entails its individualisation: the issue of identity is taken out of the powers of tradition, history, and communality and placed instead, existentialist-like, as a task and burden on the shoulders of the single individual. This shift carries a moral message, or perhaps more precisely, it articulates a metaphysical conviction with moral import: the identities that matter are chosen ones, not derived ones.

National, religious, and ethnicist ideologies pursuing genocidal aims join company in rejecting wholesale the optionalisation-cum-individualisation of identity. What is rendered dynamic, a matter of changeability, in the modern notion, is instead maintained as static and given once and for all in the anti-modern notion. For *anti-modern* this latter notion of identity clearly is. The differences making a difference in moral terms between individuals are not individual differences, in the sense of individually *authored* differences; instead they are differences awaiting the individual upon his or her birth into some specific collective.

We should beware of conceiving the two notions as simply contradicting and excluding each other. The relationship between them is precisely not static, but dynamic. What does this mean?

There is a dialectic between individualism and collectivism, between optionalism and essentialism at work in various phases of epochal modernity. I may state the moments of the dialectic in awkward terms, but for all that, the idea I have in mind should be eminently familiar. Take Hannah Arendt's (or Erich Fromm's) attempt to understand the triumph of totalitarian fascism and Nazism as examples. Their claim is that the atomism of modern secularised mass society reaches a point where the isolated and alienated individuals crave for belongingness to some sort of organic community in which they, among other things, will be relieved of the super-heavy burden of having to create all meaning, identity, and moral values out of themselves in their sheer capacity as distinct and unique individuals. Put differently, as soon as the existentialist individual portrayed by early Sartre and Camus starts to become a historic reality, with all the metaphysical loneliness that goes with such a development, it is only a question of time before a reversal sets in: feeling *überfordert*, such atomised individuals start craving for the return to what they increasingly feel deprived of, namely a community which would furnish the individual with a substantial package of ready-to-use meaning, identity, and moral values. Individuals liberated from the shackles of tradition arrive at a point where they stop cherishing their newly attained freedom and instead start fearing it; the fear of freedom in its turn leads to the attempt to escape from freedom, to allude to Fromm's book title. The rest, one is tempted to say, is history: along comes a charismatic leader claiming to represent an organic *Volksgemeinschaft* of one version or the other, and instead of feeling bewildered and astray, the individuals are given a unitary direction in which they may collectively march, being many yet feeling as one.

To be sure, one may doubt the validity of this dialectic as brought to bear on what took place in former Yugoslavia. For one thing, the nationalism of a leader such as Slobodan Milosevic needs to be put in inverted commas; it is but mere pretence, a card he repeatedly has found it useful to play – not, as it were, for the sake of the collective he claims to be intent on protecting, but rather for the sake of his own concern with staying in power at all costs. On the other hand, the popular *success* with which he has played the card of nationalism – be it as anti-Croat, anti-Muslim or anti-Kosovo-Albanian nationalism – highlights the vast political potential collectivism-qua-nationalism undoubtedly appears to carry in the Balkans – in the recent past as well as in the present. Highlighted in the events in former Yugoslavia is a "revaluation of communal identity as national, and of national identity as congruent with that of a state".[14] Moreover, the identities rendered all-important in these events function as categories for the mobilisation for action – always portrayed as warranted self-defence, regardless the degree of aggression directed at the target group in question – and as categories for the distribution of fear, whereby the genocidal frenzy is

---

[14] ALLEN, B., 1996, p. 133.

fed by one identity fearing annihilation by another. The sheer existence, or co-presence, of alien identity is pictured as a lethal threat.

A lot has been said in the international media about President Milosevic – about his unhappy childhood, about how both of his parents committed suicide, about his careerism and opportunism, about his brilliant strategic intellect and his boundless cynicism and obsession with maintaining personal power. Milosevic is regarded as the embodiment of late 20th century evil, as the mastermind of ethnic cleansing in Bosnia-Herzegovina and in Kosovo, as the leader pulling the strings, orchestrating genocide as a means to instilling fear and staying in power.

But why do these people – in particular, extremist Serbs – kill? Can we answer this question simply by pointing upwards to Milosevic as the one calling the shots? There are both general and specific responses to this question.

A general, if not to say sweepingly universal and a historical response can by found in the writings on evil of Ernest Becker. Becker writes:

> In his confrontation of Le Bon and Trotter, the early theorists of "mental contagion" and the "herd mind", Freud asked the question, Why the contagion from the herd? And he found the motive in the person and not in the character of the herd. [...] Freud had explained how the mob identifies with the leader. But beyond that we also saw that man brings his motives in with him when he identifies with power figures. He is suggestible and submissive *because he is waiting* for the magical helper. He gives in to the magic transformation of the group *because he* wants relief of conflict and guilt. He follows the leader's initiatory act because he needs priority magic *so that he can delight* in holy aggression. He moves in to kill the sacrificial scapegoat with the wave of the crowd, not because he is carried along by the wave, but because *he likes* the psychological barter of another life for his own: "You die, not me." The motives and the needs are in men and not in situations or surroundings.[15]

In a later passage in *Escape from Evil*, Becker continues his argument:

> It is true [...] that most men will not usually kill unless it is under the banner of some kind of fight against evil; in which case one is tempted, like Koestler, to blame the banner, the propaganda and artificial belief system, and not the men. But banners don't wrap themselves around men:

---

[15] BECKER, E., 1975, pp. 138f.

men invent banners and clutch at them; they hunger for believable words that dress life in convincing meaning.[16]

Becker also comments on Arendt's thesis about the banality of evil:

The ease and remoteness of modern killing by bespectacled, colourless men seem to make it a disinterested bureaucratic matter, but evil is not as banal as Arendt claimed: evil rests on the passionate person motive to perpetuate oneself, and for each individual this is literally a life-and-death matter for which any sacrifice is not too great, provided it is the sacrifice of someone else and provided that the leader and the group approve of it.[17]

The intellectual debt of Becker's understanding of evil is to Otto Rank and Elias Canetti. Rank observed that

The death fear of the ego is lessened by the killing, the sacrifice, of the other; through the death of the other, one buys oneself free from the penalty of dying, of being killed.[18]

Taking his lead from Rank, Becker states that "all wars are conducted as 'holy' wars" and that "all ideology is about one's qualification for eternity"; and "so are all disputes about who really is dirty"; "the target of one's righteous hatred is always called 'dirt'".

From Canetti, Becker appropriates the view that "what each person wants is to be a *survivor*, to cheat death and to remain standing no matter how many others have fallen around him".[19] In his *Crowds and Power*, Canetti puts it as follows:

Fortunate and favoured, the survivor stands in the midst of the fallen. For him there is one tremendous fact; while countless others have died, many of them his comrades, he is still alive. The dead lie helpless; he stands upright amongst them, and it is as though the battle had been fought in order for him to survive it. [...] All man's designs on immortality contain something of this desire for survival. He does not only want to exist for always, but to exist when others are no longer there.[20]

The idea is simple: man kills in order to feel alive; in killing, he cheats his own mortality and vulnerability.[21] It is significant that such

---

[16] *Ibid.*, pp. 141f.

[17] *Ibid.*, p. 122.

[18] *Ibid.*, p. 108.

[19] *Ibid.*, p. 132.

[20] CANETTI, E., 1973, p. 266-265.

[21] ALFORD, C. F., 1997.

killing happens not as a spontaneous act on behalf of the acting individual, but as part of his group's endeavour to attain immortality. This brings us to see that the sought-for commonality of meaning, values and goals characteristic of the in-group is attained at the price of directing all aggression outward, toward the out-group: "To achieve this intimate identification it was necessary to strike at strangers, pull the group together by focusing it on an outside target."[22]

Becker quotes Hugh Duncan to make this point:

We *need* to socialize in hate and death, as well as in joy and love. We do not know how to have friends without, at the same time, creating victims whom we must wound, torture, and kill. Our love rests on hate.[23]

In his recent work, the American philosopher C. Fred Alford explores the nature of evil along lines clearly inspired by Becker, Rank, and Canetti. In a thought-provoking review of Goldhagen's book, entitled *What does "Willing" Mean?*, Alford urges that we

should consider whether much of what passes as the orders of leaders is actually leaders granting permission to their followers to do what they want to do anyway, but are too guilty and embarrassed to know. Could it be the psychological function of leaders to provide plausible psychological deniability to their followers, as well as shelter them from the consequences of their desires?[24]

In his tentatively formulated theory about evil, Alford puts special emphasis on sadism:

What distinguishes sadism from aggression is not the sexualisation of domination and destruction, but the sadist's intense identification with his victim. Sadism is the form aggression takes when it seeks to inflict its doom on others.[25]

Evil in general and sadism in particular are about the relief sought in placing the feeling of doom and the fear of dread onto another person, so as to be rid of it and be able to control it, having rendered exterior what used to be interior: *Entlastung durch Veräusserung*. In a

---

[22] BECKER, E., 1975, p. 134.

[23] *Ibid.*, p. 116.

[24] ALFORD, C. F., 1997, p. 732.

[25] *Ibid.*, p. 732.

nutshell, then, sadism is "the joy of having taken control of the experience of victimhood by inflicting it upon another".[26]

In his Holocaust book, Bauman quotes a statement made by Dwight MacDonald in 1945 to the effect that we must now – *i.e.*, after Auschwitz – fear the person who obeys the law more than the one who breaks it – from which Bauman concludes that it is time we started talking about the moral requirement (or duty) of "resisting socialisation"; far from cultivating moral impulse, modern society undermines it or instrumentalises it for purposes all its own and siding more often with immorality than morality in a positive sense. Alford's perspective is a different one. Criticising Milgram's claim that his famous experiment had shown that evil is a function of authority, that is to say, of adopting an agentic state devoid of autonomy, Alford maintains that

> those who obey the law are not just following orders. They are being given the opportunity to express, channel, and implement society's sadism, its lust for destruction.[27]

Violating a social and moral taboo – and the one against killing defenceless persons surely is recognized as supreme in nearly all known cultures – "may be experienced as equally thrilling, a transgression of the most sacred boundaries".[28]

Whereas Bauman takes the Holocaust to demonstrate that evil acts are not necessarily the deeds of evil men ("that evil men commit evil deeds we have known all along"), Alford, in summarising the vast literature in the wake of Milgram's experiment, is struck by one thing: "how difficult it is for social theorists to call humans evil, even – or especially – when they do evil things". This being so, he finds that

> the assumption that normal men might be evil is the hidden variable, the most straightforward and obvious explanation of all, the one that cannot be uttered.[29]

Again, Bauman's argument in the case of the Holocaust is that evil impulses in the individual perpetrator – such as sadism in Alford's sense – are not required in carrying out large-scale mass murder, stronger still, such affect-based impulses are downright undesired; they

---

[26]   *Ibid.*, p. 733.
[27]   *Ibid.*, p. 735.
[28]   *Ibid.*, p. 755.
[29]   ALFORD, C. F., 1997.

would only interfere with and so hinder rather than further the killing. Alford's reply is that even in a thoroughly "modern" society such as the Germany of the thirties and forties or the U.S. of the nineties, evil – the will to make others suffer – has lost none of its force and centrality as a motive in human behaviour. Far from being a structural attribute (Hilberg) or a situational one (Milgram, Bauman), evil, insists Alford, is a characterological or more precisely anthropological attribute, an attribute of man which as such cannot be "modernised-cum-rationalised" to the point of losing all motivational impact – and be it with regard to mass murder modern style. But whereas Bauman risks neglecting the deep-seated existential basis from which man's evil-doing springs, Alford risks eternalising evil inasmuch as he views it *sub specie aeternitatis*, as a feature of man as such, thereby ignoring the structural and situational conditions of specific cases of large-scale evil where in-group pressure and the like effect a side-stepping and so neutralisation of the individual-existentialist twist to partaking in evil that Alford takes as his principal focus. The one approach succeeds where the other fails, and vice versa: Bauman is good at throwing light on evil as rendered impersonal and carried out at a distance; Alford helps us recognise the nature of evil as performed person-to-person and in conditions of proximity. In the first case, evil is about destroying the uniqueness of the persons involved; in the second, about maintaining it.

Can the perspective shared by Becker and Alford – as relentless and grim as it is sweeping – throw any light on genocide in Bosnia? I take it that I am not alone in being struck by the euphoria displayed in the expressions of Serb militiamen: Arkan's "Tigers", Seselj's "White Eagles". Not to mention the radiant smile on General Ratko Mladic's face as he toasts, on one occasion, with British UN General Michael Rose, or, on a much more famous – and notorious – occasion, with Dutch UN Lt. Colonel Ton Karremans upon Mladic's seizure of Srebrenica in mid-July 1995, one of the six UN-declared "safe areas"; Srebrenica, the location of the worst massacre on European soil since World War II, an area for whose civilian population the UN had gravely declared "guarantee of life and security".[30] In particular, one is struck by Mladic's remark, upon entering a bus of Muslim men just taken captive and about to be taken to the killing field in Bratunac, the soccer stadium chosen for the killings of more than 7,000 unarmed civilians just outside the town of Srebrenica, that "I am your God

---

[30] See BOTH, N. and HONIG, J. W., 1996; ROHDE, D., 1997.

now": an appearance and a remark displaying not only recklessness (the scene was in fact filmed and will be used as evidence in court if Mladic is ever brought to trial) but exuberance: it was an act of excess. It was Mladic believing himself invincible, master of life and death.

Apart from the person of Mladic, I suspect that a more general feature of genocide as ethnic cleansing is revealed in incidents such as this one. This is the astonishing lack of secrecy. True, the so-called Ram Plan (dating back to August 1991), later referred to as the Brana Plan, headed by General Blagoje Adzic (formerly commander in chief of the Yugoslav Army and chief of military security, and a long-time close associate of Milosevic), were drawn up in secrecy in closed meeting in Belgrade; in this they resemble the Wannsee Conference chaired by Heydrich in Berlin in January 1942, the meeting when the decision about an *"Endlösung der Judenfrage"* by means of physical extermination in death camps was taken.

A central passage of the Ram Plan is worth quoting at length:

> Our analysis of the behaviour of the Muslim communities demonstrates that the morale, will, and bellicose nature of their groups can be undermined only if we aim our action at the point where the religious and social structure is most fragile. We refer to the women, especially adolescents, and to the children. Decisive intervention on these social figures would spread confusion among the communities, thus causing first of all fear and then panic, leading to a probable [Muslim] retreat from the territories involved in war activity. In this case, we must add a wide propaganda campaign to our well-organized, incisive actions so that panic will increase. We have determined that the co-ordination between decisive interventions and a well-planned information campaign can provoke the spontaneous flight of many communities.[31]

This passage is, verbatim, as close to a blueprint for genocide as a document of this type may come. The actions planned clearly fall within the Geneva Convention on genocide; article II, it will be recalled, refers to "acts committed with intent to destroy, in whole or in part, a national, ethnical, racial or religious group as such". As we know, mass rapes from early on formed a crucial and meticulously thought-out part of ethnic cleansing. A letter from the commander of the third battalion of the Serb army, Milan Dedic, to the chief of the secret police in Belgrade, Mihajlo Kertes, contains the following information:

---

[31] ALLEN, B., 1996, p. 57.

Sixteen hundred and eighty Muslim women of ages ranging from twelve to sixty years are now gathered in the centres for displaced persons within our territory. A large number of these are pregnant, especially those ranging in age from fifteen to thirty years. In the estimation of Bosko Kelevic and Smiljan Geric, the psychological effect is strong, and therefore we must continue [the practice of genocidal rape].[32]

Whereas the Nazis took great pains to remove all signs of the extermination they had carried out (to the point of faking the gas chambers as designed for taking showers), extremist Serbs, in making mass rapes a programmatic goal and a systematic part of their genocide (and precisely not a by-product of it) appear to have sought a prolongation of the suffering they brought upon their victims: the rapists, in making sure that the enforced pregnancies of their victims were brought to completion, meaning that the raped women were compelled to give birth to what this ideology designated as a *Serb* son or daughter, that is, to suffer the utmost humiliation of giving birth to and thus sustaining their tormentors (whereby, illogically, the identity of the mother that marked her as a victim – an ethnic alien – in the first place is effaced, reducing her to a mere sexual container[33], seem to have been bent upon leaving *"lebendige Zeichen"* of their genocidal doings for years – generations – to come. This aspect of genocide as ethnic cleansing, pointing to its sexist character (scarcely less crucial than the emphasis on ethnicity), may represent a novelty when compared with other recent instances of genocide.

I shall not go into the details of the atrocities committed in particular – but not only – by extremist Serbs. A few observations must suffice. As many noted early on, the genocide that took place in Bosnia was not high-tech, it did not rely on mechanisms setting perpetrator and victim apart and increasing the distance between them in so many senses of that word. To the contrary, atrocities performed as part of Ethnic Cleansing took place in a setting of proximity between perpetrator and victim: the former wanted to be seen and heard by the latter, the more up-front, the better. It is telling that, when the survivors of rape camps began to reach Zagreb from the hinterlands of Bosnia-Herzegovina in the spring of 1992, one of them made it very clear that "we have fled not from bombs and bullets but from rape and the knife".[34] Ethnic cleansing is not about killing at a distance, it is not

---

[32] ALLEN, B., 1996, pp. 59f; VRANIC, S., 1996.

[33] See ALLEN, B., 1996, pp. 97ff.

[34] *Ibid.*, pp. 81f.

about killing persons never met, never known. Rather it is about killing neighbours, colleagues, friends, lovers, family members. How can this happen? Whence the intensity of such person-to-person violence? Does this intensity emerge *despite* the closeness between perpetrator and victim, or *because* of it? Perhaps the latter. The "otherness" of the enemy needs to be asserted, nay displayed and quasi proven more vehemently in cases where at the start the differences between "us" and "them" are hard to spot. Demarcation then has to be established and maintained all the more visibly and violently: the so-called "impure" must prove his or her purity by renouncing that in himself or herself which points to impurity, even if, in cases that were not rare in a multi-ethnic and multi-religious society such as Bosnia, this meant being prepared to kill members of one's own family, or lovers, friends or neighbours. Explains Espen Barth Eide:

> By killing a member of the other group, one may kill a small part of oneself, but what will emerge is a purer, more whole person, more worthy not only of the respect of others in one's "own" group but also more worthy of self-respect. One has actively drawn a line in blood, not only *between* two groups, but in *oneself* – and in an irrevocable manner.[35]

Analysts of genocide tend to say that distanciation (be it by way of technology, bureaucracy or ideology) produces dehumanisation and deindividualisation, and the latter in turn insensitivity to the suffering of the victims and so a readiness to take part in causing it.[36] I take this to express a widely held view, one not exclusive to, say, the structural approach of Raul Hilberg.[37] But does the process from distanciation hold for Bosnia?

To ask this question is to ponder whether it is plausible that individuals with whom one for years, or a lifetime, has been close in all the sociological senses of that word, all of a sudden come to be seen as depersonalised "representatives" of a group now said to pose a deadly threat to one's own. Can we really believe that stereotypes of the crudest sort in almost no time at all reigned supreme and effaced all dimensions of long-recognised human individuality and uniqueness, so that a Serb would only see a Muslim, not his former classmate Amira or his brother-in-law Ramiz? Or is the real horror of ethnic cleansing that the known individuality of the victim at hand *remained*

---

[35] *Ibid.*, p. 83.
[36] See VETLESEN, A. J., 1994, Ch. 5.
[37] HILBERG, R., 1985.

acknowledged, giving a truly personal twist to the atrocities to follow where in the case of the Nazi genocide we have been used to thinking that the murder had depersonalisation – of perpetrator no less than victim – as a crucial condition? I am unable to answer these questions. I only note that, though undoubtedly highly ideologised from above, meaning top-down, the genocide that took place in former Yugoslavia was highly personalised on the ground.

Put crudely (and *pace* Goldhagen): the Nazi genocide of the Jews carried out in the extermination camps in Poland shunned proximity and, whenever proximity was met upon, replaced it by mechanisms of distanciation so as to annul it completely. Robbed of all traces of individuality, perpetrator and victim ended up as equally alienated and exchangeable.[38] Ethnic Cleansing, by contrast, seizes upon and *maintains* existing conditions of proximity between perpetrator and victim and in fact creates such conditions if they are not present and prolongs them as a matter of principle when they seem to wane. In this super-personalised violence, whole families were forced to be witnesses to torture, rapes, and killings; Serb militiamen often made a point of singling out for particularly cruel mistreatment persons known to them beforehand; and the utter kind of humiliation was to enforce relatives to rape, wound or kill each other. Such enforced *inter-familial* – hence intra-victim – violence was in fact a speciality among extremist Serbs, and to my knowledge we find no parallel to this, evolving into a routine, in the Nazi genocide; a systematic feature of the latter was precisely the separation of family members (husbands and wives, parents and children) immediately upon arrival in the death camp. In keeping with this difference of method, secrecy seems to have been much more important to the Nazis than to the extremist Serbs. Whether the role played by seeking to prove purity where impurity has long prevailed, of attaining homogeneity where there is mixture, simple identity where there used to be a plurality, is what fosters the deliberate sadism and sheer perversion of much of the up-front, person-to-person, village-to-village killings in Bosnia, I can only speculate.

Is there a link from this to certain principles set out by the Enlightenment? In his important book *Act and Idea in the Nazi Genocide*, Berel Lang argues for a strong continuity between Kant's Enlightenment and the Nazi genocide against the Jews. Lang singles out Kant's well-known principle of universalisation for special

---

[38] ARENDT, H., 1951.

attention here. Kant links the test of universalisation to the traits that distinguish human beings as human beings (and so as ends in themselves; it is on the basis of those traits – *i.e.* of the "noumenal" or extra-historical self – that man's claim to moral status depends. On this basis, too, human beings are by definition alike in their essential nature. Thus, for Kant, "any differences which foster apparent distinctions among human beings are thus at best morally irrelevant; at worst, insofar as they may obstruct the process of universalisation, they are moral liabilities". In short, "Kant makes universalisability into a condition of moral value, overriding any apparent differences in circumstance".[39] Now, as far as the application of the categorical imperative is concerned, individual or group differences are at best irrelevant; at worst such differences become hindrances or obstacles which then have to be overcome.[40] Lang's claim is that

> it is the theme and thesis of universalism [...] which in its later structural turns would be incorporated in the structural framework of the phenomenon of genocide.[41]

According to Lang, then, the critical light cast upon Kant's celebrated universalistic ethics by the Nazi genocide is this. Universalism is opposed to all claims for particularism. To the extent that the Enlightenment focuses on what all men have in common so as to ensure freedom and equality for everyone, all citizens are subjected to

> an obligation to commit themselves to those (universalistic) ideals by renouncing the differences that had characterized (whether as cause or effect) their previous tutelage.

Lang observes,

> To choose to maintain differences of cult or custom – and thus, more fundamentally, of identity – in the face of an offer of commonality could itself serve as evidence that the offer had been misconceived.[42]

What happens in the wake of the intellectual hegemony of the ideas of universalism and universalisation in moral reasoning is that individuals and groups who henceforth wish to retain for themselves a distinct identity, meaning a particularity *vis-à-vis* what is deemed common and universal, thereby assume the burden of justification –

---

[39] LANG, B., 1990, p. 175.
[40] *Ibid.*, p. 177.
[41] *Ibid.*, p. 178.
[42] *Ibid.*, p. 184.

and this burden, Lang wants to show, cannot be redeemed, given the intellectual and historical reign of Enlightenment universalism:

> In a social or conceptual structure which stresses equality of rights as a function of the equality of persons, individual differences and *a fortiori* group differences become suspect and the rights that would "normally" be ascribed to them, problematic.[43]

Since the Jews after the Enlightenment hardly less than before it retained an identity set in their own terms", this "was bound to test severely any prescription for universalism".[44] In concrete terms:

> The "difference" of the Jews was judged by the Nazis to be fundamental – and with this decision, there was nothing to inhibit the decision subsequently made about what followed from that judgement: there was no "reason" *not* to destroy the difference.[45]

Lang's conclusion is unequivocal:

> The Jews were all to clearly a test of what the impulse of universalization, detached from history and radically extended, would tolerate.[46]

In other words, the fateful bias of Kantian universalism is that it guarantees universal rights for all universalists – be they individuals or groups, customs or cultures – but provides no barrier against the effacement (to the point of physical extinction) of stubborn particularities.

I think that Lang's attack misses the mark. In a (further) criticism of Kant reminiscent of Sandel's criticism of the "unencumbered self" in Rawls's contract theory, Lang writes that

> Whatever else membership in a group or polity does for or to the individual, it does not constitute him as a person [...] it follows, then, that group identity – religious, social, political – is accidental and, where it exists, always defeasible.[47]

Indeed, this is Kant's view, representative of the Enlightenment. And on this point, history – especially the history of genocide – has taught us that Kant is right. For what would be the logical antiposition to the one correctly attributed to Kant here? It would be that

---

[43] *Ibid.*, p. 186.
[44] *Ibid.*, p. 204.
[45] *Ibid.*, p. 195.
[46] *Ibid.*, p. 205.
[47] *Ibid.*, p. 180.

membership in some particular group does indeed constitute the individual as a person, and as a moral person, at that. Furthermore, this position would hold that group identity is not accidental and, therefore, never defeasible; instead, group identity is essential, there exists no option to overturn it, and it determines the moral standing of the individual. *This* view, with which we have grown only too familiar as of late, is that adhered to by collectivist ideologies of the kind staging genocide – genocide against individuals not *as* individuals but as members of some particular group to whom certain rights are denied by virtue of that membership. This being so, Lang has a strong case for the threat against particularity with which Kant's formal universalism is pregnant. But Lang perpetuates rather than negates the thinking behind genocide when he rejects the Kantian primacy of individual autonomy and responsibility over collective identity.[48] The enduring strength of Kant's position consists in holding the *Würde* of the human person as intrinsic to the person, hence as absolute and so not as dependent on the particularity, and contingency, of the person's belongingness to some collective.

We need to appreciate more exactly how identities were constructed and acted upon in the historical context that facilitated (I do not say produced) ethnic cleansing. To my knowledge, Michael Sells is alone among academic analysts of the Bosnian genocide in placing his major emphasis on the *religious* dimension. His book's focus is on "a national mythology that portrays Slavic Muslims as Christ killers and race traitors".[49] Sells' claim is that

> Those who have been singled out for persecution have fallen on the wrong side of a dividing line based solely on religious identity.[50]

According to the religious ideology in question, Slavic Muslims, by converting to Islam, "turkified". "To convert to a religion other than Christianity was simultaneously to convert from the Slav race to an alien race".[51]

In the novels of Ivo Andric, Nobel laureate in literature, the Bosnian Slavs who converted to Islam represent the corrupted "Orient" that cut off the Slavic race from the "civilising currents" of the West. The major premise in this outlook is that Slavs are racially Christian; a

---

[48] *Ibid.*, p. 193 (bottom).

[49] SELLS, M., 1996, p. 27.

[50] *Ibid.*, p. 13.

[51] *Ibid.*, p. 45.

Slav who converted from Christianity to Islam must have done so out of greed or cowardice. Sells terms "Christoslavism" the ideology that Slavs are by essence Christian and that conversion to another religion is a betrayal of the race or people. Christoslavism

> places Muslims and any Christian who would tolerate them in the position of the Judas figure of the battle at Kosovo Polje, Vuk Brankovic. Brankovic is the Serb who betrayed the battle plans to the Ottoman army and who is held responsible for the killing of Prince Lazar, the head of the Serb army. Hence Braskovic becomes the Christ killer within. In the Serb nationalist myth, he represents the Slavs who converted to Islam under the Ottomans and "any Serb who would live with them or tolerate them".[52]

According to Sells, the six hundred year old ideology of Christoslavism effectively

> sets the Slavic Muslims outside the boundaries of nation, race, and people [...] it demonstrates what can be done to those defined as nonpeople and what is, under certain circumstances, a religious duty and a sacred, cleansing act.

As brought to bear on our issue:

> In their acts of genocide from 1992 through 1995, Radovan Karadzic and his followers integrated the Kosovo tradition, as it was handed down through Vuk Brankovic and transformed by Njegos and Andric, into the daily rituals of ethnoreligious purification.[53]

The same ideology was applied to the situation in Kosovo from 1985 onwards. The charge of cultural genocide against the Serbs in Kosovo was a signal that the Serb nation was again being crucified; as Sells notes,

> the archetype of national myth was tied into the actual situation in Kosovo province. The relics of Lazar were paraded around the province of Kosovo as a reminder of the killing of the Christ-Prince and as a territorial claim.[54]

What we see at work here – and immensely forcefully so – is the crucial ideological importance of the *chosen trauma*. In particular, the lost battle at Kosovo Polje in 1389 was to serve as the prime symbol of the afflictions dealt the Serbs by the "Turks" throughout the last six centuries. The wrongs allegedly suffered in the past are evoked again

---

[52] *Ibid.*, p. 31.

[53] *Ibid.*, p. 51.

[54] *Ibid.*, p. 59.

and again so as to elicit fear of present or future threats from the same enemy. Memory is selective; but here remembrance of things past is employed in the service of retaliation not forgiveness or reconciliation. Kosovo Polje 1389 is made into an event that is not allowed to fade away; it is recalled for the sake of mobilisation for what is to ensue: recollection of "favourite" wrongs serves to legitimise the wrongs of tomorrow, only this time around the roles of aggressor and victim will be reversed. This bespeaks the simple logic of retaliation. It seems to me that especially in cases of highly ideologised warfare, memory is limitlessly exploitable.[55] For the Serbs addressed by Milosevic's and Karadzic's propaganda, it became a "duty not to forget" (Bauman). And now, after Srebrenica, we may expect that Bosnian Muslims have got an object for *their* version of the duty not to forget. Forgetting can be dangerous, just as not-forgetting. As journalist David Rohde remarks, "A young Ratko Mladic may have been born during the fall of Srebrenica".[56] In an ideological atmosphere pervaded by the idea of retaliation, the generations to come on both sides are likely to be brought up on tales of atrocities committed against his people. Here again, the group is made to answer for what the individual did, just as the individual is made to answer for what the (his or her) group did – or allegedly intends doing.

Readers of Sells' book who are not knowledgeable about Bosnian culture and society might easily get the impression that in everyday life and prior to the so-called civil war that broke out in April 1992, Bosnia was a society where religion constituted an all-important identity mark among the people. Not so. It is a fact that this conflict occurred in a largely secularised society where religious practice had been declining steadily for half a century. Slavic Muslims are in fact the most secularised and integrated Muslims on the European continent; less than 3% attend prayers in the Mosques. The Islam of Bosnian Muslims experiencing the events from 1992 onwards no doubt is that of a people in distress, feeling increasingly abandoned by a Europe which, for its part, increasingly started to buy into the Serb ethno-nationalist propaganda that "the Turks" were about to gain cultural and religious hegemony in the heart of Europe. In this way, as we have seen, the Slavic Muslims were played against the West, with the Serb leaders presenting themselves as defenders of Western values and "Civilisation" now being threatened by a wave of Islamic fundamentalism in

---

[55] KASCHUBA, W., 1999.

[56] ROHDE, D., 1997, p. 375.

Bosnia. However, there is little evidence to suggest that this revived emphasis on Muslim identity actually made a significant number of Bosnian Muslims vulnerable to the call of Islamic fundamentalism.[57]

Thus, when Sells maintains that the primary victims of the genocide have been Bosnian Muslims, "selected for destruction because of their religion"[58], the reference to religion must be understood correctly. The actual element of religious faith in the individual, expressed in his observance of rituals and prayers, in abstaining from drinking alcohol, and the like, makes no difference here as far as the ethno-religious ideology depicted by Sells is concerned. What matters is, again, the generic attribution: the attribution of collective guilt to a whole group for Christ-killing and religious and race betrayal. Considered historically, within the context of developments in Yugoslavia, what gives the "Muslims" their group identity as Muslims is not the religious faith and expression of such among individuals forming this group; rather, it is something negative and extrinsic: namely, failing to identify as Orthodox Serb or Catholic Croat. The background is this. In the wake of the break-up of the Yugoslav federation following Tito's death in 1980, a common identity as simply "Yugoslavs" became problematic. For the Orthodox in Bosnia, this meant increasingly identifying as Serbs, and for the Catholics, identifying as Croats; but for the Bosnian Slavs who had become Muslims, the only thing to fall back on was their cultural identity of Islam. But, as we observed above, this identity as provided by Islam was more of a cultural kind than a strictly religious one. Likewise, in the Yugoslav census of 1971, many Bosnians of Muslim background who considered themselves atheists or sceptics had declared themselves "Muslim" to avoid the categories of "Serb" and "Croat", both of which had religious implications. While this classification gave Bosnian Muslims an independent political voice alongside Catholics and Orthodox Serbs, it did so, explains Sells, "at the cost of further reinforcing the identity between religion and nationality".[59] It is precisely this identity that was to prove lethal from 1992 to 1995 in that it served to define friends and foes, and in an ineluctable and irreversible manner, at that.

Hence the "Muslims" singled out for genocide by extremist Serbs are a truly heterogeneous group. In actual fact it is made up of faithful believers, religiously indifferent, and atheists. The homogeneity of this

---

[57] ASPEN INSTITUTE, 1996, p. 18.

[58] SELLS, M., 1996, p. xiii.

[59] *Ibid.*, p. 15.

target group is not artificial; it is a fiction, a construct of extremist Serb (later also extremist Croat) propaganda.

What is the point of enforcing such homogenisation upon a group of people? The point is to ensure that there be no exit option from the group. A hallmark of genocidal ideology is that individuals are at a loss to *act* in such a way as to evade persecution. To act is to make a choice; it is to express an identity as unique author to the world, to be a *beginner* in the world in Arendt's sense of agency as natality. Now political modernity, as spurred by the normative ideas of the Enlightenment (in particular, of Kant), prides itself on placing primacy on individual agency, especially in the moral dimension, thus pointing to the autonomy of the individual qua moral agent. On this view, an individual is responsible for his actions; actions are properties of individuals who could have chosen to act otherwise.

As we know, a Bosnian Muslim was brought to a Serb or Croat killing centre not because of any particular act, expression, or thought. His "guilt" was not a product of his actions; instead of post-dating his actions, his guilt preceded them and thus rendered them impotent and insignificant as far as determining his guilt is concerned. Again, this is genocidal logic. But it does not express the logic of political modernity, nor of the European Enlightenment. If anything, the latter two flatly contradict the former.

But this is only the logic, and logic isn't everything. Historically and sociologically, it is possible that political modernity places such a demanding burden upon the shoulders of individuals that they feel incapable of carrying it all by themselves and start looking for options to throw it off, or delegate it to sources outside themselves. Here the group offers itself in its capacity as determining the proper place and task of the individual, or, rather, is offered to the individuals as such by the leader. If authors such as Arendt and Fromm are right that this is what helps explain the popular triumph of totalitarianism in our century, the implication is that *modernity produces its negation*: the collective – or mob, or crowd – promises "authenticity" for its members by way of extinguishing everything in each of them that would point to their being – precisely – autonomous individuals instead of interchangeable group-members.

I am aware that the dialectic of modernity described here is neither very subtle nor particularly original. What is more, I am uncertain as to how much light in succeeds in casting on the horrorful events in former Yugoslavia. A young woman who had fled Yugoslavia just before ethnic cleansing began taking place, and who has returned many times to visit relatives and friends of all the three ethno-religious identities involved, told me that the kind of approach I take in trying to understand the conflict puts an emphasis on the impact of ideology that is hopelessly out of touch with how people thought and acted at the time. People, she maintains, saw through the stereotypes spread by Milosevic-controlled television. When they endorsed the removal of former Muslim neighbours – friends, colleagues, even close relatives – from their flats, only to move in and take over all properties that had hurriedly been left behind, they did so out of pragmatic, material self-interest, not out of ideological conviction concerning the threat of being taken captive in Muslim harems, and the like. The Muslim flat was bigger than their own. Simple as that.

This explanation is fine as far as it goes. But there is more involved than cynically taking the opportunity to improve on one's flat or acquiring a bigger car. We know that between them, Croat and Serb nationalists destroyed an estimated fourteen hundred mosques throughout Bosnia-Herzegovina. In many cases the mosques have been ploughed over and turned into parking lots. Graveyards, birth records, work records, and other traces of the Bosnian Muslim people have been eradicated, and systematically not randomly so. As the mayor of the newly "Cleansed" and 100% pure Serb Orthodox city of Zvornik said, after all the city's mosques had been dynamited, "There never were any mosques in Zvornik".[60] Such a statement is evidence of the wilful extinction of a culture. It is similar to Hitler's dream of one day being able to say, "There never were any Jews in Europe". In killing people, genocidal perpetrators mean to wipe out an entire culture. It is difficult to see that setting out to do so can be explained by purely pragmatic, non-ideological reasons.

In the autumn of 1998, Milosevic switched tactics. Needless to say, his obsession with staying in power at all costs is undiminished. As a means of doing so, however, Milosevic increasingly attempts to pose before his people as a leader bullied by the West. The more unanimous the world's condemnation of Serbian repression of the ethnic Albanian majority in Kosovo, the more the Serbian people comes to assume the role as the world pariah number one; and the more the multi-deprived population comes to make this identity their own (be it in defiance or in resignation), the more Milosevic hopes to gain in terms of domestic

---

[60] *Ibid.*, p. 150.

support for being unrepentant when faced with charges of genocide – yet again.

So the positioning of Serbia (or rump-Yugoslavia) as belonging to the West and to the proud history of Civilisation and the celebrated tradition of modernity turns out to have been but mere posturing. If this is so, the argument for complicity on the part of the Enlightenment for the genocide that took place in former Yugoslavia loses plausibility. I hope we can observe this much without encouraging yet another round of Balkanisation to the effect that "they" – meaning (it is, significantly, not clear) the Serbs, or the Muslims, or the Albanians, or all of them together – are so different from "us" (meaning the indeed civilised West) that what comes to pass among them reflects on them alone and, though regrettable and tragic, is none of our business.[61]

Part of our being enlightened is our commitment to the ideals of tolerance and pluralism. The question raised by genocide – regardless where and against whom – is whether these ideals are well-equipped to guide our judgement when the phenomenon at hand is that of evil – in this case, genocide.

Let me turn to Berel Lang's book once again. Teaching a course with the title "The Concept of Evil", Lang made a shattering experience quite unlike all others made as a teacher: namely, that his group of students (well-meaning, decent, intelligent all of them) in discussing the literature given for the course (including Arendt's *Eichmann in Jerusalem* and Simon Wiesenthal's *The Sunflower*) proved

> simply blind to the appearance of evil when it actually appeared, substituting for what was plainly there before their eyes a set of oblique replacements.[62]

The students, that is, devoted their intellectual energy to inquiring whether the trial of Eichmann was not actually illegal and to denying the question asked by Wiesenthal by insisting that the SS man in his book had acted as a soldier and that there could thus be no issue *either* of forgiving him or of not doing so. To Lang, the students' responses

> disclosed a pattern that was, it seemed to me, nothing more than a reluctance to admit the necessity imposed by moral choice altogether – an

---

[61] This chapter was composed prior to the "Ethnic Cleansing" in Kosovo and the Nato intervention that it provoked.

[62] LANG, B., 1990, p. 236.

impulse to replace those demands with the deferrals of tolerance and understanding. Where, as for the actions of (Wiesenthal's) SS man, there seemed no way of judging him without condemnation, exclusion, then the judgement must itself be flattened, denied.[63]

And with regard to Eichmann, where the moral enormity was more difficult to avoid, the question for discussion became whether Eichmann, after all, was so different. Lang, in keeping with his critique of Kantian Enlightenment thought, reflects as follows:

> What stirred these reactions could best be understood as an enlargement of the principle of tolerance: from a precept governing relations *among people* to a precept governing judgement *within the individual*.[64]

Lang reminds us that tolerance appeared in John Stuart Mill as a social ideal. But now, as brought out in the young students discussing evil – or rather not-discussing it – the ideal of tolerance becomes internalised

> as if the individual person, in the attempt to be fair and just, had the obligation also to see *himself* as a society, as if he should renounce his own agency, admitting all possibilities and declining to make judgements or discriminations on the ground established by the principle of tolerance, namely, that all potential actions share equally the right to be summoned.[65]

Lang concludes:

> The point here is, not that tolerance and pluralism are not authentic values, but that *by themselves* they cannot do the work of moral judgement or action. [...] What tolerance and pluralism teach is mainly how *not* to choose, how *not* to discriminate; [...] they offer no basis for the positive choices that – often in the same moment – have to be made.[66]

The institutions of education, historically informed as they are by the Enlightenment ideals pointed to – induce in all of us, teachers and students alike, a respect for the many and a keen eye for the universal – inducing, on the other hand, no determined commitment to the one and so being "reluctant, almost disabled, to confront the one and the particular".[67]

---

[63] *Ibid.*, p. 237.
[64] *Ibid.*, p. 237.
[65] *Ibid.*, p. 237.
[66] *Ibid.*, p. 238.
[67] *Ibid.*, p. 239.

On this score, Lang is right. Add impartiality and neutrality to tolerance and pluralism and what you get is the proud ideals to which nearly everyone among Western politicians, diplomats, and military officers paid lip-service day and night for four years while genocide was being carried out in Bosnia the selfsame days and nights for the selfsame four years. Like Lang's students but with incomparably more sinister consequences, these leaders used every opportunity, meaning every documented atrocity, to try and take the sting, the absoluteness, out of what was right before their eyes but somehow went unseen. They wished to replace the sting with some balance about to be lost but always, in principle, open to restoration, provided only that the "parties" to the "conflict" all could be kept at the conference table, of course. But the conflict was actually planned genocide, and you do not negotiate genocide because genocide is evil at its evilest and hence beyond the weighing of interests and the restoration of balances lost. There is a hopeless mismatch between ongoing genocide on the one hand and the *Haltungslosigkeit* of the compromise-seeking attitude on the other. When the phenomenon to be judged is evil, judgement directs itself at something absolute – not complex, not ambiguous, not fascinatingly multifaceted etcetera. Here disinterested reflection will not do. The phenomenon to be judged is one craving action, intervention, so as to stop it. Evil is not for contemplation, which takes time, which would only prolong the object contemplated in taking it in and letting it be as it is so as better to grasp it. With evil as real, hence as suffered, hence as situated and particular, *experience* forces itself upon us in all its one-sidedness, partisanship, individuality. And, to end on an Aristotelian note as familiar as it is anti-universalistic, "a training in generality affords little preparation for a grasp of particulars or the decisions which they require".[68]

---

[68] *Ibid.*, p. 239.

CHAPTER 7

Stalinism in Context and Perspective: Sources of Permission to Hate in Europe

Robert THURSTON

Russian thinkers often comment on the large measure of support or even adulation for Stalin among Soviet citizens both during the dictator's lifetime and, for older people, to this day. L. Gordon and E. Klopov wrote in 1989 that Stalin was widely seen as a

> demi-god, possessing superhuman abilities and superhuman wisdom. For tens of millions of people [...] he was the symbol of the motherland, Soviet power, socialism.[1]

Perhaps unwittingly, Gordon and Klopov had paraphrased an earlier assessment by the writer Ilya Ehrenburg of Stalin's popularity on the eve of the German invasion:

> In the minds of millions of people Stalin had become a sort of mythical demi-god; everyone uttered his name with awe and believed that he alone could save the Soviet State from invasion and disruption.[2]

Other memoirs of the period often note similar sentiments. Anton Antonov-Ovseyenko indicates that both he and his father strongly supported the regime into 1937; the son clung to this attitude until years later.[3] Eugeniia Ginzburg encountered various fellow prisoners who continued to worship Stalin.[4] The recent films *Burnt by the Sun* (directed by Nikita Mikhalkov, 1994) and *The Inner Circle* (Andrei Konchalovsky, 1991), while presenting chilling images of Soviet

---

[1] GORDON, L. and KLOPOV, E., 1989, p. 143.

[2] EHRENBURG, I., 1964 [1921-1941], p. 426.

[3] ANTONOV-OVSEYENKO, A., 1981, p. 19.

[4] GINZBURG, E., 1967, p. 214 for example.

repression, also depict adoration for Stalin among ordinary people during the 1930s and 1940s.[5]

Among Russian historians of the USSR, Roy Medvedev argues that,

[t]he longer Stalin ruled the Soviet Union, cold-bloodedly destroying millions of people, the greater seems to have been the dedication to him, even the love, of the majority of the people. When he died in March 1953 the grief of hundreds of millions, both in the Soviet Union and around the world, was quite sincere.

More specifically, Medvedev argues that

in 1936-1938 the overwhelming majority of Soviet citizens, not only industrial and office workers but intellectuals as well, had no doubt that real enemies of the people were seated on the defendants' bench in the Moscow show trials.[6]

Dmitri Volkogonov, thus far Stalin's major Russian biographer, believed that "people took Stalin as the symbol and human embodiment of socialism". During the Terror Stalin "received the whole country's blind adulation".[7]

Why, in the opinion of these observers, did such support for the dictator exist? Medvedev, following the tradition of Russian intellectuals' disdain for the mental level of the people, imputed to them a low level of culture and cited the negative, degrading effects of Russian history.[8] Volkogonov's use of the word "blind" reflects similar attitudes: the "masses" supported Stalin because they were "misinformed", while the peasants had a "predisposition to cult worship", and the "cries of support were the voices of ignorance, lawlessness, and intimidation". Volkogonov made his condescension toward the common folk clear by quoting from the *émigré* philosopher Nikolai Berdiaev:

the Russian Revolution [...] confirmed an old idea of mine [...] freedom is not democratic, but aristocratic. The rising masses are not interested in

---

[5]   In a poll taken in April 1989, 48% rated Stalin positively. In another conducted in June-July 1992, 27% agreed completely with the statement that "Stalin was a great leader", 22% more or less agreed; in my THURSTON, R., 1996, p. 231.

[6]   MEDVEDEV, R. A., 1989, pp. 617, 375.

[7]   VOLKOGONOV, D., 1991, pp. xxiv, 188.

[8]   MEDVEDEV, R. A., 1989, p. 711.

freedom and they don't need it, nor are they up to bearing the burden of freedom.

Volkogonov commented that this is "a debatable idea, no doubt, but it was true when applied to both the masses and the old guard who were incapable of coping with freedom".[9]

Volkogonov and other Russian writers sometimes suggest that factors such as the spread of education and industrialisation within the USSR, together with its precarious international situation, produced some reasoned support for Stalin, based on more than fear or self-interest.[10] Yet, despite the different political outlooks of the Russian historians and biographers noted here, they maintain that Stalin's rule rested on gullibility, lack of understanding, and a low cultural level of the Soviet people.[11]

By emphasising such factors and appealing to certain strains of Russian history, especially reverence for the tsar (a much more complicated subject than Volkogonov *et al.* suggest) at the expense of other patterns of the past, namely the periodic tendency to flee from onerous circumstances or to revolt, Russian intellectuals try to explain away the great involvement and support in Stalin's crimes that they often perceive. One does not blame a donkey for carrying heavy loads, after all; the donkey's mental and cultural level fit him quite well for the task. This analogy is not far-fetched: it is common for the Russian elite to refer to ordinary citizens as "dustpan" or "*liumpen*" (from the German word *Lumpen*, "rags").[12] Thus the Soviet people are exonerated from all crimes or complicity in evil, but at the cost of denying their humanity.

Classic western accounts of Stalinism emphasise fear and not voluntary support as the basis of Stalin's rule.[13] In the western press

---

[9] VOLKOGONOV, D., 1991, pp. 98, 209, 267 and 308.

[10] *Ibid.*, pp. xx, 194.

[11] *Ibid.*, 122; and RADZINSKY, E., 1996, p. 90, where, in reference to common people in 1917, he calls them "slaves". On p. 424 the people are termed "docile", in the 1930s, convinced by Stalin that they were "victors". KHLEVNIUK, O. V., 1992, p. 7, finds that the people were naive. Like other Russian writers on the period, Khlevniuk recognizes only resistance to the Terror, never participation in it, as action.

[12] *The New York Times*, March 28, 1993. "Sovok", can also mean soviet, but that was not its usage here. On "liumpen", see DAVIES, R. W., 1997, p. 62.

[13] For example, CONQUEST, R., 1968; CONQUEST, R., 1990; ULAM, A. B., 1973.

and films, a metanarrative of Stalinism predominates in which the dictator rules as a superhuman, fully evil figure; occasionally Stalin is depicted literally as a devil.[14] Even if there is little discussion of the population's capabilities in such treatments, people other than executioners never assume an active role in the story. This judgement seems important in the West's construction of itself as the region of agency, superior to other parts of the globe.[15]

However, this metanarrative has come to the fore, at least in western scholarly writings, only fairly recently; other approaches played a major role in western thought until the late 1960s. The *émigré* sociologist Nikolai Timasheff's *The Great Retreat: The Growth and Decline of Communism in Russia* appeared in 1946. Timasheff saw the communist regime as savage and bloody, but also emphasised the ways in which it returned to "national tradition", which engendered support for it.[16] In 1958 Merle Fainsod, then dean of Soviet studies in America, published *Smolensk under Soviet Rule*, an investigation of one region of the USSR. He believed that the Soviet system was totalitarian and dominated by terror in the 1930s[17], but he also stressed the right of ordinary citizens to complain about their situation to officials; their letters were read and often resulted in investigations and judgements in favour of the protester.[18]

In 1957, Joseph Berliner published *Factory and Manager in the USSR*, based on interviews with *émigré* Soviet managers and engineers. Berliner went beyond Fainsod in his depiction of a crucial arena of Soviet life characterised by compromise, negotiation, and attempts to satisfy complaints. Managers, far from being cowed by the pressure and threats directed at them from above, had to take risks in order to survive. To keep up production, they had to try to meet some of their workers' concerns. Berliner belittled the notion that the regime

---

[14] For example, at the beginning of each instalment of *Stalin*, a film by Thames Television, London, 1990; cover of the *New York Times Book Review*, May 5, 1996.

[15] This construction of the "West", and its "civilization", as opposed to the barbarism of other regions, was a key project of the Enlightenment: see WOLFF, L., 1994. I would quarrel with Wolff's argument only in that forerunners of Enlightenment ideas in this respect date back at least to the sixteenth century, especially among accounts by travellers like Sigismund von Herberstein.

[16] TIMASHEFF, N., 1946.

[17] FAINSOD, M., 1958, pp. 379 and 12.

[18] *Ibid.*, esp. Chapter 20 "The Right of Petition".

controlled everything and commented on the "all-pervasiveness of the personal factor in the determination of the allocation of resources".[19]

David Granick echoed many of Berliner's judgements in his *The Red Executive: A Study of the Organization Man in Russian Industry*, 1960. Granick even described the Communist Party as an "old-fashioned US city political machine". Politics was not something far off in the Kremlin, it was local. The party served among other things as a giant complaint bureau across the country. Workers took the initiative in proposing many ideas, and no factory manager could afford to ignore their criticism.[20]

The Soviet Citizen: Daily Life in a Totalitarian Society, by Alex Inkeles and Raymond Bauer, appeared in 1961. They stressed terror in understanding the 1930s yet detailed other important sources of compliance, including support for policies in education and the economy.[21] In short, a number of studies published in the West well into the 1960s argued for a lively society motivated to work and to comply with the government for many reasons. This society was beyond the control of the state in important respects.

However, the tendency in western writing to acknowledge at least some voluntary support for Stalin and some involvement in his policies on the part of ordinary people virtually disappeared by the late 1960s. Why that happened is a question largely beyond the scope of this article. But certainly one reason for the change was the powerful prose and dramatic picture of massive, undeserved suffering in Robert Conquest's *Great Terror*, 1968[22], which gave his book wide appeal.

Aleksandr Solzhenitsyn's *Gulag Archipelago* made headlines all over the West when it appeared in English and other languages beginning in 1973.[23] Earlier accounts of how factory managers had worked outside of Stalinist legality hardly had the same impact on readers as Solzhenitsyn's tales of starving prisoners in the Gulag gobbling up the remains of a frozen mammoth they had found. His portrayal of the USSR was received in the West as one of unremitting suffering inflicted upon the helpless people; this was ironic in view of the author's insistence that the Soviet political police (called the

---

[19] BERLINER, J., 1957, pp .18, 26-30, 54, 56 and 68.

[20] GRANICK, D., 1960, pp. 197, 231 and 229.

[21] BAUER, R. and INKELES, A., 1959.

[22] CONQUEST, R., 1968.

[23] SOLZHENITSYN, A. I., 1973.

NKVD in the late 1930s) was "from our own roots" and "our own blood". He also recorded his own personal happiness as the terror of 1937-38 raged and the sense that the arrests were few in number and far away: "All the provincial leaders had been removed, but as far as we were concerned it didn't matter. Two or three professors had been arrested, but after all they hadn't been our dancing partners."[24] Yet once again, images of torture, injustice, and death completely overrode Solzhenitsyn's comments about popular response to and even involvement in the terror.

As the Cold War became hot in Vietnam, more one-dimensional treatments of Stalinism probably appealed to the western, especially American, public more than nuanced studies did. American soldiers went to Vietnam to fight not flesh-and-blood peasants but communism, in the new literature depicted as a thing which crushed the innocent people. Starkly drawn images of communist rule as coercing entire populations into obedience also helped explain why, although the United States killed thousands upon thousands of Vietnamese, there were always more to join the fight.

The mass victimisation argument also fits neatly with a key theme in Russian culture, the tendency to see the people's story as unremittingly tragic. Russian thinkers regularly present their own lives and their country's past in a series of litanies of suffering and death.[25] Russians emphasise their own ability to withstand suffering as a central, perhaps essential part of a highly developed, collective identity. This self-image is held to mark Russia off from the West, considered materialistic and shallow, a place whose people have not been tempered in the flame of suffering on anything like the Russian scale. For hundreds of years, Russians have often seen themselves as behind the West in material terms but superior in their ability to feel emotions and keep in touch with the most important things of the natural world, which have nothing to do with indexes like the number of computers *per capita* or standard of living.[26] However, this outlook raises the difficulty that, as Russians construct their past, they emphasise its darker moments and the purported ubiquity of suffering.

---

[24] *Ibid.*, "Gulag I" pp. 160-161.

[25] RIES, N., 1997, especially Chapter Three, "Litanies and Laments: The Discursive Act of Suffering".

[26] For a recent treatment of this theme, with an emphasis on the Russian emphasis on suffering as part of the national experience and character, see RANCOUR-LAFERRIERE, D., 1995.

Moreover, it is the torment endured by innocents, those not involved in wielding power in any way, which is most laudable. Thus the Russians are ennobled at the same time that they are described as lesser beings than other peoples.

For foreign commentators, the USSR sometimes becomes a fantasy realm. It is not a country of widely varied individuals but a kind of canvas whose deeply shaded background is already painted as pain and suffering. Only the details need be added. Thus in a recent novel by the American David Plante, a major character announces that

> I knew everything I was ever capable of imagining that was true had already happened, in documented black and white, in Russia, because Russia was, is and will be the country of the greatest suffering in the world, beyond anyone's imagination.[27]

No serious writer wishes to minimise the truly awful suffering that has occurred in Russia. Estimates of the death toll for any of the major catastrophes of the twentieth century, from the 1905 Revolution through the famines which followed World War II, evoke a heart-rending bafflement upon seeing them even for the hundredth time. But if we wish to analyse and understand at any but a superficial level why such devastation has taken place in Russia, and why so many people were heavily involved in persecuting so many others, we need to attempt to strip away the seductive appeal of litanies of suffering.

The experience of someone in the Gulag does not help us understand why the camp system arose and flourished, or why its history is so full of rapid shifts in policy, numbers of prisoners, and so forth. There were many different types of experiences in the hands of Stalin's political police and, of course, in Soviet society as a whole. Fear of the regime and disloyalty provoked by its violence did exist in large measure in the USSR, but reference to them by no means approaches a full explanation of how Stalinism operated. Persecution was not the central experience of Stalinism for many millions who lived through it.

Some recent western scholarship has begun to challenge all of these views and to argue that much of the terror of the mid – to late 1930s had a strong populist component. Such work describes ways in which ordinary people participated as actors in the Terror, not simply as

---

[27]   From David Plante, *Age of Terror* (New York, St. Martin's Press, 1999); quoted in an approving review by Richard Bernstein in *The New York Times*, January 20, 1999.

victims, and how they found that the arrests of others resonated with their grievances and sense of justice.[28] These discussions of Stalinism do not depend on or stress any assumed low level of culture among the populace. New studies, reiterating themes of some older western analyses while moving beyond them in other respects, instead note that the regime provided the citizenry with certain meaningful avenues of complaint and influence. Soviet people used these means widely, especially during the Terror. While there was nothing like freedom of speech in the western sense, still ordinary folk could make their voices heard, often obtain some positive response to their grievances, and even secure the dismissal or arrest of superiors who displeased them.[29] In this situation people behaved honestly, villainously, or in any other possible way: they acted across the whole range of human emotions and motivations.

Not all recent western studies of Stalinism adopt these emphases; some are strong restatements of victimology.[30] Among works which do see agency during the terror among the Soviet people, major differences of opinion certainly exist. What is held in common is a rejection of the view that the mass arrests were something that "the state" or "regime" did to "the people".[31] Students of Western Europe increasingly provide complex descriptions of the state which stress its broad connections with society throughout history;[32] observers of the USSR need likewise to move beyond invocations of the state as a mechanism somehow independent of its people.

Finally, part of the process of restoring complexity and multiple foci to any examination of Stalinist terror must involve close attention to the broad historical factors which helped produce it. This point would seem to be perfectly obvious, yet accounts like *Le livre noir du communisme* manage to present the mass arrests of the 1930s as though they took place almost in an international and historical

---

[28] See, for example, my THURSTON, R., 1996; FITZPATRICK, S., 1994; and DAVIES, S., 1997.

[29] See DAVIES, S., 1997; KOTKIN, S., 1995. Kotkin, it should be noted, does not see popular participation in the Terror.

[30] See, for example, VIOLA, L., 1996. The book begins with a poem by an unknown Russian which laments collectivization and sets the tone for a treatment of the peasantry as victims in a dramatic tragedy.

[31] This is the view of Conquest and Ulam, for instance, and of countless textbooks.

[32] See, among many works, STRAYER, J. R., 1970; HENSHALL, N., 1992.

vacuum.[33] To treat the Terror without emphasising the dangers confronting the USSR from abroad or without serious attention to the searing experience of the Russian Civil War, which ended only in 1920-1921, is absurd. For no other country – or, more precisely, perhaps for no other western country – would such an approach to history be deemed adequate.

At a time when scholarship on Nazi Germany has come increasingly to emphasise popular, willing involvement in the state and its crimes[34], the USSR now stands virtually alone in writings about the Christian-based world in one respect: in the public mind and the mass media, Soviet terror is held to be absolutely unpopular. Stalin is put into a category with non-western figures such as Mao Zedong, Idi Amin, Pol Pot, and Sadaam Hussein. In this distinction between the "West" and the rest of the globe there appears to be considerable condescension and Orientalism at work; Russia is often seen as a bloody, mysterious place inhabited by people of lesser capabilities.[35]

Given the old and thick cultural filters in place for Russians and foreigners as they examine Stalinism, a comparative approach may open some useful perspectives. How does Soviet repression compare to earlier mass persecutions in regard to the long process of identifying or even creating "enemies" within a society? How do the dynamics of arrest and mistreatment compare, and in what ways were the declines of persecution similar? Space does not permit consideration of the second question; this essay will concentrate on the background to Western European and Stalinist persecution and to popular involvement in repression. Stalinism has been identified for so long as a unique phenomenon – a point of pride in the Russian culture of suffering – that many readers will probably resist the idea that terror in the USSR may be compared to anything except Nazi behaviour. But there is much to be gained from thinking about what was not unique in Stalinism.

---

[33] COURTOIS, S. *et al.*, 1997. The section of the book on the Soviet Union reveals its thrust in its title: "un état contre son peuple". Although the book pays some attention to historical context for the period 1917-1921, this concern disappears thereafter.

[34] Among many works see BROWNING, C., 1992; GOLDHAGEN, D. J., 1996; LIFTON, R. J., 1986; KOONTZ, C., 1987.

[35] On Orientalism see SAID, E. W., 1979; on the application of some of Said's concepts to views of Russia, see WOLFF, L., 1994.

In April 1545 a French force comprised of soldiers and local peasants devastated several villages and their inhabitants in an area of Provence to the north of Avignon. This campaign aimed to destroy the Vaudois heretics, or, in some accounts, "Lutherans". The attackers wreaked havoc and death in villages like Luberon, Mérindol, Orgon, and Sénas. Peasants from outside the region who joined in the campaign were distinguished by their ardor in hunting down the "Vaudois"; these persecutors were "worse than the gendarmes", one observer reported.[36] The troops "could only pillage, burn and kill" all those they caught who had fled from the assault. Of course rapes accompanied the campaign. At Cabrières on April 20 the only Vaudois who had tried to defend themselves surrendered on the promise that their lives would be spared; but the soldiers promptly executed several and confined others, including women and children, in the local church. Apparently those prisoners gave some indication that they would try to flee, or the soldiers thought they did, for the troops then entered the church and put everyone inside to the sword.[37] Francis I himself, pointing to reprehensible acts supposedly committed by the Vaudois, had ordered the massacre "to extirpate this evil plant of heresy".[38]

It is difficult to estimate the toll of victims. All the people of Cabrières either fled or were killed; 2,700 dead for the whole of Provence was a contemporary guess.[39] All this was done in the name of the king, the pope, and defence of the true Christian faith.

Several decades later and a few hundred kilometres to the north-west, another spate of blood-letting was under way. In July of 1629 a grandmother and widow, Catharina Ringelspach, was arrested on the charge of witchcraft in the district of Ban de la Roche or Steinthal, in Alsace. The specific accusation was that she had used an ointment given to her by the devil to murder her grandson. Within a few days the presiding judge ordered that "with the help of torture the truth be brought out from her".

Ringelspach was tortured at least eight separate times, probably with a variant of the *strappado*, which involved tying her arms behind her back and hauling her up off the floor. In many cases heavy weights

---

[36]   VENARD, M., 1993, p. 373.

[37]   *Ibid.*, p. 372.

[38]   *Ibid.*, p. 370; AUDISIO, G., 1984, p. 359.

[39]   AUDISIO, G., 1984, p. 386-387.

were attached to the victim's legs to increase the pain. Ringelspach must have been a tough person, but eventually she confessed to murder. We do not know her fate, but probably she was executed; at least fifty other women, and thirty men, were burned for witchcraft in Ban de la Roche between 1620 and 1630. At the time the total population of the nine villages in the district was only about 1200.[40]

What might serve as an organising concept in the analysis of these early modern events and in comparing them to Stalinism? In discussing the coming of legal racial segregation in the United States, C. Vann Woodward wrote that the North gave "permission to hate" to the South.[41] At various times and in multiple ways western culture, governments, and people have granted permission to hate within their societies, facilitating mass persecutions under certain circumstances. The withdrawal or the muting of permission to hate can then be seen as the major ingredient in bringing mass violence to an end.

Of course, it may be that no particular world view or set of cultural constructs is necessary to produce large-scale murder; perhaps it has been sufficient in Kosovo or Rwanda to say, "they are different from us, so let us kill them". After all, the distinction between "us" and "them" can be found in the earliest written records, from Sumer.[42] Tribes in various parts of the world refer to themselves as "man" and neighbouring peoples as "monkeys, crocodiles, or malign spirits".[43] The urge to distinguish one's own people from the "other", dehumanising it in the process, seems basic to early social organization.

Yet in the history of a considerable portion of Europe it is possible to see a long development of particular, focused permission to hate directed not only toward others who live elsewhere but others within mainstream society. In a well-known passage, Norman Cohn writes of a "specific fantasy in Europe", that

> there existed, somewhere in the midst of the great society, another society, small and clandestine, which not only threatened the existence of the great

---

[40] "Originale Hexen-Protokolle aus dem Steinthal", Manuscripts in the Rare and Manuscripts Collections, Carl A. Kroch Library, Cornell University [hereafter Steinthal mss.], 197-210 on Ringelspach, 19-260 on witchcraft charges and executions in the area. For a discussion of the region and its population, see LEYPOLD, D., 1989.

[41] WOODWARD, C. V., 1974, p. 81.

[42] SMITH, J. Z., 1985, p. 15.

[43] GREEN, W. S., 1985, p. 49.

society but was addicted to practices which were felt to be wholly abominable, in the literal sense of anti-human.[44]

And it is possible to give rough dates and broad reasons for the appearance of this fantasy, in new and highly developed forms, in Western Europe. In R. I. Moore's view, during the late Middle Ages Western Europe became a "persecuting society" in which

> deliberate and socially sanctioned violence began to be directed, *through established governmental, judicial and social institutions*, against groups of people defined by general characteristics such as race, religion or way of life; [...] membership of such groups in itself came to be regarded as justifying these attacks.[45]

Elite members of western society became prone to see dangerous deviants at work from within and without.

This change in attitudes and practices is clear in numerous respects. From the late fourth century to the early eleventh century, heretics had not been regarded as a particularly grave danger in the West and were not executed;[46] the early church was "full of optimism, still sure of its faith and of the triumph of that faith".[47] Then came the first mass execution of heretics known to scholars, at Orléans in 1022. The charges included holding diabolic orgies and burning babies.[48] What had happened to shake the confidence of the clerical and secular authorities and to cause them to seek out – or to create in the first place – enemies within?

Among the reasons for the formation of a persecuting society was surely state-building, which can be dated well back into the Middle Ages[49], and which sometimes involved charges of anti-human practices in order to give central authorities the opportunity to discredit their

---

[44] COHN, N., 1975, p. xi.

[45] MOORE, R. I., 1987, p. 5 his italics.

[46] Moore notes that there is only one example of the burning of a heretic in western Europe before 1022; it occurred in 383: MOORE, R. I., 1987, p. 12.

[47] COHN, N., 1975, p. 67.

[48] MOORE, R. I., 1987, p. 15.

[49] STRAYER, J. R., 1970.

powerful internal opponents. This would appear to explain why the trial of heretics in Orléans in 1022 was a political affair.[50]

Another cause of rising persecution was a new determination in the church to reform itself and to realise more coherence and influence as an institution. Into the early Middle Ages the church

> had not yet developed the means, or, some would say, the inclination, to demand uniformity of worship and practice throughout Western Christendom.[51]

Until about 1100 "Christian cosmology was not considered a literal blueprint of God's creation".[52] But now religious authorities in the West identified enemies within, much as the gospel authors had, in all likelihood to strengthen Christian solidarity by defining the acceptable community and its beliefs more clearly than ever before.

Surely a sense of a growing external threat from two quarters also figured in the new western anxieties and determination to increase solidarity. The Arabs had captured Jerusalem in the seventh century and continued to maintain a strong presence in Spain. Meanwhile, a split was looming between the eastern and western churches, to burst into the open and into mutual anathema in 1054. All these factors combined to produce new western Christian zeal, expressed in the First Crusade, 1095, and also in new and virulent persecution of Jews, who had heretofore lived relatively peacefully among Christians in many areas of the West.[53] This was the context in which, in the second quarter of the eleventh century, the Cluniac chronicler and church reformer Ralph Glaber produced a book which detailed Satan's release into the world in the year 1000. Another book produced in 1115 retailed anecdotes of Jews' outrageous sexual behaviour and ties to the devil.[54]

A perceived threat from the East now became personified in one of the first major heretical groups of the period, the Bogomils. By 1143 western "native dissent", labelled heretical, "was being joined by emissaries of the heretical communities of the Byzantine world" who

---

[50] MOORE, R. I., 1987, p. 15; The first known European witch trial, that of Alice Kyteler in 1324, also appears to have been politically motivated; see DAVIDSON, L. S. and WARD, J. O., 1993.

[51]. MOORE, R. I., 1987, p. 69.

[52] KORS, A. C. and PETERS, E., 1972, p. 6.

[53] For a recent treatment of this topic see SWANSON, R. N., 1995, p. 290.

[54] MOORE, R. I., 1987, pp. 13-14 and 35.

had come from Thrace and Bulgaria. No matter that these were "probably refugees" who had been persecuted in eastern Christendom;[55] they were deemed infiltrators in league with Satan, all the more frightening because they came from a strange, powerful, and hated empire. Heretics could be anywhere, and so to western authorities the Bogomils were more menacing than the Muslims, who remained a regional problem.

The old sexual charges soon reappeared:

bugger: [ME bougre<OF bolgre<ML Bulgarus, lit., a Bulgarian; orig., 11th-c. Bulgarian heretic] 1. a sodomite 2. a contemptible person [...] verb transitive to commit sodomy with.[56]

"The other" had to be described as depraved in order to drive home the point that he or she was a threat to basic human values.

By about the year 1500, a series of setbacks for western faith increased the general level of anxiety and undoubtedly contributed to the hunt for enemies. The crusades, for example, begun as an effort to reconquer land from the infidels, had become merely an attempt to keep them out of Europe. The fall of Constantinople in 1453, even though it marked the end of a despised empire, was another major advance for Islam.

Missionary efforts in Asia had largely petered out; heresy had struck hard in central Europe; converts from the non-Christian minorities within Europe were feared as a fifth column undermining the purity of the faith; Antichrist was at the gates and Satan's minions within them.[57]

Needless to say, after 1517 the Protestant Reformation and the Catholic (Counter-)Reformation greatly heightened tensions and combat in the West.

It is not possible here to examine in detail the spread of dire accusations against Jews, homosexuals, lepers, Muslims, heretics, and finally "witches".[58] This widening of the circle of suspected anti-

---

[55] *Ibid.*, p. 22

[56] WEBSTER'S, 1982, p. 185.

[57] SWANSON, R. N., 1995, p. 260.

[58] This progression has been noted by various authors; see, for example, COHN, N., 1975 and GINZBURG, C., 1992; MOORE, R. I., 1987, p. 65, remarks that, "[f]or all imaginative purposes heretics, Jews and lepers were interchangeable. They had the same qualities, from the same source, and they presented the same threat: through

humans in Western Europe was more or less complete by the late fifteenth century. Except for the Muslims, the targeted groups were within the great society and were considered more dangerous because of that fact. Anyone might be a heretic or a witch posing as a normal person for the purposes of infiltrating and wrecking the Christian community. Even Jews and lepers might pass for a time as good, righteous citizens.

However, while these trends led to expulsion of the Jews from various countries, mass murders of Jews in other areas, segregation and maltreatment for lepers, and deadly attacks on heretics, the persecuting society produced only highly erratic hunts for witches. The persecutions did not reach major proportions in Italy or Spain, for example, and were localised in France and Germany. Not a single witch was condemned to death in Frankfurt, but in neighbouring villages and in the principalities of Mainz and Nassau many were burned.[59]

The witch trials often spread through cultural influences and the proximity of other hunts. The persecutions had little to do with goals often ascribed to them, for example to reaffirm social boundaries, control deviance, frighten and subjugate women, assert the authority of towns over villages, or any other "functional" explanation.[60] Instead, the persecutions reflected fear of perceived internal enemies.

In any event, it is now difficult to reconstruct the witch hunts or the persecution of heretics without considering, as accounts of the Provençal killings in 1545 indicate, popular hatreds and participation at work. The fears outlined in the previous discussion, as well as those induced by the French wars of religion, help to explain why ordinary folk might have agreed with their leaders that the Vaudois merited extermination. The witch hunts depended upon voluntary denunciations and testimony to magistrates by peasants, who, according to many accounts, widely believed in the ability of some of their neighbours to employ evil magic.[61]

---

them the Devil was at work to subvert the Christian order and bring the world to chaos." Obviously the same thought applies to "witches".

[59]   ESCHENROEDER, W., 1932, p. 13.

[60]   This is the conclusion of recent work by BRIGGS, R., 1996 and CLARK, S., 1997.

[61]   The classic account of such beliefs is THOMAS, K., 1971; on denunciations by peasants see BRIGGS, R., 1996, pp. 406-08, among many passages on this point.

The Russian Revolutions of 1917 occurred after three years of extremely costly fighting in the world war, which at the very least dulled people's sensitivity to violence. Then with the October Revolution, as much its cause as its effect, came the Russian Civil War. In that chaotic conflict terror, torture, and murder, including mass atrocities, were practised on all sides. Probably the worst set of incidents, among many horrific choices, was the killing by forces under General Anton Denikin of perhaps 100,000 Jews in Ukraine in 1919 alone.[62] The rapid changes in areas controlled by the various armies; the length, geographical scope, and devastation of the fighting; and the unsurpassed brutality of the period made the Civil War the great Russian formative experience of the whole period from 1905 to 1941.

Even as internal warfare unfolded in 1918, the Soviet regime did not devote considerable attention, resources, or personnel to the secret police until Lenin himself was shot and wounded in August.[63] Before and after September 2, when the "Red Terror" was proclaimed as official Soviet policy, much pressure for bloodshed against the upper classes and army officers came from ordinary people, not the authorities.[64] A severe critic of the Bolsheviks noted that as the Red Terror developed, local jurisdictions tended to be more violent than central officials were.[65] Soviet bloodshed occurred, moreover, in a context of economic collapse, foreign invasion, and severe food shortages; in this maelstrom none of the sides involved, whether Red, White, or Green, avoided using terror.[66]

The next great wave of Soviet violence, collectivisation of agriculture, also began during a desperate economic situation. By 1927

---

[62] On these and other killings by non-Bolshevik forces see, for example, KENEZ, P., "The Prosecution of Soviet History: A Critique of Richard Pipes", *The Russian Revolution, Russian Review* 50, No. 3 (1991); BROVKIN, V. N., 1994 and RADKEY, O. H., 1976

[63] As late as August 28, 1918, just before Lenin was shot and badly wounded, there were only 75 *Cheka* organizations at the country *(uezd)* level; at the time the Bolsheviks probably controlled no more than half of the old empire's 815 European *uezdy*. Therefore probably some 252 *uezdy* had no political police units in place at that point.

[64] Among many examples, see COCHRAN PONFADINE, E., 1931, pp. 131-138; SOROKIN, P., 1950, pp 7, 16, 17, 31 and IZGOEV A. S., 1923, pp. 25-26.

[65] See, for example, MELGOUNOV, S. P., 1925, p. 37.

[66] For other discussions of terror used by various sides in the Civil War see FIGES, O., 1989 and BROVKIN, V. N., 1994.

a combination of factors, including a poor harvest in important regions of the country, a war scare, and high unemployment, made the Bolshevik leadership inclined to seek harsh solutions to the problem of low grain collections. The twists and turns of policy as the state tried to get grain are now fairly clear: Stalin urged seizing grain and punitive measures against peasants who resisted, but he was outvoted in the Central Committee (CC) in 1928. However, as fighting between villagers and the state's forces increased in the countryside, the CC changed course and supported Stalin's line.[67] Under different circumstances, Stalin and the leadership might have behaved much differently. In addition, the CC could have blocked him repeatedly and even removed him from power. But once fighting over grain began in 1927, an "us" against "them" psychology – Stalin's outlook, in a word – took hold, prompting officials at various levels to apply dehumanising labels to resisting peasants: "kulak", "enemy of the people", "White Guard element", and so on. These were enemies within, a concept made plausible for many citizens by the experience of the Civil War, in which many inhabitants of the former Russian empire had collaborated with foreign forces.

As for the famine of 1932-1933, we now know that, contrary to long-standing charges, the state did not possess a large supply of grain which it refused to give out to starving people. The famine was not directed at Ukrainians: the death toll was high across the country, and in Ukraine was worst in Russian-speaking areas.[68] If genocide is

---

[67] The CC voted against Stalin's policy of seizing grain and making wide arrests on April 6, 1928; in July the CC voted again, over Stalin's objections, to discard "extraordinary measures". But the situation in the countryside continued to deteriorate, and peasants met state procurement groups, police, and communist officials with considerable violence. Finally in April 1929 the CC reversed itself and supported Stalin's use of coercion – which itself drew upon considerable support within officialdom, urban dwellers who were suspicious of the peasantry, and Red Army men who presumably saw the needs of the country for grain as higher than the villages' demand to be let alone. See MANNING, R., "The Onset of the Stalin Revolution in the Countryside: the Grain Crisis, the Extraordinary Measures, Peasant Rebellions, and the Stuggle over Repression within the Soviet Leadership, 1927-1928", paper presented to the AAASS Annual Meeting, Boca Raton, Florida, September 1998.

[68] For recent literature on the famine see, among many works, see R. W. Davies, M. B. Tauger, and S. G. Wheatcroft, "Stalin, Grain Stocks and the Famine of 1932-1933", *Slavic Review* 54, No. 3 (Fall 1995), which finds that there was no significant grain reserve which could have been distributed; and Mark Tauger, "The 1932 Harvest and Famine of 1933", *Slavic Review* 50, No. 1 (1991), which argues

defined strictly as its root words would indicate, an attempt to destroy a gene pool, that is, an entire people, no policy of genocide versus Ukrainians or other groups existed. That is not to say that many did not suffer and die; recent estimates of the toll in 1932-1933 of "excess deaths"– those above what one would expect from "normal" mortality rates – run from three to five million for the entire USSR.[69] In the spring of 1933 relief finally flowed to the stricken countryside, too late for many.[70]

Famines are usually caused to a substantial degree by state policy. Stalin and the other leaders are to blame for the Soviet disaster in that without collectivisation and the state's demands for grain, the population would probably have found ways to overcome the food shortage with a much smaller loss of life. However, the events of 1932-1933 also occurred in a context which deserves attention. First, the harvest of 1930 had been good, leading central authorities to believe that collectivisation had worked. Second, officials and peasants were locked in an age-old struggle in which the former tried to get more food from the villagers, while the latter tried to hide some of what they had produced. This contest had occurred over tithes and taxes in Europe for centuries and was related to the traditional contempt that the elite felt for peasants.[71] Third, as Sheila Fitzpatrick points out, "the 1932 harvest was only the third since collectivisation, and the state was

---

that the primary cause of the famine was a poor harvest, though "organizational and political factors" also played a role; p. 85. WHEATCROFT, S. G., 1993, pp. 282-283, details the high mortality in Russian-speaking Ukraine.

[69] For an estimate of four to five million deaths in the famine, not just in Ukraine but across the whole country, see WHEATCROFT, S. G., 1993, p. 280. For a recent estimate by a Russian scholar of "over three million", famine deaths, based on archival materials, see OSOKINA, E. A., "The Victims of the Famine of 1933: How Many?", *Russian Studies in History* 31 (Fall 1992), No. 2, p. 13.

[70] Documents on display at the Library of Congress exhibit "Revelations from the Russian Archives", 1992 [hereafter LC Documents], a top secret order to the Communist Party of Ukraine, "On the elimination of food shortages in the collective farms, areas of acute malnutrition, and cases of famine", February 22, 1933, LC number A.19.10. It is not yet clear how much relief flowed to the stricken areas; probably not much, given the lack of food reserves. For more information on the relief efforts, see TAUGER, M., "The 1932 Harvest and Famine of 1933", *Slavic Review 50*, No.1 (1991), p. 88.

[71] For the European elite's traditionally negative views of peasants see, for example, BURKE, P., 1978, pp. 27, 163.

still trying to find out just how much it could extract from the peasants under the new order".[72]

Fourth and most important, Soviet officials bore recent and bitter memories, highly skewed by their own ideology and interests, but real nonetheless, of violence committed by peasants. Party and government cadres at various levels regarded peasants as enemies and rejected reports of a poor harvest as more lies from those enemies.[73] Many officials had dehumanised the peasants and could not, or would not, cut through the cultural barrier they had erected between themselves and the villagers until the situation reached hugely lethal proportions. Understandably, this dehumanisation has now been turned back upon Stalin and his regime – but it explains as little now about what happened as it did about the food supply in 1932-1933.

"Stalinism" was responsible for the famine deaths, just as the British government bears much responsibility for Irish deaths in the potato blight and the French authorities for Vietnamese deaths during the post-war famine. However, Stalinism entailed participation and judgements by many people. Not only officials but urban dwellers as a group were deeply mistrustful of peasants, to a great degree because of the perception during the Civil War that they grew wealthy at the expense of urban lives.[74] At the same time, there was no essential, murderous Stalinist impulse which produced the Soviet famine of 1932-1933. After another poor harvest in 1936, the state reacted quickly to prevent starvation; this time, it had grain reserves.

The Terror of 1936-1938 also has a history that requires close examination. Elsewhere I have provided a detailed account of the regime's chequered behaviour as it moved to implement police and judicial reform in 1934-1936, then turned in a rapidly rising tide of frenzy to mass arrests, then lurched back and forth in 1938 between repression and condemnation of unfounded persecutions. Finally in November 1938, Nikolai Ezhov lost his post as head of the NKVD, and arrests and the use of torture, widely adopted in 1936 and 1937, declined dramatically. The courts reduced many sentences, switched a large number of cases from the charge of sabotage or "wrecking" to

---

[72] FITZPATRICK, S., 1994, p. 70.

[73] *Ibid.*, pp. 70 and 74. And see the documents suggesting the same attitude in LC Documents, numbers A.19.5a and A.19.6a, for example, dating from December 1932.

[74] See MCAULEY, M., 1989, on the Civil War resentments. For similar feelings at the end of the 1920s among urbanites, see HINDUS, M., 1931, p. 114.

lesser counts, and placed great emphasis on tangible evidence in deciding prisoners' fates. The police after late 1938 looked hard for such evidence and largely jettisoned their earlier reliance on confessions obtained through torture.[75] In many of these respects the end of the Terror parallels the erratic end of the witch hunts.

As all this occurred, neither the size of the NKVD nor its situation in Soviet life permitted it to operate independently of society. In 1939 the NKVD numbered 366,000 people, including border guards, internal security troops, the regular police *(Militsiia)*, fire brigades, and the security police.[76] Considering all the responsibilities assigned to the NKVD, it was not a particularly large organization in a country with a population of about 170 million.

A former colonel of the border guards reported that a typical *raion* (district) had between six and fifteen police employees.[77] In another *raion* the NKVD team consisted of eight people, of whom one was a building inspector and another was probably a secretary.[78] About 91,000 people lived in this district before the war[79], so the ratio of police officials to inhabitants was approximately 1 per 6,000; this was certainly not profound penetration of the population.[80]

Police informers were neither particularly numerous or independent of society. One former NKVDist believed that in the city of Kuibyshev in 1938 the *Militsiia* had "approximately 1,000 informers at a minimum"[81], which would mean 1 police spy per 400 people. Two *émigrés* said that they knew who the local, "secret" police spies were, and that these agents wanted to protect their co-workers, not harm

---

[75] I tell this story in some detail in my THURSTON, R., 1996.

[76] NOVE, A., "How Many Victims in the 1930s?–II", *Soviet Studies*, 42, No. 4 (1990), p. 813.

[77] A. Repin, Manuscripts, Bakhmetieff Archive of Russian and East European History and Culture, Columbia University [hereafter BA], p. 254. Repin had been a colonel in the NKVD border troops.

[78] MANNING, R. T., "Government in the Soviet Countryside in the Stalinist Thirties: The Case of Belyi Raion in 1937", *The Carl Beck Papers in Russian and East European Studies)*, No. 301, (1984), p. 9.

[79] *Ibid.*, p. 2.

[80] For other examples of the low ratio of police to people, see my THURSTON, R., 1996, pp. 70-71.

[81] "NKVD SSSR", Hoover Institution Archives [hereafter HI], box 294, folder 2, 273. This anonymous report appears to be by someone familiar with the inner workings of the NKVD; the author's remarks are echoed in other sources, for instance Repin.

them.[82] These *émigrés* as well as a third did not feel threatened in any way by the spies.[83] Many other *émigrés* were also sure that the secret informers could be identified and that it was easy to avoid them.[84]

The police had to have some ready assistance from society in order to operate. An incident from Murmansk recounted by an ex-NKVD officer illustrates the connections between authorities and the populace which helped fuel the arrests. Reports from informers about a port employee led the local police to investigate him. But after working on the case for almost a year, the officer in charge found no stains on the suspect's record; he was "completely loyal to the Soviet regime". The investigator realised that a trial, even in a special closed court or "troika" of three officials, would fail. The case was closed.[85] The story also reveals a police concern for evidence that, however abused and weakened at the height of the Terror, nonetheless continued to appear.

On the other hand, ordinary people sometimes successfully resisted police pressure to denounce. For instance, in 1937 an army captain was arrested in Kiev. His wife was ordered to move 100 kilometres away. The chief of the Kiev passport bureau, a *Militsiia* officer, accused the woman of being an enemy and required her building manager and a neighbour to see him; both spoke in her favour. Finally the official gave her a permanent residence permit for Kiev and even said he greatly appreciated her frankness; "his office only saw people with long stories and lies".[86] The support of her neighbours and the

---

[82] [Harvard] Project on the Soviet Social System, Widener Library, Harvard University [hereafter HP]. "A" schedule interviews were life stories; "B" schedule interviews were on specialized topics. If available, short biographical data will also be provided, using the project's designations. The interviews were translated into occasionally awkward English. HP No. 139, A, vol. 11, p. 9. This female Russian psychiatrist was born in 1886 into a middle class family. No. 353, B11, p. 14; a medical student, no other biographical data.

[83] HP No. 139, p. 9; No. 353, p. 14; and No. 131, B10, p. 38.

[84] HP No. 424, B11, p. 18, no biographical data available. No. 423, A, vol. 21, p. 14. This respondent was a female Ukrainian teacher born about 1893 into the old middle class. No. 131, B10, p. 38; No. 454, A, vol. 23, p. 20, a male Ukrainian professor born about 1879, also from the middle class. No. 1313, A, vol. 33, p. 12, an female Armenian bookkeeper born about 1901 into the upper middle class.

[85] DENISOV, V. A., "Organizatsiia, metody i tekhnika sledstviia v organakh gosbezopasnosti SSSR", Nicolaevsky Collection, HI, Box 293, folder 7, pp. 1-2.

[86] HP No. 1296, A, vol. 33, pp. 6 and 21. This Russian female singer and blueprint copyist was born about 1910 into the family of a tsarist colonel.

woman's frankness saved her; the worst "crime" of the Terror was to lie about one's circumstances.[87]

A case in the life of General Petr Grigorenko further illustrates the possibility of deflecting police accusations. Grigorenko was a student at the General Staff Academy in the fall of 1937. A colonel in his class, M. N. Sharokhin, was accused by the political commissar and the chief of military counter-intelligence (Smersh) of the academy of having worked previously with people convicted of anti-Soviet activity. At that point in the Terror, this charge usually resulted in arrest. But two other officials, the party cell secretary of the class and his assistant, made sure that repressions "simply were not permitted to develop and gain momentum" within the group. At a meeting of the cell a heated discussion occurred in which the party secretary and his assistant resisted the attempts of the commissars to fasten a charge of political crime on Sharokhin. When the Smersh chief refused to share the information he supposedly knew about Sharokhin with the meeting, the party cell condemned the chief's behaviour and sent a copy of its decision to his party organization. He was disgraced and soon disappeared from the Academy. Grigorenko's party cell did not have a single case of links with enemies of the people, and no one in his class was arrested.[88]

The security police did not ruthlessly ignore the public's wishes. Especially when a charge concerned someone with a good work record, the NKVD responded to pressure from outside its ranks. The opposite also happened, that is, in numerous cases the police did not initiate charges against people, but reacted to accusations of criminal acts lodged by ordinary citizens.

What can be said about popular belief in and support for the Terror, as indicated by the comments of writers like Medvedev and Volkogonov cited above? Space permits only a few examples from a vast array of sources.[89] Workers in Magnitogorsk, where the American John Scott was employed as a welder, sneered at their supervisors: "You're a wrecker yourself", they would say. "Tomorrow they'll come

---

[87] Repin, Manuscript, 243-244. And see also his "Na sluzhbe v sovetskoi razvedke", Nicolaevsky Collection, HI, box 233, folder 7, where he uses the name A. Almazov.

[88] GRIGORENKO, P. G., 1982, pp. 79-84.

[89] For more cases, see my THURSTON, R., 1996, Chapter 5.

and arrest you. All you engineers and technicians are wreckers."[90] The rank and file troops under Grigorenko demanded, "Who is commanding us! Enemies of the people are intentionally putting us in danger of slaughter. All the officers ought to be punished."[91] These incidents indicate support for the arrests among ordinary people and also their sense that only the elite was targeted for repression.

Even when Anton Antonov-Ovseyenko's father was arrested in 1937 and executed the following year as an "enemy of the people", his son's faith did not waver. He recorded general approval of the campaign against spies and saboteurs and his own attitude that

> for me, a youth of nineteen, Stalin's name was sacred. As for the executions of enemies of the people, what could you say? The state had the right to defend itself. Errors were possible in such matters, but Stalin had nothing to do with it. He had been and remained the Great Leader.[92]

Antonov blames his lack of understanding on indoctrination, but the fact remains that he accepted the necessity for the purges. Nothing shook that faith until his own arrest in 1940. Usually only personal experience of detention shattered this outlook – but even that disaster did not always change views.

General A. V. Gorbatov recalled his reaction after the announcement that Marshal Tukhachevskii and other top officers had been executed on the charge of treason in June 1937:

> "How can it be", I thought, "that men who took such a part in routing foreign interventionists and internal reactionaries, men who have done so much to improve our army, Communists tested in the leanest days – how can it be that they have suddenly become enemies of the people?" Finally, after mulling over a host of possible explanations, I accepted the answer most common in those days. "No matter how you feed the wolf, it will always look towards the forest", as the saying goes. There was apparently some justification for this, since Tukhachevsky and a number of those arrested with him came from rich families, and had been Tsarist officers. "Obviously", many people said at the time, trying to puzzle out an answer,

---

[90] SCOTT, J., 1973 [1942], p. 195. Scott had been a student in Wisconsin before traveling to Magnitogorsk to work as a welder.

[91] GRIGORENKO, P. G., 1982, p. 75. And see VON HAGEN, M., "Soviet Soldiers and Officers on the Eve of the German Invasion: Towards A Description of Social Psychology and Political Attitudes", *Soviet Union/Union Sovietique* 18, No. 1-3 (1991), pp. 92-93.

[92] ANTONOV-OVSEYENKO, A., 1981, p. 231.

"they fell into the nets of foreign intelligence organizations while abroad on duty or to take a cure."[93]

Office workers responded similarly to the arrest of their boss in Lydia Chukovskaia's novel *Sofiia Petrovna*. She wrote the story in 1939-1940 as an attempt "to record the events just experienced by my country, those close to me, and myself.[94]

Nicholas Prychodko reacted the same way in late 1936 or early 1937 to the arrest of a professor he knew. "I began to wonder whether there really was something wrong, for surely the NKVD would not do this to an innocent man!"[95]

When the *Politburo* member Stanislav Kosior was arrested in 1937, General Grigorenko approved:

> I blamed everything I discovered about the Ukrainian famine on Kossior [...] I considered it [his arrest] just retribution for his activities against the people.[96]

An *émigré* also believed that the famine had been caused by enemies.[97] Thus for some people – speculation about how many would be pointless – the disaster of 1932-1933 may have evoked not disloyalty but support for the regime later in the decade, if they believed that the government was arresting those responsible for the famine.[98]

Pavel Kuznetsov's father, who had quit the party in disgust over collectivisation in 1930 but was never arrested, "believed the repressions were the machinations of enemies of the people; he wasn't the only one who thought this way.

---

[93] GORBATOV, A. V., 1964, p. 103.

[94] CHUKOVSKAIA, L., 1965, pp. 52 and 59. See also 50. The novel is also called *Sofiia Petrovna*. Chukovskaia's father was the translator and writer Kornei Chukovskii.

[95] PRYCHODKO, N., 1952, p. 21. Prychodko worked in education; his father had been a well-off peasant.

[96] GRIGORENKO, P. G., 1982, p. 36.

[97] HP No. 9, A, vol. 1, p. 45; this Belorussian woman, who was born about 1920 into the family of a mechanic, was a student before the war. A friend who had served in grain collections told her stories of people dying.

[98] In addition to the materials just cited, during provincial show trials of rural officials in 1937-1938 peasants often accused defendants of having helped worsen or cause the famine; see FITZPATRICK, S., 1994, p. 305. This sort of accusation may well mean that the peasants believed that the rural officials were guilty regarding the famine; after all, they were put on trial, and plenty of very real abuses by them were exposed in the process.

This reverses the usual identification of enemies but nonetheless recognizes their role. Moreover, the elder Kuznetsov accepted the necessity for "vigilance" and for harshness: he had the "conviction that whoever ran counter to the regime should be exterminated for the good of the community".[99]

Belief that spies and saboteurs had penetrated the upper echelons of Soviet society was common. *Émigrés* who had left the country during or shortly after the war and were later interviewed in the West regularly expressed certainty that Tukhachevskii was guilty of plotting with the Germans.[100] John Hazard, an American Sovietologist who studied law in Moscow in 1937, remembered that the students he knew usually believed that the marshal was guilty.[101] If citizens considered one of the country's best-known officers a traitor, they would have felt great unease about saboteurs among other strata as well.

A young naval intelligence officer had eagerly looked for foreign agents in 1935-1938, he told a post-war interviewer. "At that time Japanese agents were very active on the Pacific", he still thought.[102] Valentina Bogdan's maid sincerely believed in enemies of the people in 1937 and considered that domestic servants had a duty to listen to conversations and report events such as the burning of papers. Servants were willingly recruited for this monitoring in the city of Rostov.[103] Markoosha Fischer, the Russian-born wife of an American journalist, also employed a domestic servant who believed in "enemies"

> truly represented the mentality of the woman and man in the street [...] she was not bothered by political doubts and accepted every official utterance as gospel.[104]

---

[99] KUZNETSOV, P., "Why I did not return to the USSR", David Dalin file, BA, 3.

[100] HP Nos. 149, 147, 11, 1684, 1664, 395 AS (NY) 1760, 135 B5, and others.

[101] Interview with John Hazard, Oxford, Ohio, May 11, 1991. Jack Miller, a British economist who lived in Moscow in 1936-1937, reported that students in a planning institute, who were mostly in their 1930s, were not at all worried about the arrests, either in terms of their own safety or out of pity for those taken. There were no arrests among these students before Miller left the institute in September 1937. See his MILLER, J., 1964, p. 118-119. I thank Lars Lih for this citation.

[102] HP No. 105, A, vol. 8, pp. 3, 4, and 11. This was a male Russian born about 1918 or a little earlier; his father was a nobleman but a middleclass civil servant.

[103] BOGDAN, V., 1982, pp. 108-111.

[104] FISCHER, M., 1944, pp. 151, 163-165.

Such statements may be found in many other sources; the degree of support for the Terror was indeed substantial. This factor helps explain later events which must otherwise be baffling, in particular the massive outpouring of grief for Stalin after his death in 1953 and the high approval rating for him mentioned above in polls taken in the late 1980s and early 1990s. Soviet people's belief in enemies within society and the need to eradicate them begins to make sense when considered in the long context of threats to the country from foreigners, greatly heightened in the 1930s by the rise of Nazi Germany on one flank of the USSR and Imperial Japan on the other. A few years earlier, the presence of foreign troops on Russian soil during the Civil War and the support they gave to White forces helped produce a widespread sense that treason was occurring within the country. Before that were the great losses of World War I and other invasions stretching back through Napoleon, repeated attacks by the Poles, Swedes, and Germans, to the Mongol conquest of 1240. The long history of death at the hands of foreigners, often with the help of Russians, helped produce a venomous mindset among Stalinist leaders and followers. This background, together with particular deeds and words adopted by the regime, granted permission to hate to millions of Soviet citizens in the 1930s.

The German public, though not the country's professional historians, enthusiastically welcomed Daniel Goldhagen's *Hitler's Willing Executioners* because it seemed to show how different the people are now from those who readily killed Jews under the Third Reich.[105] Germany had a miserable and deadly history of anti-Semitism, but Goldhagen seems to say that it could be, and has been, overcome; the Germans have changed and achieved a higher level of civilization and compassion.[106] Russian commentators on Stalin also frequently offer a simple way out of the dismal past: become educated, cultured, and western, and all will be well.

Yet such glossy optimism says little about why German, Soviet, or other peoples became involved in mass persecution in the first place. The tendency to dehumanise one's enemies is probably inherent in all early forms of social development, and it has had a long history in western culture. The Bible demeans entire groups at numerous points; the Gospel according to Luke blames the death of Christ on the Jews as a people, for example. But Western Europe remained fairly tolerant

---

[105] GOLDHAGEN, D. J., 1996.

[106] See Goldhagen's remarks in GOLDHAGEN, D. J., 1998, especially p. 143.

of groups outside the mainstream until about the year 1000, when various factors began to create a persecuting society, with deadly results. The Enlightenment added fuel to any possible fire by providing a supposedly scientific rationale and hierarchy to discussions of the world's peoples; one key project of eighteenth-century western thinkers was to define "civilization" and contrast it to "barbarism", which supposedly characterised entire nations located outside of an area from Berlin to Dublin.[107] Karl Marx was a worthy product of the Enlightenment in his yearning to rearrange society for the better and in his tendency to categorise and rank people according to their inner worth: some classes are better than others.

But the Soviet Terror of the late 1930s was hardly "Marxist" or "socialist", since the arrests were linked not to social categories but to the perception that suspects had committed real crimes. In a frenzy of suspicion promoted from above and below, Soviet citizens widely believed that saboteurs or "wreckers", aided by foreigners, were mounting a desperate attack on society from within.

Mass murder of witches, heretics, or enemies of the people, for instance, appears to depend on this kind of fear, itself produced by a combination of some general outlook and a specific set of circumstances. It is not of much use to point to ideology or world view as the culprit: Christianity in a broad sense could produce an impetus to greater civilization but also ferocious attacks on heretics and aboriginals. Marx could mention the "dictatorship of the proletariat" – a few times and only in passing – and also believe that socialism could come to power democratically in certain countries.[108]

Mass persecution develops when both the authorities of an area and the local population come to believe that internal enemies pose a grave threat to the larger society. Examining how and why this happens requires a close look at the ways in which permission to hate has been elicited from above, from below, and by circumstances.

---

[107] WOLFF, L., 1994.

[108] See "The Possibility of Non-violent Revolution", a speech Marx delivered in Amsterdam on September 8, 1872, in MARX, K., 1978 [1872], pp. 522-524.

CHAPTER 8

The Cutting Edge:
A Sterilisation Campaign in Sweden

Elin FRYKMAN

Beginning in 1935, over a period of forty years, 62,888 Swedes
were sterilised. A law passed in 1941 clearly states that the Swedish
Board of Medicine could order sterilisations by force. Under certain
particular circumstances two physicians could decide upon the
operation and realise it without the consent of the Board of Medicine.
And they did.

This text tells a story of the sterilisations in Sweden. In a very
down-to-earth manner it attempts to give an account of the reasons and
the ideas behind the laws of sterilisation, the debate and its practice.
Without a thorough understanding of what happened during that
Golden era of the Swedish welfare state, one is too easy a victim of the
frequent over-simplifications that flourish in the press and the less
serious academia. A very political Swedish debate in 1997 gave rise to
a tidal wave which hit the shores of Europe, Japan and America alike.
The debate, though important to Swedish society, suffered from a lack
of historical perspective which alienated serious academics. It is
crucial that an understanding of the historical context accompanies any
account of the sterilisations to prevent them from an entirely political
interpretation.[1] This text will attempt a historical understanding of the
sterilisations with reference to Zygmunt Bauman's analysis of the
Holocaust.

---

[1] The journalist who initiated the debate, Maciej Zaremba, has recently published a
book about his cause, called *De rena och de andra: om tvångssteriliseringar,
rashygien och arvssynd*, Stockholm, DN, 1999, read also Broberg, Gunnar and
Tydén, Mattias "När svensk historia blev en världsnyhet", *Tvärsnitt*, no 3, 1998 for
an account how the debate of 1997 was received and depicted in other countries.

The Swedish welfare state that emerged during the 1930s and 1940s became a model for many industrialised states. These were years when the Swedish social engineers Gunnar and Alva Myrdal advised social workers of the United States about how to avoid racial conflicts and inspired European administrators to emulate Swedish child-care policies. Marquis W. Childs wrote *Sweden, the Middle Way* in 1936. The world watched in awe as the Swedish state took on the problems of the working-class and the economy "scientifically". More than anything else, the Swedish experts were the ambassadors of a modern, rational state with the best of intentions towards its citizens. It excelled in administration and efficiency, often calling upon academic experts to make sure the solutions found to the problems of the recently industrialised country were really the best.

Having introduced the ins and outs of the sterilisations and their scientific authority, this text will go on to address the question whether the Swedish welfare state can be used as an example of the swift and efficient modernisation, legitimised by scientists and experts, that Zygmunt Bauman uses as an ideal type to describe genocide as preconditioned by modernity.[2] We will compare the logic behind the sterilisations with that of genocide to look for explanatory similarities as a new way of understanding why the sterilisation of 62,888 persons met so little resistance.

Through Tinted Glasses

Racial hygiene, or the dream of improving man through the control of reproduction is far from new or unique to 20th century Sweden. In 1686 epileptic sufferers were forbidden to marry. When the law was reviewed in 1757 the wording was changed to explicitly state the function of preventing *hereditary disease*. This was long before Darwin publishes his *On the Origin of Spices*, but it was also thousands of years *after* man started cross-breeding wheat to improve its feeding capacities. The knowledge that qualities were hereditary was present in the everyday life of anyone living close to animals and crops, in spite of the fact that they did not have our understanding of it. The reason why marriage between individuals who might transmit a hereditary disease to their offspring was prohibited in the 17th and 18th century was the contemporary view that a country's population

---

2   BAUMAN, Z., 1989.

constituted an important national resource. It is understood that if the population was to be a resource then its quality had to be intact.[3]

The racial and later social hygiene that was to assure the quality of the Swedish citizens was practised in a modern society, the welfare society. In 1929 the Swedish model for the welfare state was labelled "the People's Home" *(folkhemmet)* by the Social Democratic leader P. A. Hansson. The concept had already been used by the young conservatives, and was developed by the conservative politician and political scientist Rudolf Kjellén at the outset of the 20th century.[4] The concept was used by all parties around 1930, but would later be associated more with the implementation of social democracy than its conservative origins. In his classic and frequently cited speech of 1929, Hansson identified the paternalistic family structure together with solidarity between the classes as the main ingredients of the *folkhem*-recipe. Together with a church that was relaxing its attitudes, the labour movement and its popular education movement, the Social Democratic politicians beginning in the early 1930s guided Sweden into a new era. The Stockholm Exhibition in 1930 launched functionalism, promoting simple, rational design. The strides made in popular education promoted a belief in the future and in rationalism within the labour movement. Scientists and experts including Gunnar and Alva Myrdal called attention to political questions of men and women alike, advocating the "reform eugenics" that Gunnar Dahlberg would introduce at the Institute of Race Biology. The new era that the term *folkhem* represented was a time of social engineering and state-oriented solutions to political and social problems. It was an era where rational, scientific facts were to be the guidelines of change, and where the social engineer as well as the medical, physical, economical or technical researcher would guide society.[5] One of a number of questions of the new era was the declining birth-rate. The threat of a dying nation seemed more real than ever: at the turn of the century an average family had four children, when Gunnar and Alva Myrdal's report on the problem was published in 1934, the average family had two children. The reproduction became a matter of state concern. Fertility became politics.

---

[3] KÄLVEMARK, A.-S., 1980, pp. 23-24.

[4] STRÅTH, B., 2000a, pp. 386ff.; STRÅTH, B., 2000b.

[5] By this era Swedish social scientists firmly established themselves as empirically guided social engineers, contrasting clearly with the development of social sciences in Germany and Italy. See WAGNER, P. and WITTROCK, B., 1992.

The history and development of sterilisation in Sweden can be studied through a variety of perspectives from the turn of the century up until 1975 (when the laws were abolished). Certain scholars have thus applied gender perspectives, and found that women were targeted for special reasons.[6] Others have studied the sterilised groups liminal state and found that social groups that threatened the equilibrium of society, like itinerants *(tattare)* or prostitutes, were targeted for other reasons.[7] Others, again, have focused on the governmental political influences and the close connection with scientists, physicians and social engineers, mainly through studying the history of science and ideas.[8] The perspective this study will employ is that of genocide.

Genocide, as defined in the UN convention of 1948, means killing or harming (mentally or physically) members of a group. It also means preventing them from reproducing or forcibly transferring their children from them. To subject a group to living conditions aimed at physical destruction is also classified as genocide.[9] Genocide, however, needs a somewhat thicker definition then the strictly ethical and legal definition of the UN convention. One possible definition revolves around the legitimisation of political power. New regimes need to construct ideologies creating "Others" by stigmatising or excluding groups that are depicted as the enemy of the regime. See here the chapter by Robert Thurston in this volume. These groups are often victims of genocide, according to Robert Melson who has isolated four genocides following revolutionary upheavals and the need to legitimise new regimes: the mass murder of Armenians by the Young Turks of the 1910s, Stalin's purge of the kulaks in the Soviet Union of the 1930s, the Holocaust and finally the genocide of the Khmer Rouge in 1970s Cambodia.[10] For a more balanced understanding of genocide we need to consider the individual actors and their convictions as well as the structures within which they act, as Klas-Göran Karlsson has stated.[11] A thick definition of genocide needs to take into account the intention behind the action, and we need to be familiar with the

---

[6]   See HIRDMAN, Y., 1989; HIRDMAN, Y., 1994 and RUNCIS, M., 1998.

[7]   SVENSSON, B., 1995; SÖDERBLOM, T., 1992.

[8]   BROBERG, G. and TYDÉN, M., 1991 and BROBERG, G. and TYDÉN, M., 1996.

[9]   Convention of the prevention and punishment of the crime of genocide. Resolution 260 (III) A, 9 December 1948, U.N.T.S., 1951, p. 277. The convention was not ratified until 1951.

[10]   MELSON, R., 1992, pp. 17-22.

[11]   KARLSSON, K.-G., 1996, pp. 134-140.

technology applied to determine whether it is a question of isolated events or centrally planned and executed actions on a large scale. Genocide is defined by Zygmunt Bauman as the killing of a group of people with the explicit intention of establishing a new and better society.[12] It is thus important to analyse the visions commonly held.

To be able to establish whether the Swedish sterilisations can be interpreted as genocide we need to go to the bottom of three matters. Firstly, what group was targeted in the supposed genocide? Were they seen as the enemy of the state? Secondly, was the genocide centrally administered, encouraged or executed? Finally, was there an intention of establishing a better society behind the sterilisations. To do this we first need to present the history of sterilisations through "genocide tinted glasses". That means that we choose to focus on the incidents, structures and ideas that are relevant to this interpretation only. The history of Swedish sterilisations has been described by many a scholar. Gunnar Broberg and Mattias Tydéns account "Eugenics in Sweden: Efficient Care" in *Eugenics and the Welfare State* will give the English-speaking reader a more in-depth account. The following account is based on their excellent work if not otherwise referenced. [13]

Mendel, Darwin and Spencer: Entering a New Century

Between 1870 and 1914 one in six Swedes left the country. They were not the old, the weak or the infirm, but the young and enterprising. The labour movement, women's rights movements, free-church movement and temperance movements pleaded for rapid changes in a still predominantly agrarian society. In 1900, 75% of Sweden's five million inhabitants still lived in the countryside. Karin Johannisson, writing on the political anatomy of the welfare state, draws a disturbing close-up of life circumstances at the turn of the century: in Stockholm 90% lived in small apartments made up of one room and a kitchen. One in every ten children died before reaching its first birthday. Tuberculosis, syphilis and rheumatism together with epidemics like polio, measles, diphtheria and scarlet fever haunted every-day life of children and grown-ups. Tuberculosis alone infected 100,000 persons every year killing 10,000 of them. Men were most commonly diagnosed as alcoholic, but occupational diseases like led

---

[12] BAUMAN, Z., 1989, p. 91.

[13] BROBERG, G. and ROLL-HANSEN, N., 1996, pp. 77-98 and BROBERG, G. and TYDÉN, M., 1991, pp. 9-14 and 26.

poisoning, silicosis and anthracosis also sent many of the young and able to premature deaths.[14] From 1900 to 1930 the capacity of the hospitals increased threefold and the number of physicians increased from 1,131 to 2,239.[15] Much of this may be derived from the fact that Sweden's late industrialisation, which started in the 1870s or 1880s, changed society rapidly.

This is part of the everyday life in the Sweden where the ideas that would later be labelled as *racial hygiene* and *racial biology* were introduced in latter half of the 19th century. Social Darwinism was at the time widespread in Europe and was influencing racial hygiene in introducing the biological determinism: the idea that man is limited and programmed by her biology, and the only way to change her is through that very biology. Social Darwinism's logic that social questions should also be determined by biological laws would be central to Swedish racism. Charles Darwin's unlucky expression "survival of the fittest" implied nothing but the survival of the species or individual that could best reproduce. This ability, Darwin wrote, was biologically inherent in an individual but also developed different-ly in each individual depending on its milieu. Certain individuals or species were better at adapting to new and different circumstances, which determined the evolutionary development in their favour.[16] Social Darwinism translated "the survival of the fittest for reproduction and adaptation" as the survival, in nature or society, of the strongest individual, a definition which fit the liberal needs of a nascent capital-ism to a T.

The discoveries of the Austrian monk Gregor Mendel were widely recognised around the turn of the century. His mapping of heredity in recessive and dominant genes was coupled with the ideas of Social Darwinism. Darwinism provided a biological determinism, Social Darwinism a conviction that this determinism favoured the successful and the Mendelian rules of heredity that the success or failure of an individual was at least partly hereditary determined. It is important to point out that these ideas were not a developed doctrine, but rather the tools of understanding society that many a European intellectual embraced at this very time. Racial hygiene, being one very practically oriented part of this entire understanding was not the unique faith of a

---

[14] JOHANNISSON, K., 1997, pp. 228-229, BROBERG, G. and TYDÉN, M., 1996, p. 78.
[15] HISTORISK STATISTIK FÖR SVERIGE, 1960, pp. 157-159.
[16] DARWIN, C., 1859.

certain political or scientific group, but part of a commonly embraced paradigm.[17]

The Threat of Degeneration and its Social Consequences

The theory of degeneration introduced by Bénedict Morel in the 1850s depicted the bad and unwanted sides of industrialisation in a very biological way. Its ugly face was a degenerated hereditary disposition and increasing sickly predisposition in the growing population. Degeneration was threatening to the individual as it lead to mental and physical illness as well as social disorders such as the abuse of alcohol, sexual perversions or criminality. Thus, the degeneration inherent in industrialisation also threatened society as a whole.[18] Luckily enough Morel had an idea of how to prevent total collapse. One of the powerful antidotes that was to be taken into account was *hygiene*. The measures that were to be taken concentrated on physical hygiene. They included good nutrition and cleanliness to stem the spread of disease, as well as the elimination of crowded housing conditions and physical exercise. They also concentrated on social hygiene in so far as voicing the view that society had to be made up of genetically adequate components: good citizens. Where hygiene in other countries was going to focus on racial hygiene, Swedish eugenics were from the onset more focused on the social side of eugenic hygiene, and its role in the social body. Swedish racial biology was question of class and social groups rather than races.[19] The conviction that certain parts of society were, eugenically, better citizens than others would help make Swedish politicians and scientists close their eyes to the facts that science presented for a number of years.

An Unsuccessful Attempt at Measuring the Skulls of the Swedish Race

The average Swede may not have experienced degeneration in a rapidly changing world. The average Swede may not even have noticed that industrialisation led to higher costs for society in increasing the number of mentally ill and retarded. But some intellectuals, like the author Viktor Rydberg and the conservative political scientist

---

[17] BROBERG, G. and TYDÉN, M., 1991, pp. 9-14.

[18] JOHANNISSON, K., 1997, p. 231; KOCH, L., 1996, pp. 30-32.

[19] FRYKMAN, J. and LÖFGREN, O., 1985, pp. 60-61.

Pontus Fahlbeck did, and they voiced their concerns.[20] The end of the 19th century idea that the Swedish society and the Swedish "race" was threatened by degeneration called for a definition of what was really Swedish. One of the answers to that question was to be searched in phrenology: the measuring of skulls. In 1897 and 1898 the 45,000 young Swedes were measured for the work of Gustaf Retzius which was published in 1902, under the title of *Anthropologia suecica*. Retzius was one of the leading members in the Swedish Society for Anthropology and Geography which was founded in 1882. In his works, the Swedish race was found, to the great disappointment of the society to be less "Nordic" than they had expected and hoped.[21] As early as 1902 the results implied that there was nothing distinct about the Swedish race. Yet, the concept of the Swedish race would be rhetorically used as late as the 1940s to legitimise the sterilisations act.

The anthropological, skull measuring tradition in Sweden was to be eclipsed by the advance of genetics. An institute for plant breeding was established near Lund in 1886. The Svalöf institute became important for the introduction of Mendelism in to Sweden. At the University of Lund, the botanist Herman Nilsson-Ehle developed Mendelian genetics. The first Swedish genetics association, called the Mendel Society, was subsequently formed in Lund in 1910, with Nilsson-Ehle as a central figure. Around this time the eugenic movement appeared. It established connections with anthropological research promoted by Herman Lundborg (see below). Fundamental to the movement was the understanding of hereditary matters that stemmed from the recent spread of Mendel's findings. The society favoured the idea of the Nordic race even though the investigations published in the *Anthropologia suecica* had pointed in a totally different direction. Many of the central characters would be physicians. Their arguments revolved around terms like "hygiene", "natural selection" and the anatomist Vilhelm Hultcranz, who had previously worked with Retzius at *Anthropologica suecica*, argued for putting a halt to "the generation of the unfit, the parasites of society".[22] It is quite clearly this kind of rhetoric that inspired the assumption that the sterilisations that happened between 1935 and 1975 were aimed at a "parasitic" group of society whose genes must be eradicated to prevent the threatening degeneration to the Nordic race and break-down of industrialised

---

[20]   BROBERG, G. and TYDÉN, M., 1996, pp. 78-79.

[21]   BROBERG, G. and TYDÉN, M., 1991, p. 26.

[22]   BROBERG, G. and TYDÉN, M., 1996, p. 83.

society. It was not, as we will see further on, the ethnical racism pronounced in those early years and resounding throughout the 1940s that was going to shape the sterilisations acts or their implementation, but the social side of eugenics, the reform eugenics.

About the same time in Stockholm, in 1909, the Swedish Society for Racial Hygiene was founded. The society joined the German *Gesellschaft für Rassenhygiene*. Though in membership the society was never large (it was never to exceed hundred members), its members were more often than not highly esteemed academics.[23] Lectures were given and research funded on a small scale. The society never had much influence on the public opinion, although its mere existence shows the biomedical reform ideas during the first decades of the 20th century. The main character in Swedish race biology was a psychiatrist and physician, Herman Lundborg. He, not the Mendel Society, the Swedish Society for Anthropology and Geography, nor the Swedish Society for Racial Hygiene was going to be the one to spread the message about the influence of heredity and the fear of degeneration to the public.

Documenting Medical History:
The Importance of Classifying

Herman Lundborg saw himself as the leader of the Swedish eugenic movement. Charismatically, he evoked an apocalyptic atmosphere and appealed to the agrarian romanticism that was so familiar to the turn-of-the-century Swedish citizen.[24] Lundborg applied his renowned colleagues Dugdale's and Davenport's methods of studying pedigrees with a historical-genealogical approach, investigating hereditary disease in a farming family from the south of Sweden. He was thus able to prove that the disease of *mycoconus epilepsy* was transmitted in the family according to Mendelian laws. The family in question did not only degenerate rapidly, but also brought down the entire region of the peninsula of Listerlandet, due to the traditions of intermarriage in Lundborg's assessment. The unfortunate genetic material and thoughtless customs had not only biological but also social consequences that threatened society. Throughout Lundborg's writings, racial biology was used not to label people as races but as classes. The hope of the nation was located to

---

[23] BROBERG, G. and TYDÉN, M., 1996, 1996, pp. 83-84.

[24] BERGGREN, H., 1995, TOLER, J., 1992.

the middle class. The middle class was, according to Lundborg, made up of farmers, urban bourgeoisie and the skilled part of the working class: a wide definition of middle-class that embraced the striving parts of the working class and welcomed them in to the welfare society. The real "élite" of the society was deemed suspect as degenerate. Needless to say, degeneration lodged there as well as in the lower strata of the working class.[25] Jonas Frykman and Orvar Löfgren have described how the rapidly growing middle-class in the emerging Swedish welfare society came to be the norm of normality. The position of the middle-class no longer had to be granted by means of political representation of economical interests, but was to be based on the fact that they represented what was "normal" and "Swedish" in the welfare state.[26] Lundborg's classification placing the best genes in the middle class gave the desired answers: Swedishness was really to be found in the middle-class.[27]

Lundborg went on to publish a popular series on the aims and methods of eugenics, the sterilisation issue and modern genetics where he propagated for The Swedish Society of Racial Hygiene. In 1918 he organised an exhibition to enlighten the masses about the different racial types, linking Swedish history to modern science in a very patriotic fashion. The Swedes seemed to enjoy the race rhetoric: the exhibition was visited by many and received considerable publicity. In Denmark as in Sweden the promoters of racial biology addressed the public to win their confidence and thus being taken seriously as a science.[28]

But Herman Lundborg also represents an idea less known to the posterity. He represents the idea that labelling and classifying the individual parts that were to make up the *folkhem* was necessary. This categorising of the world is partly to be seen as one of the fundaments upon which the labellers; the social workers, priests and physicians were to build their shrine. By labelling others they were going to make themselves indispensable, as the upkeepers of the seemingly crucial borders drawn between groups. The collecting of data on individuals

---

[25] FRYKMAN, J. and LÖFGREN, O., 1985, p. 61.

[26] FRYKMAN, J. and LÖFGREN, O., 1987 [1979]; FRYKMAN, J., 1993, pp. 259-274.

[27] Welcoming the ambitious representatives of the working-class in to the middle-class was nothing unique to the Social Democratic *folkhem* period. Göran B. Nilsson has showed that the idea was promoted by Swedish liberals as early as the 1850s. NILSSON, G. B., 1995, pp. 136-140.

[28] KOCH, L., 1996, pp. 115, 176.

and on biological phenomena also made way for a comparison between results and between groups. This, in turn could be related to a norm, which for the first time was possible to create from collected data. We know from Herman Lundborg that this norm was the middle-class. It was later going to be used efficiently as a means of controlling the ones that fell outside of the norm.[29]

Early Sterilisations, a Few Rare Cases

The first recorded sterilisation in Sweden dates back to 1895. The professor of medicine, Elis Essen-Möller, performed at least sixteen sterilisations between 1906 and 1915, some on eugenic grounds and others on medical grounds. Since there was no legislation pertaining to sterilisation, the operations performed on other than purely medical grounds were formally illegal. Throughout the 1910s the attitudes toward eugenic sterilisation in Sweden as well as Denmark were marked by uncertainty and scepticism. Scientific knowledge on heredity was insufficient, and scientists repeatedly testified to its uncertainty. The Scandinavian authority on race biology, the Dane Willhelm Johanssen knew by this stage that negative eugenics (like sterilisation) could never change the gene pool of a people. The only way to do that was through positive eugenics (*e.g.* breeding institutions for the best suited).[30] But Swedish politicians seemed determined to use eugenics in their reforming of society according to the middle class, and thus (as in the case of the findings of the *Anthropologia suecica*) choose to ignore this scientists voicing signs of hesitation. Even though he had performed a few eugenically motivated sterilisations, Elis Essen-Möller did not speak in favour of a sterilisation law in 1915. Public opinion was not quite ready for that. In stead, the debate on eugenic legislation was to begin with the impediments to marriage. The marriage laws instituted in 1915 aimed at preventing transmission of believed hereditary diseases such as mental illness, mental retardation and epilepsy. They opened the door to a legislative solution to the seemingly biological problems of industrialised modern society.

---

[29] QVARSELL, R., 1991, p. 79.

[30] In Denmark, politicians realised in the early 1920s that scientists refused to support a sterilisation legislation based on eugenics, as they had no evidence in support of the social questions that the politicians wanted to address. The politicians thus abandoned eugenic arguments and focused on economical, humanitarian and moral arguments. KOCH, L., 1996, pp. 57-87.

Racial Biology Goes Political and Becomes Racial Hygiene: Foundation of an Institute for Race Biology

In 1921 a bill was introduced in both chambers of the Swedish parliament, signed by members of all parties. The bill promoted a state institute for race biology. The proposals of the bill were submitted to the universities. Amongst universities and political parties the representatives were unanimous in recommending the establishment of an institute. When the Swedish Institute for Race Biology was set up in Uppsala in 1922 it was the first such state institute in the world. Herman Lundborg would be the dominant force at the institute. The very act of Parliament provided Swedish eugenics with the status and the institutional basis that the new science needed to be officially accepted. Another important motivation for the institute was the recently appearing reference to science as a means of transforming society and of moral improvement. The traditional nationalistic stance and the more modern stance of the newly discovered race biology as a means of transforming society thus joined together in an easily accessible rhetoric which the public could easily follow. The public connection was particularly important to the institute, which continued the work for "popular education".[31]

At the institute Herman Lundborg followed in the footsteps of *Anthropologia suecica*. About 100,000 "Swedes" were measured, statistics collected and photographs taken. By the end of 1926, the result was published under the title *The Racial Character of the Swedish Nation*.[32] The findings were very much the same as those of the *Anthropoligia suecica*. The work having won a lot of international attention and praise, Herman Lundborg went on to attempt a complete inventory of the race biology of the Swedish Sami. The work concentrated on the consequences of one people merging with another. The investigation would not be presented until ten years later and received very limited public attention. The institute enjoyed international recognition. Lundborg co-operated with Charles Davenport in Cold Springs Harbour and S. J. Holmes at Berkley. The institute was also working

---

[31] BROBERG, G. and TYDÉN, M., 1996, pp. 87-88; RUNCIS, M., 1998, p. 173; KOCH, L., 1996, p. 87.

[32] LUNDBORG, H., 1927 and 1928.

closely with their German colleagues, and a certain amount of co-operation existed between the Scandinavian countries.[33]

As Nils von Hoffsten pointed out in his textbook on the science of heredity in 1919, genetics still did not offer any clear guidelines for eugenic sterilisation.[34] The proponents of sterilisation solved this problem by turning to social and economical arguments, but the vocabulary of the racial biology was used throughout the 1940s. The irony behind the sterilisations is that while the principles of race hygiene were enthusiastically embraced by politicians and public alike, science would never prove that sterilisations on eugenic grounds could be genetically motivated.

The first proposal for a bill of sterilisation was introduced in 1922 by a psychiatrist, Alfred Petrén. Although not arguing for compulsory measures, the bill (which was signed by Social Democrats, Liberals and one representative from the Agrarian Party) argued for systematic sterilisation of the mentally retarded. Epileptics, mentally ill and sexual offenders were also included in the bill. Like those who shared his opinion, he had to argue for the sterilisations from economical and social points of view.[35]

A Turning Point in the History of Swedish Race Biology

In 1933 the institute and with it the Swedish race biology, reached a crisis point. The director, Herman Lundborg was, like the academic circles in Sweden from the 19th century up to World War II, pro-German. He had invited numerous German speakers to the public lectures given by the institute beginning in 1922. Lundborg was not only active in the public through his series of public lectures, but also himself personally as an orator of great skill and intensity. In 1933 the press had turned against him as it might against a very charismatic person, and public opinion was questioning the existence of his institute. Lundborg, an intransigent character, was to be replaced by the

---

[33] In Norway an Institute of Racial Hygiene had opened at Oslo University in 1916. In Denmark Copenhagen University opened its Institute for Human Eugenics and Hereditary Biology sponsored by the Rockefeller Foundation as late as 1938, but an annual grant for research on racial biology had been granted since 1920 by the Anthropological Committee. KOCH, L., 1996, p. 137-138.

[34] HOFFSTEN, N. V., 1919, pp. 493-494.

[35] Swedish Parliament records 1922, *Forsta Kammaren Motioner*, No.188.

Left wing candidate, Gunnar Dahlberg.[36] He is the marker that traces a break with the "old eugenic school". The "old" mainline eugenics that Lundborg represented, believed in the decisive role of heredity, the limited effect of environmental influence and thus the immediate usefulness of a eugenic reform. Lundborg was convinced of the advantages of the Nordic race (in spite of the fact that Retzius findings showed there was no such thing), he opposed industrialisation and would later profess anti-Semitic views and declare himself a Nazi. Herman Nilsson-Ehle did the same thing.[37] The "new eugenic school" which Gunnar Dahlberg represented, stressed environmental influences rather than hereditary, and heralded social medicine as the successor of the outdated racial eugenics. Gunnar Dahlberg shared the political views of the Social Democratic party, and was close friends with Gunnar Myrdal. Dahlberg and Myrdal as "social engineers" represented a Social Democracy which emphasised the importance of economical and social sciences in restructuring society rather than biological.[38]

The Swedish Institute for Race Biology would follow the visions of the *folkhem* closely. The new era appearing in the 1930s would, as stated in the introduction, concentrate on social medicine where racial eugenics had once inspired. A corner-stone in the politics of the *folkhem* was state-oriented solutions to political and social problems. Through legislation the principle of state intervention was going to enter the private sphere of sexuality.

Social Hygiene Replaces Eugenic Hygiene

The first law of sterilisation would come in to existence in 1935. By then Swedish Social Democracy was beginning to stabilise, and no longer concerned itself exclusively with the working-class. When the basic demands of the workers were satisfied, newer Social Democrats (if not the old ones) directed their argumentation and tactics towards a growing middle class. The monetary and social politics of the Social Democrats represented a significant break with conservative politics. To be able to achieve the desired break they had had to co-operate with the Agrarian Party, and their politics met with considerable hostility

---

[36]   The Social Democrats had just formed a government which would usher in a long era of Social Democratic rule in Sweden.

[37]   BROBERG, G. and ROLL-HANSEN, N., 1996, p. 93.

[38]   BROBERG, G. and ROLL-HANSEN, N., 1996, p. 94.

and distrust from the conservatives as well as criticism from within the ranks. This new regime needed to legitimise its politics and maintain confidence. The Social Democrats were to focus very firmly on a few questions, and create nation-wide concern for these questions. Population policy and the politics of health was but one question on their programme. The state and the public sector were strengthened, increasing the rights of the state towards the individual and at the same time showing great respect for her. The strong centralisation was seen as a prerequisite for freedom of choice, granting the rights of the weak. This complex way of viewing things is best described by Gunnar Broberg and Mattias Tydén: "Although such a policy may be based on the best of intentions it never quite works [...]."[39]

The Sterilisations Act of 1935 was to be preceded by intensive debate. The first Commission of Sterilisation, made up of two professors of medicine, one lawyer and one psychiatrist proposed in 1929 a very restricted law limited to voluntary sterilisations on genetic grounds. Their report was vehemently criticised because of its focus on voluntary sterilisation and on strictly hereditary matters. In 1933 Alfred Petrén convinced the Parliament to review the matter, and one single professor of criminal law, Ragnar Bergendal, prepared a second proposal. His proposal opened the door to sterilisations of legally incompetent individuals without their consent, to guarantee that sterilisations that were in the interest of society should not be stopped.[40] The bill was passed on 1 January 1935. It did not accept the forcing of a person to the operating theatre, but recommended persuasion of unwilling patients. This "persuasion" has been much debated, and even though no physical violence was allowed, many of the sterilised testify to different ways of being coerced into undergoing the treatment. According to the bill there were two reasons for sterilisation. Either the person in question was incapable of taking care of their child *(social indication)* or if the person through their hereditary disposition risked passing mental deficiency or mental disease to their offspring *(eugenic indication)*. If the person was legally incompetent the operation could be done against their will (but without the use of force). With the bill of 1941 the indications for sterilisation were substantially widened. *Eugenic indication* came to include carriers of malignant diseases and grave disabilities as well as the mentally ill and mentally retarded. *Social indication* extended from previously concerning mainly

---

[39] BROBERG, G. and ROLL-HANSEN, N., 1996, p. 98.
[40] Swedish Parliament records 1933, *Forsta Kammaren Motioner*, No.188.

mentally ill and mentally deficient to include any "asocial way of life". A third indication exclusive to women was added. *Medical indication* was reserved for women who's health was endangered through pregnancy.

A Targeted Group?

The sterilised individuals shared only one experience: that of having their Fallopian tubes or spermatic ducts cut. The one thing they had in common was that they themselves, or representatives of the Swedish state found them incapable either of having well-born children or of looking after them properly. They came from a number of different groups; they were often women, sometimes mentally retarded or mentally ill, often poor, criminal, alcoholics or living on the fringes of society like itinerants, sometimes their only crime was a large sexual appetite or elevated fertility. Many were dependant upon social welfare, and unemployed. There was no opportunity to create a common identity between these heterogeneous groups that could have been activated in a resistance or the shaping of a group with common interests.

When the journalist Bosse Lindquist did the research for his book and radio-programmes on the sterilisations in the early 1990s he found that the sterilised were very reluctant to speak about their experience. He had great difficulties finding the two persons, Astrid and Torbjörn, who were willing to talk publicly about it.[41] The people he had contacted were ashamed to have been labelled as unworthy of motherhood or fatherhood, and some had not informed anyone but their very closest family. There never has been any organisation where the victims of the sterilisations could meet and talk about their common experiences. Being singled out as a bad mother or father was in itself so stigmatising that it effectively deterred the victims from creating or exploring a common identity after the incisions. There is no common identity as "victim of the scalpel" that could be used to define the individuals as a group even after the incision.

The modern welfare state creates Otherness.[42] The existence of groups of people living on the margins of society is not particular to any modern or post-modern society though. Any historian having read Aron Gorwitsch or Bronislaw Geremek's enquiries in to the emergence

---

[41] LINDQUIST, B., 1991, p. 10.

[42] BAUMAN, Z., 1989.

of the individual in medieval Europe and the marginal groups in 13th century Paris will find it hard to contest the fact that early Christian and urban society defined itself in opposition to its liminal groups.[43] The kind of otherness the modern welfare state created was of a very specific type. Believing that there was only one rational way of organising Swedish society, anyone not suited to this rational life by necessity had to be defined as the "Other". From a genocide perspective the "Other" would have been the enemy, within or without, who threatened the regime and with it the prosperity of the majority. So what did the "Other" really look like? Let us have a closer look at the different groups.

Fifty Eight Thousand Five Hundred Women

Women comprised 93% of the sterilised. The fact that men reproduce exactly as much as women (because it takes two to make a baby) was of little importance when sterilisations were being discussed and implemented. For a short time span statistics tell us that the eugenic effect of serialisations played some role in the decision making. Between 1935 and 1948 when eugenically motivated sterilisations made up a substantial part of or dominated the interventions, 19% of the sterilised were men. From the time when medically motivated sterilisations dominated (1949-1975) only 3% of the sterilised were men.[44] It is quite obvious that when sterilisations were eugenically motivated men were targeted as well as women although to a much lesser extent. When medical motivations dominated, women were almost exclusively targeted. We do not know exactly what hides behind the eugenic, medical and social motivations. These are mere bureaucratic labels that would have been used differently by different actors. We do know, thanks to Maija Runcis, that two thirds of the

---

[43] GEREMEK, B., 1987; GURWITSCH, A., 1997.

[44] Between 1935 and 1941 (the period when the initial law was applied) 12% of the sterilised were men. Mattias Tydén and Gunnar Broberg, on gathering the statistics, found that it was impossible to know from the application forms of this time if the sterilisations had medical, eugenic or social motivations. I believe it is reasonable to assume that a substantial part were eugenically motivated. In the period that follows, 1942-1948, eugenic sterilisations formed the dominant category, only to decline to about 10% from the mid 1950s to a stable 1-5% in the 1960s and 1970s. From the time when eugenically motivated sterilisations dominate over the other categories (1941-1949), 22% of the sterilised were men. From the time when medically motivated sterilisations dominated (1950-1975), only 3% of the sterilised were men. BROBERG, G. and TYDÉN, M., 1991, p. 99.

mothers mentioned in the applications following the initial law of 1934 were single mothers whose children had been taken away from them by the local social welfare.[45]

The all-encompassing motivation for the sterilisations had to do with the visions for the welfare state. When the laws were introduced the political arguments very much centred around social problems. One of the questions addressed was the reproduction of new citizens. Although the making of children obviously requires both sexes, the reproduction sphere was strictly woman's responsibility. In her much debated study *Att lägga livet till rätta* (Laying Life in Order) Yvonne Hirdman analyses the development of power relations between women and men in Sweden between 1930 and 1990. Her study has been summed up and translated in to English in the research report *Women – From Possibility to Problem?*, which I will refer to below.[46] She refers to the different stages of development as contracts between men and women. During the time the sterilisations act was being debated and introduced, the 1920s and 1930s the contract revolved around the women performing their duties as housewives. The social engineers of the 1930s articulated the gender conflict as a purely political problem, namely "Why and how were women (and to a certain extent, men) needed in modern societies?".[47] Their answer was quite simply: to form one unit, the family, apart from the other (larger) unit, society, but to work in both. Women's roles were, according to Hirdman, threefold: to produce children, to consume the various utilities that modern life and the economic policy of the welfare state required and finally to foster the new human beings in line with a modern, socially developed and technically adjusted society.[48] The unit of the family, which was so important to the development of the Swedish welfare state, was strictly woman's responsibility. It was also this unit that was going to be the centre of attention for the social engineers and the social politics of the 1930s.

The fact that women were targeted probably reflected their situation as wardens of the reproduction. They were targeted because of that function, not as an enemy within society that must be eliminated for

---

[45] RUNCIS, M., 1998, pp. 117-139. Runcis' statistics were collected from 499 applications between 1935 and 1941. Not all of these resulted in actual sterilisations.

[46] HIRDMAN, Y., 1989; HIRDMAN, Y., 1994.

[47] HIRDMAN, Y., 1994, p. 14.

[48] *Ibid.*, p. 19.

the comfort of the majority. It was not all women that were targeted, just those who did not fulfil the contract, as stipulated in the view of Yvonne Hirdman, the women who were bad mothers and thus could not secure their roles as producers and fosterers of the children of the nation.

Living on the Margin of Society: Itinerants and Prostitutes

Another way of perceiving the targeted group is to define them as those who choose to live on the margins of society. From Mary Douglas we know that those who live on the margins or the *limes* of a certain society appear threatening to those who live within.[49] When the welfare state defined what was marginal it also defined itself. Through defining "them", the outline of who "we" were became all the clearer. The "we" was, as we have seen, modelled on the middle-class.

Birgitta Svensson has studied the Swedish *"tattare"* (itinerants). Living on the fringes of society, they were one of the groups that was actually most likely to come under the scalpel. Her study focuses on the marginal status they enjoyed, and the amount of freedom that that status gave them in relation to the state, compared to those living within the margins.[50] There is no way we can know how many itinerants were actually sterilised. The administration paid no attention to which group they represented. Rather then being classified as itinerants, they are more often described as asocial, a label often used for those who strayed from the norms.

Another group which had chosen to live on the margins of society and enjoyed its relative freedom were prostitutes. Thomas Söderblom has studied prostitutes and state power in Sweden between 1920 and 1940. They were often targeted in the sterilisations. Sexuality belonged, according to the logics of the welfare state, in the sphere of reproduction which was the family. In a way, Söderblom argues, the controlled sexuality belonged to the Swedish state. All other sexuality threatened the project of modernisation, and was seen as dangerous.[51] Maija Runcis found that in no less than 43% of the sterilisation applications, sexual abnormality was mentioned as single reason or one of several reasons. For women the abnormality often represented a

---

[49]   DOUGLAS, M., 1966.

[50]   SVENSSON, B., 1995, p. 114.

[51]   SÖDERBLOM, T., 1992, pp. 197-204.

large sexual appetite which often resulted in the very visible unwanted pregnancies. For men the sexual abnormality did not concern a large sexual appetite (which Runcis suggests was seen as only natural), but rather sexual violence directed at women, children and animals or homosexuality.[52]

A life at the fringes of society may have had its fascination, but it was very much the subject of interest of the rational state. By suggesting an alternative way of living outside the modern project, they became utterly threatening to those struggling inside the project. Had the marginal individuals such as itinerants and prostitutes been the only groups targeted, we might have been looking at a perceived enemy within the state through our genocide tinted spectacles. But that was not the case. They were but two out of many sub-groups. As entire groups they were not really targeted. The aim to sterilise every single itinerant or prostitute was never pronounced. Only the individuals who got in to trouble with the law or social welfare were subject for sterilisation applications.

Mentally Deficient

Many of the sterilised were classified as mentally deficient *(sinnesslö)*. The implementations of the sterilisation acts were made possible by the mapping of social as well as psychological and medical lives of individuals. This mapping was, as Herman Lundborg has demonstrated, not unique to sterilisations, but part and parcel of the developing social politics of the welfare state. An individual classified as mentally deficient was an easier target for coercion than one who was not: the mentally deficient did not have to consent to the incision themselves. Maija Runcis discusses how the concept of *mental age* became of importance in the practice of the sterilisations: with *mental age* it became possible to measure the deviating and label it. With the label mentally deficient, which could thus be objectively measured, the state could strip the individual of his or her civil rights.[53] Runcis thesis may be that of a conspiratory against the outcasts of society, but she has actually showed that the category *mentally deficient* (which made up 20% of her cases) in no way corresponded to *mentally retarded*. The diagnosis was used for all of those transgressing the norms rather

---

[52] RUNCIS, M., 1998, pp. 121-122.

[53] *Ibid.*, p. 211.

than those with a poor psychological development.[54] Women with high fertility were for instance frequently labelled as mentally deficient, and so were women with a large sexual appetite.[55]

In the journalist Bosse Lindquist's book we meet Astrid, who was sterilised in her late teens before leaving an institution for delinquents. Astrid now works at a large hospital, and lived with her husband until he recently passed away. We also meet Torbjörn who was supposed to be sterilised before leaving an institution for delinquents, but managed a close escape by smuggling out a letter to his foster-parents asking them to refuse to approve. Torbjörn and Astrid represent a large group of young delinquents who were sterilised before being allowed to leave the institutions where they lived or were kept for shorter periods. These youngsters were not usually mentally retarded, but kids who had got a bad start in life, involved in petty crimes or just showed common unruliness in school. The one thing most of them had in common was that they were quite simply poor.[56] Maija Runcis has showed how those who were reported as mentally deficient often were screened as early as primary school, where very concrete instructions for the teacher's evaluations in such cases existed.[57]

The Centrally Planned, Legitimised and Executed Sterilisations

The sterilisations were but one in a long list of scientifically engineered and motivated solutions that were voiced and implemented in the 1930s and 1940s. And it was in no way the reform that had the greatest impact on the everyday lives of the Swedes. Other questions, such as the housing question, the labour unions, the unemployment and inflation met rational recommendations from economical and political science.[58] The sterilisations were carried out in a modern society where it was second nature to turn to science for solutions. Science could provide the answers to any question asked by the politicians, and the

---

[54] *Ibid.*, p. 138.

[55] *Ibid.*, pp. 117, 133-141.

[56] LINDQUIST, B., 1991, pp. 9-23, 94-102, 147-150.

[57] RUNCIS, M., 1998, pp. 200-202.

[58] See Torbjörn Björkman's critical review of Yvonne Hirdman's interpretation of racial hygiene and family planning as the most important question of the 1940s. Björkman, T., 1991, in *Tidskrift för Arkitekturforskning*, volume 4, No. 2, pp.129-136.

politicians could be sure that this was the one correct and objective answer. When Alva Myrdal published *Nation and the Family* in 1941, she quite naturally introduced the goals for her (and her husband, Gunnar Myrdal's) population policy thus:

> The Scandinavian countries have been fortunate in that they have achieved a closer collaboration between social science and politics than other countries. It is natural, therefore, to expect from them a contribution toward the clarification of the methodological problems of framing a population policy that will comply with scientific standards. The fact that academic experts are consulted on political questions on investigation and expert influence on public opinion and politics is one of the characteristics of our type of rationalistic democracy.[59]

The logics of the modern welfare state put the interest of the state over those of the individual.[60] Very few statements against the encroachment of the individual's personal rights to the benefit of the state were to be heard.[61] However, the sterilisations were justified from the individual's point of view as well as society's. The reader will recall that until 1934 it was illegal to perform any sterilisations that were not medically motivated (*i.e.* to prevent the mother-to-be from dying at childbirth). Thus all the people that were seen as unfit mothers and fathers (here mainly the epileptics and the only slightly mentally retarded) had to be protected from parenthood in one of two ways: either kept under control at institutions (at the expense of the taxpayers). It was seen as a humanitarian act to sterilise these people as that would allow them to live together "as God had intended" without risking the unwanted consequence of pregnancy.[62] Even though the reasoning was founded on the fact that these people were unable to decide for themselves what was best for them, there was a profound concern for their well-being behind it. Another reason may be suggested, here voiced by the director of the largest home for mentally deficient in Sweden, Vipeholm Hospital in Lund. If these persons, only

---

[59] MYRDAL, A., 1968 [1941], p. 100; Cf. WAGNER, P. and WITTROCK, B., 1992.

[60] This was not a particularly Swedish pattern. The exact same logic was to be found in the neighbouring country, Denmark. KOCH, L., 1996, p. 78.

[61] The ones that did appear, such as the professor of forensic medicine, Gunnar Hedrén, were, according to Broberg and Tydén, stray remarks except one group of radical lawyers that Maija Runcis describes, who heavily claimed the rights of the individual over that of the state. BROBERG, G. and TYDÉN, M., 1996, p. 104 and RUNCIS, M., 1998, pp. 75-82.

[62] KOCH, L., 1996, p. 71-78; RUNCIS, M., 1998, p. 216.

slightly mentally retarded, could re-enter society they could contribute to the production of welfare. The director pondered, they would be fit to do the kind of "monotonous, simple and boring work that no other person is willing to undertake".[63] It was, in a time of stagnating growth of population and up coming production, in the interest of society that all able hands were busy in the production of welfare.

Another factor inherent to modern society was the incessant categorising of people. From the turn of the century the biologically and racially centred sciences were founded on a categorising and way of seeing people, reducing them not to the product of their actions but of their beings. Herman Lundborg was one of the representatives of the labelling frenzy. Collective labels such as "Caucasians" "itinerants" or "laps" were used as a fix set of qualities in races. This way of thinking was, according to Mattias Tydén, still part of the reasoning in the 1930s and 1940s when politicians and laymen alike express the "natural roles" of men (as providers) and women (as mothers).[64] The categories used in the application of the sterilisations were not the racial categories, but social categories such as "mentally deficient", "sexually abnormal" and "asocial".

The Visions of the Social Engineers

It would be difficult to imagine a project like the *folkhemmet* without visions. The visions for the welfare state were multifarious. The voice of Alva Myrdal will testify to the role of social engineering in utilitarian politics: "Politics has, to a considerable degree, been brought under the control of logic and technical knowledge and so has been forced to become in essence constructive social engineering."[65] She then goes on to argue that scientists must distinguish clearly between "factual relations they can establish" and "the value judgements they will have to assume". The value judgements relevant to the population policy that she writes on, are very practical, hands-on values. The first one being "freedom for the individual that is compatible with social orderliness". Next she postulates the "positive valuation of a high level of living" which she labels as an "undeniable striving toward the elevation of living conditions". One way to reach that elevation that had been tried by a great number of people was the

---

[63] FRYKMAN, E., 1998:1, p. 82.

[64] TYDÉN, M., 1996, pp. 57-58.

[65] MYRDAL, A., 1968 [1941], p. 100.

reduction of family size, which was just the opposite of the goals of Alva Myrdal's suggested policy. Alva Myrdal wanted a higher birth rate. The "positive valuation of economic equality" holds another key role, and steps taken in this direction testified to the existence of these values: not only the equalising of incomes, but also the "levelling the effects of regional advantages and disadvantages, pooling of risks and co-operating in stead of profiteering". The institution of reproduction, the family, holds a special role in these positive values:

> Finally, there is in the general value sphere of Swedish democracy an undeniably positive valuation of children, family and marriage. [...] Between these basic values [referring to the values mentioned above] there will in actual life be many occasions for conflict. But one judgement is unanimous, namely that quality of children should not be sacrificed to quantity. The desire for children, both as a private attitude and still more as a political attitude, will have to yield if it is a conflict with the desire to defend standards, particularly the welfare standards of the children themselves. There can be no approval, therefore, of childbearing that infringes on the welfare of the children.[66]

Alva Myrdal is in no way an uncontested representative of the value in the politics of the 1930s and 1940s. Gunnar and Alva Myrdal have often been depicted as influential pioneers of the social engineering that radically dictated the social and partly the economical politics of the nascent welfare state. Yvonne Hirdman knighted the Myrdals "the ideal model of the art of Swedish social engineering" in 1989.[67] The appointment was soon to be contested. Bo Rothstein five years later showed that the Myrdals may have said what they pleased, but the actual laws and implemented social politics bore little resemblance to the ideals they promoted. The right of the state to interfere with the individual's very personal spheres was rarely practised, it belonged to the category of "mere rhetorics" of a group of social engineers that thought themselves more important than they really were.[68]

Neither Hirdman nor Rothstein has been proven wrong. The research published and the ideas promoted by the social engineers, out of which the Myrdals' voice rang most clearly, probably represented the basic attitudes of most intellectuals involved in shaping the welfare society. But politics never was reduced, as Alva Myrdal suggested, to a

---

[66] All quotes from MYRDAL, A., 1968 [1941], pp. 101-103.

[67] HIRDMAN, Y., 1989, p. 98.

[68] ROTHSTEIN, B., 1994, pp. 208-216. See also BJÖRKMAN, T., 1991, "Review of Hirdman" in *Tidskrift för Arkitekturforskning*, vol. 4, No. 2, pp.129-136.

mere "essence of social engineering". Rather the politics of the welfare state can be seen as a coat of many colours representing a number of equally important questions: international neutrality relations, internal military politics, monetary politics national and international, relations to the industry and social politics.

The Moral of the Welfare State

The politicians, administrators and researchers promoting and implementing the sterilisations obviously thought of their activity as good and necessary. There were few qualms about the implementation of the logic of the welfare state. Was there a moral philosophy behind their seemingly total conviction? The answer is yes, there was. The most influential Swedish moral philosopher of the 1950s and 1960s has described it and argued for it in a number of popularly read books. In *Liv och nytta* (Life and Utility) Ingemar Hedenius described utilitarian moral as the leading principle of the welfare state. Its essence was to create a maximum of comfort and happiness for a maximum of people, and nothing else. If this goal demanded the sacrifice of a few to the benefit of the majority, then the sacrifices were in order. This moral included the plight to sometimes perform actions that went against prevailing morals. When different duties clashed the governing principle must always be, he argued, to inflict the lesser evil. The utilitarian ideal, furthermore, was closely intertwined with rationalism. Only scientific research and common sense could motivate measures taken to assure common welfare. The problem was, of course, that consequences can not always be foreseen or even imagined.[69]

I would like to suggest that it is possible to isolate a common interest in the state sanctioned politics and the visions of the engineers. They both strove towards a better society. The more often repeated arguments of the social engineers makes the utilitarian logics seem to be striving for happiness and comfort for a maximum of people. The intentions of the state representatives are harder to pin point, but may be described as a utilitarian logic aimed at a maximised production, whose benefits should be distributed to a maximum of people. Keeping institutions running was expensive and social welfare for those unable to look after their children was forking out a hole in the already strained social budget. Lene Koch writes on the similar development of

---

[69] HEDENIUS, I., 1961, pp. 11-24, 139-141, 156-160.

237

sterilisations in Denmark. Behind them she isolates the same explicit utilitarian philosophy and a valuation of people based on their productivity and usefulness to society. With economical calculations the cost of these people's care and their contribution to society was measured.[70]

Conclusion

This text has tried to draw some of the parallels between the logic behind Zygmunt Bauman's modern genocide and the Swedish sterilisation policies of 1934 and 1941, by attempting an interpretation of the sterilisations as genocide. According to the UN convention of 1948, sterilisation of a group is labelled as genocide. However, a number of additional facets of the definition have been stressed. The need for new regimes to legitimise their politics has been one factor taken in to account. So has the visions of the actors behind the genocide, and the centrally administered and executed genocide. Through genocide tinted glasses we have re-read the history leading up to the bills of 1934 and 1941. The difficult everyday life of the turn-of-the-century Sweden has been depicted to show that there was indeed a call for strong reforms. The threat of degeneration of society as well as the individual was perceived as immediate to many living in the phase of early industrialisation. Degeneration per definition needs to be a change from some kind of original state: a state of good and healthy Swedishness. The search for that Swedishness was going to land in the eugenic characteristics of the middle class, which was to promote itself as the norm of the emerging welfare society. Anyone not fitting this norm was going to be labelled as "different" or "other". Labelling and categorising was the very important heritage from the racial biology in Sweden. But racial biology was going to take a slightly different turn than other countries: it was going to focus on social categories more than racial categories.

The first recorded sterilisations in Sweden date back to 1895. Until the legislation of 1934 it is difficult to judge weather the sterilisations performed were legal or illegal. When the Institute for Race Biology was founded in 1922, it was true to the categorising intentions of the racial biology. The fact that no research could actually prove that sterilisation was efficient as a means of eugenic hygiene was initially ignored. When the politicians realised they had no support in science,

---

[70] KOCH, L., 1996, p. 233.

they turned to humanitarian and economical argumentation to motivate the bills of sterilisation. A caesura can be found in 1936 when eugenic hygiene was replaced by social hygiene. From then on social medicine and economics would be the main inspirations of the social reforms. This was part of a new kind of politics that the Social Democrats energetically promoted. A new kind of politics that needed approval and legitimisation for the Social Democrats to stay in power.

We have then looked at the targeted groups, only to find that there was no common identity between the sterilised. They represented a wide range of groups that did not fall in to the middle-class model of "normality", with only one common characteristic. The representatives of the welfare state did not think them fit to be parents. Mainly women were targeted, and almost always those who fell outside of the norms of "normality". Other groups living on the fringes of society were itinerants and prostitutes, whose lives posed a threat to those living inside the margins of society. The fact that they lead an alternative ways of life outside of the *folkhem* project was threatening to those struggling inside the project. Another group was the mentally deficient, a category which proved to include anyone living an antisocial life rather than mentally retarded people.

The sterilisations were centrally planned and executed. But they were part of a much wider politics where the questions of society's problems were repeatedly left to science to answer and the state to implement. The sterilisation question was but one – and not the greatest one – in a line of questions that the Swedish welfare state had to deal with at this time. The visions of the social engineers have been described as very hands-on values, resting securely on a utilitarian moral advocacy of the quest for maximum comfort for a maximum number of people at all times. If certain sacrifices had to be made for the benefit of utilitarianism, then that was legitimised by the good intentions of the moral. The social engineer's definition of maximum comfort seemed more directed towards happiness whereas the definitions actually visible in the politics of the state seemed more directed towards maximum profit. The implementation of the sterilisa-tion politics tells the tale of economical valuation of people's costs and efforts. But the goal was constant: the best of intentions for the citizens of the *folkhem*.

The Swedish sterilisation programme represents principally a secondary phase in the history of racial hygiene, a *reformed* racial hygiene (reform eugenics, in the terminology of the historians of science) where the ethnical racism had been thrown overboard. […] The Myrdals were not

239

ethnical racists, in stead they emphasised the social aspects of the population problem. They did, however, share the contemporary view of human beings and argued on behalf of measures being taken against what would be referred to as "inferior" individuals – *e.g.* mentally retarded – *within* a population.[71]

Having studied Swedish racism as well as the sterilisations for over ten years, Mattias Tydén interprets the sterilisations as a natural course of action taken in the light of reform eugenic, the kind of eugenics that since 1936 dominated the scientific approach to eugenics in Sweden. The reform eugenics applied its conclusions drawn from the social sides of reforms rather than biological sides of reform. But, and this is the crucial "but" of this article, the reform eugenics shared the same view of human beings as the ethnical racists. A standpoint that took for granted a specific value for each and every individual and these values varied as did the individuals' roles within the welfare state.

Three conditions have made it difficult to realise and accept that ethnical racism had nothing to do with the sterilisations, according to Tydén. The first condition is the fact that the political rhetoric of the introduction of the sterilisations was seductively similar to that of the Nazis'. Influential Swedish politicians referred in 1934 to "the inferior offspring" as motivating the first act and in 1941 promoted a "decontamination of the Swedish race" through the second act. The second condition is the fact that even though central prime movers to the eugenic thinking like Nils von Hoffsten as early as 1920 admitted that it was impossible to change a population's gene pool through sterilisations because if the influence of recessive genes isolated serious academics such as Bertil Lundman in Uppsala and Arne Müntzing in Lund continued to argue for their impact and publish racial studies as late as the 1960s. Swedish encyclopaedias and schoolbooks were reluctant to let go of the racist view of eugenics, and terms like "Negro" "lap" and "gypsy" continued to testify to the ideas of the 1920s. The third condition is that the simplified version of the ethnical racism of the 1920s illustrates what we think was the racial biology of "yesterday". The schemes where healthy looking tall, blond, "Nordic" people are contrasted with shady images of poor and suspicious looking immigrants are often used in today's articles to illustrate the racism behind the sterilisations, even though it represents only one distinct part of the history of racial thinking, that of the

---

[71] TYDÉN, M., 1996, p. 59. Tydén's italics (translation EF).

1920s.[72] Because it is hard to accept that the moral behind the sterilisations was the very moral of all the positive sides of the welfare state, we want to imagine "yesterday" as the antithesis of our lives in the welfare state of "today".

It is very comfortable to view the Swedish sterilisations as an outburst of racial violence against unwanted groups. Mattias Tydén's conclusions lead us to believe that the racism behind them was of a modern type, the type that from the mid 1930s came to dominate Swedish reform politics. Reform eugenics aimed to confront the politically and economically provoked problems of the emerging modern society not in a biological way but in a social way.

Zygmunt Bauman argues that the genocide of the Nazis should be understood as the very opposite of an impulsive outburst of violence. In stead, his conclusions lead us to believe that they depended upon the rational administration of the modern welfare state for efficiency and motivation. Reform eugenics was part of an over-all rational attitude that the state could and should confront the political and social problems created by modernisation. The very modernisation was the key to the problems: by rational research and implementation, by rational bureaucracy and infrastructure and by rational reproduction and life-style the problems would be put right. The guiding principle of the welfare state was the utilitarian moral, putting a maximum gain of a maximum number of individuals first. By ascribing different values to individuals, it was possible to motivate the coercion sometimes used in the sterilisations as necessary for the best of the "victim" and the best of society as a whole.

If we accept the above, we must also accept that the sterilisation of 62,888 Swedes under the acts 1934 and 1941 can only be seen as a very specific, or "refined", form of genocide. Reform eugenics were not directed at a targeted group that was seen as an enemy but a problem within. The guiding principle was not so much to extinguish or harm any group or individual, but to help maximise happiness and profit for the majority of citizens. The "good intentions" did not murder the "victims", on the contrary, it was argued that it would actually help them to lead a "normal life", of course for them "normal life" was deemed to exclude one life function, reproduction.

---

[72] TYDÉN, M., "Rasbiologi och andra rasismer", in *Folkets Historia*, 1996:3-4, p. 59-62.

The use of Zygmunt Bauman's thesis of genocide as an extension of the logic of modern society has proven rewarding. Bauman's thesis needs to be modified to suit the Swedish conditions. The logic of modern society to create "otherness" and the "self" was the logic that conditioned the sterilisations. In defining the "other" the outlines of the "normal" were evoked. What we see here is a modern welfare state creating a new identity for its citizens. An identity based on the middle-class included many of those previously excluded from modern society. The different groups that were targeted in the sterilisations in fact held a crucial role in the creation of the new Swedish citizen identity: they were the ones who shaped it.

CHAPTER 9

The Heritage of a Century

Göran ROSENBERG

The other day I heard some people discuss the future of one or another trend in society. It was on the radio and I didn't listen very carefully and things nowadays just slip my mind, so it could have been about the future of film, or literature, or visual arts, or fashion, or soap operas, or computer games or Internet shopping. I only remember, and I remember it clearly, one person, I believe it was the moderator, say: "so what can we expect of this or that – when we move into the third millennium?"

Into the third millennium, he said. About something which it normally would be wise not to have an opinion about more than a month or two in advance. And of which we can be certain only about one thing: it will change. I try to imagine people of the last millennium – they would of course have had to subscribe to a Christian calendar which was not always the case in the heathen corner of Europe where I happen to dwell – asking themselves about the thousand years to come. But I find that the mere idea of asking such questions, questions emanating from expectations of historical change (as distinguished from changes in the fortunes of life), cannot even have been invented. And had it been invented, we know how utterly wrong the questions would have been. Not to mention the answers.

I myself rarely plan things more than a year in advance – and only after crossing my fingers and knocking on wood and inserting a good number of "ifs" and "buts" into the equation. Life nowadays is too tricky and too fragile to allow for long-term planning. Even the traditional markers of the ordinary human lifespan are rapidly being upset, moved, changed, uprooted. Childhood, adolescence, mother-hood, fatherhood, sex, family, work, career, reward, retirement, yes even death, are all changing their meaning and position and significance. A person born in 1980, like my youngest daughter, does not expect the same stability and predictability in life as a person born in 1880. She is facing more choices, more risks, more opportunities, more mobility, but also less coherence, less trust, less safety, less certainty about the society in which she lives – and about the kind of life that awaits her.

I am not saying that my daughter is worse or better off than a person who was born hundred years before her. That kind of comparison I find meaningless. We cannot evaluate or judge other people's lives in other times – by our own standards of good and bad. We can only try to understand in what way *actual* lives differ from each other, in what way one end of a century is distinguished from another. And perhaps we can do that more clearly if we try to remember what was *not* there one hundred years ago. Or perhaps, more telling, *who* was not there.

Picasso wasn't really there yet, nor Proust, nor Joyce, nor Stravinsky, nor Kandinsky, nor Schönberg, nor the founders of Bauhaus, nor Einstein, nor Kafka, nor Orwell, nor Chaplin, nor the moguls of Hollywood, nor Mussolini, nor Stalin, nor Hitler. People alive in the 1900 lived in a world without these people and without their contributions to the human imagination. I don't even think these people could have been imagined. The people of 1900 of course also lived in a world without two world wars, without totalitarian mass movements, without the terrors of xenophobic nationalism, without Gulag and Auschwitz, without the gaze of Dr. Pannwitz, the head of the Chemistry department in Auschwitz, who across his table inspected one of his offered slave labourers, a young Italian Jew and chemist by the name of Primo Levi, and gazed at him as if he were looking at a fish in fishbowl, as if this were a meeting not between two human beings but between two different biological species.[1]

It goes without saying that the people of 1900 also lived in a world without the theory of relativity, without quantum mechanics, without cars, aeroplanes, atomic bombs, genetics, DNA, cloning, personal computers, Internet, the information society, homosexual partnership, legal abortion, working women, democracy, family breakdown, welfare states. So what of all this will be considered the heritage of this century? And can one speak of such a thing? A century, one hundred years, is after all a rather arbitrary way of measuring time – although a relatively harmless one. Millennia are considerably worse. Millennium

---

[1]   LEVI, P., 1987.

is a strong and seductive and plain dangerous word. Millennium wishes to imbue history with finality, with ultimate meaning, with redemption, with messianic promises.[2] It was no coincidence that Hitler's Reich were to last a thousand years. And anyone who speaks about the coming millennium is either ignorant, cynical or dangerous. But even if a mere century, however mechanically and randomly delimited, seems more within our grasp and less imbued with hidden messages, it is not always the most natural period of time to define a historical heritage.

In 1989, when the Berlin wall came down and the Soviet empire was on the verge of collapse, I wrote an article where I argued that this was the end – not of the 20th century, but of a very long 19th century, a double-century that began in 1789, with the French Revolution and the dream of a new, secular, rational, enlightened, evermore perfect, world-order.[3] With the idea that history had a meaning, a given course of progress – and a final goal. In 1789 man himself, not God, became the great Creator. Man himself would make perfect the world and the human element in it. A distinctly Western, or rather Judeo-Christian, religious messianic idea of fulfilment and redemption was succeeded by a secular creed, promising basically the same, albeit this time through the purely rational and scientific management of Man and Nature.

Kant was of course there, promising us Rational Man. Rousseau was here, promising us *la volonté générale*, the general will, Hegel was here promising us the Meaning of History. And soon came Karl Marx and promised us the scientific key to its course. Only human ignorance now separated heaven and earth. The future became clear, bright and – inevitable. The European stage was set for revolution and redemption.

These men of 1800 were all there in 1900 as well. Physically dead, of course, but spiritually well alive. The turn of our century was a time ripe with expectation and self-confidence, *A Proud Tower*, the historian Barbara Tuchman named it, or perhaps rather a bomb about to explode. It was not a golden age, as some people in retrospect remembered it, not really a *belle époque*, it was full of tensions and conflicts and social misery, but it was also a period where all curves of

---

2   Revelations 20:1-6.

3   *Swedish Euroworld Magazine*, January 1990, reprinted in ROSENBERG, G., 1994, pp. 76ff.

human development and activity pointed sharply upwards, where radical change had become the order of the day, where machines and industries rapidly multiplied human production and productivity, where enormous social energies were accumulated, where a relentless movement ahead, progress if you so wish, the *will to power*, seemed to be the objective nature of things.

Nietzsche was there too, literally on the doorstep to our century. He died in 1900 – and with him the 19th century could indeed have ended, because unlike so many others he perceived that the end was there, that the collective messianic project of human and social perfectibility could lead nowhere but to moral and human disaster. He not only proclaimed that God was dead, but also observed that what he called,

> the Christian-ecclesiastical pressure of millennia [that created in Europe] a magnificent tension of the spirit, the like of which had never yet existed on earth: With so tense a bow we can now shoot for the most distant goals,[4]

Nietzsche wrote this in his 1885 preface to *Beyond Good and Evil*. He did not, however, live long enough to see how far the goals really were. He himself had hoped that this tension would catapult the spiritual liberation of the individual, create that free spirit in which he placed his hopes. *"We good Europeans"*, he wrote (long before the European Union),

> we still feel the whole need of the spirit and the whole tension of the bow. And perhaps also the arrow, the task, and – who knows? – the *goal* […].[5]

Yes, with Nietzsche properly read and understood, we "good Europeans" could perhaps have perceived the dangers ahead, the destructive power of the millennial bow and arrow, perhaps also the darkness of its goals.

Instead, the accumulated tensions and energies catapulted us into the war of 1914. Some argue that this war was the true beginning of our century, because it was bigger and more destructive and more irrational than all previous wars, because it ravaged so much and killed so many, because it did away with the last remnants of chivalry, because it made a mockery of so many values and beliefs.

Hannah Arendt writes about the days before and after the outbreak of this war as

---

4   NIETZSCHE, F., 1966 [1886], p. 3.

5   *Ibid.*, p. 4.

separated, not like the end of an old and the beginning of a new period, but like the day before and the day after an explosion. [6]

It was a war, she writes, that unleashed human hatred on a new scale, making the deceptive quiet years of the twenties assume

the sordid and weird atmosphere of a Strindbergian family quarrel. Nothing perhaps illustrates the general disintegration of political life better than this vague, pervasive hatred of everybody and everything, without a focus for its passionate attention, with nobody to make responsible for the state of affairs – neither the government nor the bourgeoisie nor an outside power. [...] Now everybody was against everybody else, and most of all against his closest neighbours – the Slovaks against the Czechs, the Croats against the Serbs, the Ukrainians against the Poles [...].[7]

Now, if this sounds a bit familiar today, it is because we too seem to experience what Arendt calls "a general disintegration of political life", an ongoing delegitimisation of political institutions and systems, a vague feeling of resentment, not hatred perhaps, not yet, without a proper focus, prone to sudden changes and shifting moods. I wouldn't stretch the comparison too far. Things have changed, important collective experiences have been made, history does not repeat itself, but when we wish to assess the heritage of this century, we cannot but note that the tensions we thought were history, are still with us, or can too easily be recreated.

So if we, as I do, believe that the First World War did not end the millennial project of 19th century Europe, only radicalised it, dehumanised it, armed it with ever more destructive weapons, pushed it towards a few logical and terrible conclusions, that the fascist and communist mass movements of this century were as much the children of Rousseau and Marx as of Lenin and Hitler, that both World War II and the Cold War were struggles against radical and still vital millennial forces in Western society, then we must come to the conclusion that the European century which is about to end has been a long one indeed.

On the other hand we can also argue that the ending itself has been a long process, with many apparent endings along the road. Intellectually and spiritually it perhaps ended already with Nietzsche, with Joyce, with Kandinsky, with Kafka, with Stravinsky and

---

[6] ARENDT, H., 1972, p. 267.

[7] *Ibid.*, p. 268.

Schönberg, with Musil and Broch. With, what the Spanish philosopher Ortega y Gasset called, the "dehumanisation of the Arts"[8], with the realisation that the coherence and unambiguity of the 19th Century were gone and that a new world of incoherence and ambiguity, a world without a given meaning and purpose, a world with no given moral authority, had come into being – a world that called for completely new artistic and literary expressions.

It was a world that clearly manifested itself in that first horrible "European" war and its aftermath, a world chillingly evoked by Hermann Broch in his trilogy of novels *The Sleepwalkers*, about a Europe which one day is on the verge of human perfection, and the next day is revealed as a monster. He asks, in the concluding third part:

> Is this distorted life of ours still real? Is this cancerous reality still alive? The melodramatic gestures of our mass movements towards death ends in a shrug of the shoulder – men die and do not know why; without a hold on reality they fall into nothingness; yet they are surrounded and slain by a reality that is their own, since they comprehend its casualty.[9]

Nineteenth century rationalism had attempted to create an external logic, an "objectivity" (what Broch calls *Sachlichkeit*), beyond human values and value systems. The inner rationality of mankind, its moral drive, had been systematically reduced to the effects of materialist, value-free logic. Broch's *Sachlichkeit* is the liberation of logic from all value-systems. When this *Sachlichkeit* loses itself in the evident irrationality of a world war, when the abstractions are transformed into horrifying monsters, men are left more naked than ever.

This new deformed machine-man is portrayed in the person of an amoral deserter, Huguenau, capable of adapting to whatever logic appears to hold sway for the moment, a human being for whom a murder, a rape or a stolen meal, are actions just as arbitrary or as necessary as any other actions in life. The cheated and finally destroyed newspaper proprietor, Herr Esch, throws himself into religious fanaticism in a desperate search for some values to hold on to. His adopted value system however becomes just one of innumerable, mutually incompatible value systems, each one hastening the decay of all values:

> There is the economic value system of "business is business", there is art

---

[8] ORTEGA Y GASSET, J., 1987.

[9] H. BROCH, *Die Schlafwandler: Huguenau und die Sachlichkeit*. BROCH, H., 1996 [1931-1932].

with its *l'art pour l'art*, architecture with its functionalism, there are military, technological and athletic value systems – each of them "unfettered" in its autonomy, each resolved to push home with radical thoroughness the final conclusions of its logic and to break its own record. And woe to the others, if in this conflict of systems that precariously maintain an equilibrium one should gain the preponderance and overtop all the rest, as the military system does in war, or as the economic system now is doing, a system to which even war is subordinate, – woe to the others!

But, as we know, it did not end there. Recreated, re-energised and radicalised certainties were soon to replace the shattered world of 1914. New visions of meaning and coherence, new dreams of perfect societies, biologically or socially purified and cleansed, were not only dreamed but applied – with known consequences.

Some artists and writers became the heralds, sometimes even the creators, of this brave new world. Others became its resistance fighters, defenders of what they believed to be a world of lasting human values, perhaps not a perfect world, but still one worthy of defence. Defending a half truth against a total lie, as Arthur Koestler later would write.[10] For some time, the conviction persisted that totalitarianism was an aberration, something deeply alien to the Western tradition, an exceptional break in the course of progress, a shocking remnant of barbaric ignorance in the midst of human enlightenment and scientific rationality.

Many continued to believe so even in the midst of total darkness. In 1942 the composer Victor Ullmann was deported from Prague to the Nazi concentration camp of Theresienstadt. He was 44 years old at the time and absolutely convinced that Schiller would beat Hitler, that artistic form would overcome the matter of day-to-day-life, that the creation of true aesthetic value would prevail over the creation of violence and death. With Plato he feared (in an essay written in 1937) that an increasing lawlessness in music foreboded an increasing lawlessness in society as a whole, and that subsequently the task of the composer was to search for a new order in music.[11] With the right kind of music, barbarism could be kept at bay. He continued to believe

---

[10] "The Seven Deadly Fallacies" in KOESTLER, A., 1970. Quoting himself in an article published in 1942 or 1943: "In this war we are fighting a total lie in the name of a half-truth", p. 32.

[11] ULLMANN, V., 1993 [1944], vol. 3, "Goethe und Ghetto: Von hier aus wird die 'Form', wie sie Goethe und Schiller verstehen, zur Überwinderin des 'Stoffes'", pp. 92-93.

when he should have known not to, when the frequent transports to Auschwitz in the fall of 1944 tore orchestras, choirs and chamber groups apart, cancelled rehearsed operas, terminated half-finished lectures, silenced jazz bands and cabarets.

On October 16th 1944 after having dedicated his Seventh Piano Sonata to his children and reserving for himself the right to perform the work as long as he lived, Ullmann was put on a train and transported to Auschwitz – together with other prominent musicians, artists and composers – where he was killed in the gas chamber on October 18th.

So was Auschwitz really an aberration? The killers and victims listened to and enjoyed the same music, saw the same plays, read the same books, subscribed to largely the same cultural symbols. And as we now know, the Holocaust was to a large extent perpetrated by, what Christopher Browning has called, ordinary men.[12] And was of course organised by the most modern of means and the most advanced achievements of Western science and bureaucracy. And its goal, not to forget, was that ultimate society, that ultimate solution, that final solution, however grotesque, that is the Messianic core of the Western tradition. Or, as Zygmunt Bauman cautiously has argued:

> The Holocaust was not an antithesis of modern civilization and everything it stands for. We suspect (even if we refuse to admit it) that the Holocaust could merely have uncovered another face of the same modern society whose other, more familiar face we so admire.[13]

Instead of seeing Auschwitz as an aberration, albeit a unique event in human history, Bauman wants us to discover its distinctively modern roots and features, and thereby understand it as something that could have happened – the way it happened – only in a modern society. Not that Auschwitz will repeat itself, but we now know, and continue to experience, that "ordinary men", however enlightened and educated, under the specific circumstances of modern society and under the influence of specific Western ideals, can be induced to commit horrible crimes.

So what are these circumstances of our society? And are they still with us?

One way to answer these questions is perhaps to go back to the writers of the inter-war period, to see if the world they tried to under-

---

[12] BROWNING, C., 1992.
[13] BAUMAN, Z., 1989, p. 7.

stand and describe sounds familiar to us? Do we for instance recognise ourselves in Hermann Broch's shattered world of *Sachlichkeit*, (relevance, objectivity, impartiality, realism, matter-of-factness, functionalism) where the value system of "business is business" overpowers all other values? Or where genuine human moral problems and choices have been transformed into issues of technical-scientific competence? Where human judgement has been replaced by *Sachlichkeit*? Where everybody can blame the system, but few can take responsibility?

Or how do we today perceive what the American essayist Walter Lippman wrote in 1929:

> the modern man who has ceased to believe without ceasing to be credulous, hangs, as it were, between heaven and earth, and is at rest nowhere [...]. He does not feel himself to be an actor in a great and dramatic destiny, but he is subject to the massive powers of our civilization, forced to adopt their pace, bound to their routine, entangled in their conflicts [...]. Events are there, and they overpower him. But they do not convince him that they have that dignity which inheres in that which is necessary and in the nature of things.[14]

There was a time, that now appears to have been a short interlude in a long century, where this perhaps was not an accurate description of the Western mood. When purpose and energy were again restored to the Western project, when the Barbarians again were at the gate, when the distinction between good and evil again was obvious, when the half truth of Koestler stood out in heroic contrast to the blatant lie of Nazism and Stalinism, when the West again seemed to have a fight to win and a cause to fulfil. Where the moral certainties and the confidence of the late-Victorian era before 1914, were miraculously resurrected – and personified by political leaders like Churchill, de Gaulle, Schuman, Adenauer, Kennedy, Helmut Schmidt, and – I maintain – Helmut Kohl.

A period and time, which arguably came to an end in 1989, when the Barbarians were suddenly vanquished, the European walls torn down and the final victory of the West proclaimed – and even "The End of History" proposed (by Francis Fukuyama). And in a way something important indeed ended there. Perhaps a very long century – or at least the last remnants of that Western self-confidence which for so long had papered over the shadows and the tensions and those self-destructive tendencies that once had seemed so obvious to an earlier

---

[14] LIPPMAN, W., 1929.

generation of writers and artists. After a short period of relief, and of triumphalist hubris, still perpetuated by neo-liberal ideologues and economists, the wounds in the Messianic project of Enlightenment became again visible.

Again we could read Broch and shiver. Again we could notice the painful separation of human values from perceived technocratic and economic necessities, of individual experience from the course of events, of actions from consequences, of rights from responsibilities.

I believe that what has come to an end, or rather should come to an end, although we cannot be too sure that it will, is the *March* of History. The end of the idea that history, or rather Western history, has a beginning, a meaning and eventually an end. That humanity is embarked on some kind of journey towards perfection. The ambiguities and uncertainties and paradoxes that seemed so obvious to Broch or to Kafka or even to an American intellectual like Lippman, are back again – and with a vengeance. And there seem to be no more escape routes. No new big coherence at sight. No new master story. No new 1789 or 1917.

What Zygmunt Bauman has explored in a number of books, is a modern Western world finally aware of its own shaky foundations, of the darker echoes of its own rhetoric, a world where every collective moral certainty has collapsed and given way to self-doubt, social fragmentation and moral ambiguity of post-modernity. A world where we ultimately must be responsible for our own responsibility.

Today we should better understand Nietzsche's mockery of his good Europeans – for their good conscience,

> that venerable long pigtail of a concept that our grandfathers fastened to the backs of their heads and often enough to the back of their understanding. [...] We the last Europeans with a good conscience: we, too, still wear their pigtail. Alas, if you knew how soon, very soon – all will be different![15]

We can of course ask ourselves why the 19th century didn't end with Nietzsche, why we managed to put the pigtail back on the back of our heads – and on the back of our understanding. But in asking so, we will have underestimated the seductive power of the Western idea, the idea that man is here on earth with a great purpose and a great mission, that there is a great end to our material and spiritual suffering. So

---

[15] NIETZSCHE, F., 1966 [1886], p. 145.

whenever our material and spiritual sufferings were large enough, and our existential loneliness seemed unbearable, there was a demand for ever new magicians who at each juncture of history would tell us what we so desperately wanted to hear. Provide us with a new illusion, invoking a new great narrative.

So has it really ended?

Yes, I believe so. Even if these final years of the century have an eerie ring of *déjà-vu* to them, with many people craving for a new certainty, a new mission for our civilisation, a new enemy to mobilise against, small or large, another clash of civilisations, it has become all too clear that whatever new certainties we will find they will all be on a lower level. We will have claustrophobic ethnic or national certainties, regional and local certainties, the certainties of sects and subcultures, the short-livened certainties of the media. But we will probably discover that every certainty that aspires for more, will disintegrate. The Western nation and nation-state, which for almost two centuries was able to organise and articulate collective meaning and purpose, to provide direction and goal, to carry great narratives and sustain great certainties, will not be able to do so anymore – except in a few remaining cases of national claustrophobia. Its moral and political authority is quickly waning.

The Europeans of the next century will thus be a lonely lot, looking in vain for that moral certainty, that human self-confidence, which for almost two centuries was provided by the Western project. Our questions will surely remain the same as in 1789, or in 1848, or in 1945, but a whole category of answers will have lost their authority and validity. We can no longer conceive of a single project as the solution to human conflict and suffering. We will increasingly have to accept and cope with the fact that humans strive in different directions, cherish different ideals, value different values, obey different authorities, enjoy different music, different books and different movies.

We will also have to realise that all human values eventually clash, that human life is a matter of continuous choice, not necessarily between good and bad, but more often between good and good, and that is because not all good values are commensurable with each other. Many are not. Freedom clashes with equality. Stability clashes with change. True moral choice is not a piece of cake – or following a pre-ordained recipe for baking one – but more often involves true conflict and genuine agony. The old Western idea of one true path of all good values, and one false path of all evil, is finally loosing its persuasive power.

So the heritage of this very long century – is the challenge to live without such an idea. The value pluralism of Isaiah Berlin; the inescapable fact that no coherence of values is possible, that human goals are many, diverse and conflicting, will be a defining feature of the coming society. If the eternal conflict of human values is a deeper truth than the promise of an evermore perfect and harmonised society, then this will demand a radical change in the way we try to organise our contemporary European societies; most of them originally based on the concept of a homogeneous nation – *en route* towards increasing unity of purpose and harmony of values. In his characteristically low voice, Berlin himself remarked that the most we in reality can hope to achieve "is a precarious balance" in the endless effort "to avoid desperate and intolerable choices".[16]

So what *is* the heritage of the century?

Let me say it in one word: Confusion. Schumpeter might perhaps have called it constructive confusion. Nietzsche perhaps too. But I know a good many people who see confusion as something destructive. In any case, confusion is always uncomfortable, it itches and moves and presses on. It is like non-equilibrium in nature. It seeks stability, *modus vivendi*, balance, rest. Confusion seeks certainty. The difference between this century, however you define it, and the coming, is that no certainties are at hand. Confusion has no quick fix anymore. In the passing century we had the enlightened and *the still* confused, the elite and its *not yet* educated masses. Now the enlightened *are* the confused. Or if you wish, we are *all* confused, the difference being that some are aware of it, and some not. Certainty, a short-lived and aggressive certainty, is now possible only among those so confused that they don't know that they are.

There is of course a perfectly normal state of mind between confusion and certainty, between despair and bliss, and that is – uncertainty, ambivalence, ambiguity. Which I think, happens to be the true human condition, at least more true than the long-lived Western fiction of a human march towards fulfilment and certainty. "Wishing to abolish

---

[16] In a filmed interview with this writer, the last ever to be made with Isaiah Berlin, broadcast on Swedish Television in May 1998.

this constitutive ambiguity", writes the German philosopher Hans Jonas, "is wishing to abolish man in his unfathomable freedom".[17]

The question then remains; will we be able to create decent societies without the fiction of a great human mission, a clear path of certainty and a shining end of fulfilment. Will we be able to build them on the much more difficult ideals of human diversity, conflict and change? Well, this is ultimately for our heirs to answer. But I do believe that if they shall succeed, they will need to preserve one tool from this old, tired, long, century; the only tool that permits us to think deeply, to reflect thoroughly, to listen carefully, to discuss with dignity, to discover with sensibility, to understand with both mind and heart. That tool is the written word.

It is true that the written word has seduced us to do foolish things and to dream vain dreams, but it is also true that the same written word has enabled us to discover the follies of our deeds and the vanity of our dreams. I do not believe that a society which increasingly understands and interprets itself through short-lived and skilfully manipulated images and pictures can provide for the kind of reflective human communication which I think will be needed in this new situation.

To write honestly and to read seriously and to consciously guard the sharpness and richness of the written language must then not only be an act of human creation – but also an act of defence. Not to defend old certainties, but the very possibility to live with uncertainty – without losing our human dignity.

This too then, is the heritage of a century.

---

[17] JONAS, H., 1984, p. 200.

Bibliography

AGAMBEN, G., 1997, *Homo Sacer: Le pouvoir souverain et la vie nue*, Paris, Seuil.

ALFORD, C. F., 1997, *What Evil Means to Us*, Ithaca and London, Cornell University Press.

ALLEN, B., 1996, *Rape Warfare*, Minneapolis, Univ. of Minnesota Press.

ALY, G. and HEIM, S., 1991, *Vordenker der Vernichtung: Auschwitz und die deutschen Pläne für eine neue europaische Ordnung*, Hamburg, Hoffman und Campe.

ANSELL-PEARSON, K., 1993, "Geist and Reich: Time, History, and Germany in Nietzsche and Heidegger" in ANSELL-PEARSON, K. and CAYGILL, H. (eds.), *The Fate of the New Nietzsche*, Aldershot, Averbury.

ANSELL-PEARSON, K., 1994, *An Introduction to Nietzsche as a Political Thinker: The Perfect Nihilist*, Cambridge, Cambridge UP.

ANTONOV-OVSEYENKO, A., 1981, *The Time of Stalin: Portrait of a Tyranny*, Saunders, G. (trans.), with an Introduction by Cohen, S. F., New York, Harper.

ARATO, A. and GEBHART, E., 1978 (eds.), *The Essential Frankfurt School Reader*, New York, Urizen.

ARENDT, H., 1951, *The Origins of Totalitarianism*, New York, Harcourt Brace Jovanovich.

ARENDT, H., 1958 [1951], *The Origins of Totalitarianism*, London, Allen and Unwin.

ARENDT, H., 1963, *Eichmann in Jerusalem; A Report on the Banality of Evil*, New York, Viking Press.

ARENDT, H., 1972 [1951], *The Origins of Totalitarianism*, New York, Harcourt Brace Jovanovich.

ARIÈS, P., 1975 [1962], *Centuries of Childhood*, Harmondsworth, Penguin.

ASPEN INSTITUTE, 1996, *Unfinished Peace, Report of the international Commission on the Balkans*, Washington DC, Brookings Institution Press.

AUBENQUE, P., 1972 (ed.), *Débat sur le kantisme et la philosophie*, Paris, Beauchesne.

AUBENQUE, P., 1990, "Le débat de 1929 entre Cassirer et Heidegger", in SEIDENGART, J. (ed.), *Ernst Cassirer: De Marbourg à New York: L'itinéraire philosophique*, Actes du colloque de Nanterre, 12-14 octobre 1988, Paris, Editions du Cerf.

AUDISIO, G., 1984, *Les Vaudois du Luberon, une minorité en Provence (1460-1560)*, Marseille, Association d'études vaudoises et historiques du Luberon.

BARBER, M., 1994, *The New Knighthood: A History of the Order of the Temple*, Cambridge, Cambridge University Press.

BARTH-EIDE, E., 1997, *Conflict Entrepreneurship: On the "Art" of Waging Civil War*, Oslo MS.

BAUER, R. and INKELES, A., 1959, *The Soviet Citizen: Daily Life in a Totalitarian Society*, Cambridge, MA, Harvard University Press.

BAUMAN, Z., 1989, *Modernity and the Holocaust*, Cambridge, Polity Press.

BAUMAN, Z., 1993, "Holocaust" in KRIEGER, J. *et al.* (eds.), *The Oxford Companion to Politics of the World*, New York and Oxford, Oxford UP.

BECK, U., 1998, *Democracy Without Enemies*, Cambridge, Polity Press.

BECKER, C. L., 1932, *The Heavenly City of the Eighteenth Century Philosophers*, New Haven, Yale University Press.

BECKER, E., 1975, *Escape from Evil*, New York, Free Press.

BENJAMIN, W., 1969 [1940], "Theses on the Philosophy of History", in *Illuminations*, Zohn, H. (trans.), New York, Schocken.

BERGGREN, H., 1995, *Seklets ungdom: retorik, politik och modernitet 1900-1939*, Stockholm, Tiden.

BERLINER, J., 1957, *Factory and Manager in the USSR*, Cambridge, Mass., Harvard University Press.

BIRN, R. B. and FINKELSTEIN, N., 1998, *A Nation on Historical Trial: The Goldhagen Thesis and Historical Truth*, New York, Henry Holt.

BOGDAN, V., 1982, *Mimikriia v SSSR: vospominaniia inzhenera 1935-1940 godov*, Frankfurt am Main, Avtor.

BORKENAU, F., 1976 [1934], *Der Übergang vom feudalen zum bürgerlichen Weltbild: Studien zur Geschichte der Philosophie der Manufakturperiode*, Darmstadt, Wissenschaftliche Buchgesellschaft.

BORKENAU, F., 1981, *End and Beginning: On the Generations of Cultures and the Origins of the West*, New York, Columbia University Press.

BOTH, N. and HONIG, J. W., 1996, *Srebrenica: Record of a War Crime*, Harmondsworth, Penguin.

BRIGGS, R., 1996, *Witches and Neighbors: The Social and Cultural Context of European Witchcraft*, New York, Viking.

BROBERG, G. and ROLL-HANSEN, N., 1996 (eds.), *Eugenics and the Welfare State. Sterilization Policy in Denmark, Sweden, Norway, and Finland*, East Lansing, Michigan State University Press.

BROBERG, G. and TYDÉN, M., 1991, *Oönskade i folkhemmet: Rashygien och sterilisering i Sverige*, Stockholm, Gidlunds.

BROBERG, G. and TYDÉN, M., 1996, "Eugenics in Sweden: Efficient Care" in BROBERG, G. and ROLL-HANSEN, N. (eds.), *Eugenics and the Welfare State. Sterilization policy in Denmark, Sweden, Norway and Finland*, East Lansing, Michigan State University Press.

BROCH, H., 1996 [1931-1932], *The Sleepwalkers: A Trilogy*, New York, Vintage Books.

BROVKIN, V. N., 1994, *Behind the Front Lines: Political Parties and Social Movements in Russia, 1918-1922*, Princeton, NJ, Princeton University Press.

BROWNING, C., 1992, *Ordinary Men: Reserve Police Battalion 101 and the Final Solution in Poland*, New York, Aaron Asher Books.

BUCK-MORSS, S., 1989, *The Dialectics of Seeing: Walter Benjamin and the Arcades Project*, Cambridge, MA, MIT Press.

BURKE, P., 1978, *Popular Culture in Early Modern Europe*, New York, Harper.

CAMUS, A., 1948, *The Plague*, Gilbert, S. (trans.), London, Penguin Books.

CAMUS, A., 1971 [1951], *The Rebel*, Bower, A. (trans.), London, Penguin Books.

CANETTI, E., 1973, *Crowds and Power*, Stewart, C. (trans.), Harmondsworth, Penguin.

CARR, K. L., 1992, *The Banalization of Nihilism: Twentieth Century Responses to Meaninglessness*, Albany, NY, State University of New York Press.

CASSIRER, E., 1932, *Die Philosophie der Aufklärung*, Tübingen, Mohr.

CASSIRER, E., 1946, *The Myth of the State*, New Haven, Yale University Press.

CASSIRER, E., 1951 [1932], *The Philosophy of the Enlightenment*, Koelln, C. A. and Pettegrove, J. P. (trans.), Princeton, Princeton University Press.

CHEYETTE, B., and MARCUS, L., 1998 (eds.), *Modernity, Culture and the Jew*, Cambridge, Polity Press.

CHUKOVSKAIA, L., 1965, *Opustel'yi Dom. Povest'*, Paris, Librairie des Cinq Continents.

CIGAR, N., 1996, *Genocide in Bosnia*, Texas, Texas A&M University Press.

CIORAN, E. M., 1975, *A Short History of Decay*, Howard, R. (trans.), London, Quarter Books.

CLARK, S., 1997, *Thinking with Demons: The Idea of Witchcraft in Early Modern Europe*, New York, Oxford University Press.

COCHRAN PONFADINE, E., 1931, *Russia – My Home: An Intimate Record of Personal Experiences Before, During and After the Bolshevist Revolution*, Indianapolis, Bobbs-Merrill.

COCKER, C., 1992, "Post-modernity and the End of the Cold War: Has War been Disinvented?", *Review of International Studies*, vol. 18.

COCKER, C., 1994, *War and the Twentieth Century: A Study of War and Modern Consciousness*, London and Washington, Brassey's.

COHN, N., 1970 [1957], *The Pursuit of the Millennium*, London, Paladin.

COHN, N., 1975, *Europe's Inner Demons: An Enquiry Inspired by the Great Witch-Hunt*, New York, New American Library.

COHN, N., 1993, *Cosmos, Chaos and the World to Come*, New Haven, Yale University Press.

CONQUEST, R., 1968, *The Great Terror: Stalin's Purge of the Thirties*, New York, Macmillan.

CONQUEST, R., 1990, *The Great Terror: A Reassessment*, New York, Oxford University Press.

COURTOIS, S. *et al.*, 1997, *Le livre noir du communisme: crimes, terreurs et répression*, Paris, R. Laffont.

COVIC, B. (ed.), 1993, "Memorandum of the Serbian Academy of Science and Arts", reprinted in *Roots of Serbian Aggression*, Zagreb, AGM.

CRITCHLEY, S., 1997, *Very Little... Almost Nothing: Death, Philosophy, Literature*, London and New York, Routledge.

CROSBY, D. A., 1988, *The Specter of the Absurd Sources and Criticism of Modern Nihilism*, Albany, New York, State Univ. of New York Press.

CUSHMAN, T. and MESTROVIC, S. (eds.), 1996, *This Time We Knew*, New York, New York Univ. Press.

DARWIN, C., 1859, *On the Origin of the Species by Means of Natural Selection, or, The Preservation of Favoured Races in the Struggle for Life*, London, John Murray.

DAVIDSON, L. S. and WARD, J. O., 1993 (eds.), *The Sorcery Trial of Alice Kyteler: A Contemporary Account (1324) with Related Documents in English Translation*, with Introduction and Notes, Binghamton, NY, Center for Medieval and Early Renaissance Studies.

DAVIES, R. W., 1997, *Soviet History in the Yelstin Era*, Basingstoke, England, Macmillan.

DAVIES, S., 1997, *Popular Opinion in Stalin's Russia: Terror, Propaganda and Dissent*, 1934-1941, Cambridge, England, Cambridge University Press.

DÖRNER, K., 1988, *Tödlichesmitleid, zur Frage der Unerträglichkeit des Lebens, oder: Die Soziale Frage: Entstehung, Medizinisierung, NS-Endlösung, Heute, Morgen*, Guttersloh, Verlag Jakob van Hoddis.

DOUGLAS, M., 1966, *Purity and Danger, An Analysis of the Concepts of Pollution and Taboo*, London, Routledge.

EDEN, R., 1984, *Political Leadership and Nihilism: A Study of Weber and Nietzsche*, Tampa, Florida, University Presses of Florida.

EHRENBURG, I., 1964 [1921-1941], *Memoirs:1921-1941*, Shebunina, T. (trans.) in collaboration with Kapp, Y., Cleveland, World.

EISENSTADT, S. N. (ed.), 1986, *The Origins and Diversity of Axial Age Civilisations*, New York, State University of New York Press.

EKSTEINS, M., 1990, *Rites of Spring: The Great War and the Birth of the Modern Age*, New York, Doubleday.

ELIAS, N., 1939, *Über den Prozess der Zivilisation; soziogenetische und psycho-genetische Untersuchungen*, Basel, Haus zum Falken.

ELIAS, N., 1983 [1969], *The Court Society*, Oxford, Blackwell.

ELIAS, N., 1994 [1938-9], *The Civilizing Process*, Oxford, Blackwell.

ELIAS, N., 1996, *The Germans*, Cambridge, Polity Press.

ESCHENROEDER, W., 1932, *Hexenwahn und Hexenprozess in Frankfurt am Main*, Inaugural-Dissertation, Johann Wolfgang Goethe Universität zu Frankfurt.

FAINSOD, M., 1958, *Smolensk Under Soviet Rule*, Cambridge, MA, Harvard University Press.

FEIN, H., 1993, *Genocide: A Sociological Perspective*, London, Sage.

FIGES, O., 1989, *Peasant Russia, Civil War: The Volga Countryside in Revolution (1917-1921)*, New York, Oxford University Press.

FISCHER, M., 1944, *My Lives in Russia*, New York, Harper and Brothers.

FITZPATRICK, S., 1994, *Stalin's Peasants: Resistance and Survival in the Russian Village after Collectivization*, New York, Oxford University Press.

FOUCAULT, M., 1966, *Les mots et les choses; une archéologie des sciences humaines*, Paris, Gallimard.

FOUCAULT, M., 1969, *L'archéologie du savoir*, Paris, Gallimard.

FOUCAULT, M., 1972 [1961], *Histoire de la folie à l'âge classique*, Paris, Gallimard.

FOUCAULT, M., 1975 [1963], *The Birth of the Clinic*, New York, Vintage.

FOUCAULT, M., 1977, "Power and Sex: An Interview with Michel Foucault", *Telos* 32: pp. 152-161.

FOUCAULT, M., 1979 [1975], *Discipline and Punish*, New York, Vintage.

FOUCAULT, M., 1984, "What is Enlightenment?", in RABINOW, P. (ed.), *The Foucault Reader*, New York, Pantheon.

FOUCAULT, M., 1985 [1984], "Kant on Enlightenment and Revolution", in *Economy and Society* 15, 1, pp. 88-96.

FOUCAULT, M., 1986 [1984], *The Use of Pleasure*, New York, Vintage.

FOUCAULT, M., 1987 [1984], *The Care of the Self*, New York, Vintage.

FOUCAULT, M., 1988a, MARTIN, L., GUTMAN, H. and HUTTON, P. H. (eds.), *Technologies of the Self: A Seminar with Michel Foucault*, London, Tavistock.

FOUCAULT, M., 1988b, "Politics and Reason", in KRITZMAN, L. D. (ed.), *Michel Foucault: Politics, Philosophy, Culture*, London, Routledge.

FOUCAULT, M., 1988c, "On Problematization", *History of the Present* 4, pp. 15-16.

FOUCAULT, M., 1994, *Dits et écrits*, 4 vols, DEFERT, D. and EWALD, F. (eds), Paris, Gallimard.

FROMM, E., 1960, *Fear of Freedom*, London, Routledge and Kegan Paul.

FRYKMAN, E., 1998, "Sockerförsöket", in *Scandia*, No.1.

FRYKMAN, J., 1993, "Becoming the Perfect Swede. Modernity, Body, Politics and National Processes in Twentieth-Century Sweden", in *Ethnos*, 58:3-4.

FRYKMAN, J. and LÖFGREN, O., 1985, "På väg – bilder av kultur och klass", in FRYKMAN, J. and LÖFGREN, O. (eds.), *Modärna tider, Vision och vardag i folkhemmet*, Lund, Liber.

FRYKMAN, J. and LÖFGREN, O., 1987 [1979], *Culture Builders. A Historical Anthropology of Middle-Class Life*, New Brunswick and London, Rutgers University Press.

GAUCHET, M., 1989, *La Révolution des droits de l'homme*, Paris, Gallimard.

GAY, P., 1968, *Weimar Culture: The Outsider as Insider*, Westport, Conn, Greenwood Publishers.

GERAS, N. and WOKLER, R., 1999 (eds.), *The Enlightenment and Modernity*, London, Macmillan.

GEREMEK, B., 1987, *The Margins of Society in Late Medieval Paris*, Cambridge, Cambridge University Press.

GIESEN, B., 1999, "National Identity as Trauma: The German Case", in STRÅTH, B. (ed.), *Myth and Memory in the Construction of Community*, Brussels, PIE-Peter Lang.

Enlightenment and Genocide

GILLESPIE, M. A., 1984, *Hegel, Heidegger and the Ground of History*, Chicago and London, The University of Chicago Press.

GILLESPIE, M. A., 1995, *Nihilism before Nietzsche*, Chicago and London, University of Chicago Press.

GINZBURG, C., 1992, *Ecstasies: Deciphering the Witches' Sabbath*, New York, Penguin.

GINZBURG, E., 1967, *Journey into the Whirlwind*, Stevenson P. and Hayward, M. (trans.), New York, Harcourt, Brace, Jovanovich.

GLICKSBERG, C., 1975, *The Literature of Nihilism*, Lewisburg, Pa., Bucknell University Press.

GOLDHAGEN, D. J., 1996, *Hitler's Willing Executioners: Ordinary Germans and the Holocaust*, New York, Knopf.

GOLDHAGEN, D. J., 1998, "The Failure of the Critics", in SHANDLEY, R. R. (ed.), *Unwilling Germans? The Goldhagen Debate*, Minneapolis, University of Minnesota Press.

GOLOMB, J., 1997 (ed.), *Nietzsche and Jewish Culture*, London and New York, Routledge.

GORBATOV, A. V., 1964, *Years Off My Life: The Memoirs of General of the Soviet Army A. V. Gorbatov*, London, Constable.

GORDON, C., 1985, "Kant on Enlightenment and Revolution", in *Economy and Society* 15, 1, pp. 88-96.

GORDON, C., 1991, "Governmental Rationality: An Introduction", in BURCHELL, G., GORDON, C. and MILLER, P. (eds.), *The Foucault Effect: Studies in Governmentality*, London. Harvester Wheatsheaf.

GORDON, L. and KLOPOV, E., 1989, *Chto eto bylo? Razmyshleniia o predposilakh i itogakh togo, chto sluchilos' s nami v 30-40-e gody*, Moscow, Izd-vo Politicheskoi.

GOUDSBLOM, J., 1980, *Nihilism and Culture*, Totowa, N.J., Rowman and Littlefield.

GRANICK, D., 1960, *The Red Executive: A Study of the Organization Man in Russian Industry*, London, Macmillan.

GREEN, W. S., 1985, "Otherness Within", in NEUSNER, J. and FRERICKS, E. S. (eds.), *"To See Ourselves as Others See Us": Christians, Jews, "Others" in Late Antiquity*, Chico, Calif., Scholars Press.

GRELL, O. P. and PORTER, R., 1999 (eds.), *Toleration in Enlightenment Europe*, Cambridge, Cambridge University Press.

GRIGORENKO, P. G., 1982, *Memoirs*, Whitney, T. P. (trans.), New York, Norton.

GURVITSCH, A., 1997, *Den svårfångade individen. Självsyn hos fornnordiska hjältar och medeltidens lärde i Europa*, Stockholm, Ordfront.

HADOT, P., 1995, *Philosophy as a Way of Life*, in DAVIDSON, A. I. (ed.), Cambridge, Cambridge University Press.

HANKINS, T. L., 1970, *Jean d'Alembert: Science and the Enlightenment*, Oxford, Clarendon Press.

HANNAFORD, I., 1996, *Race: The History of an Idea in the West*, London and Baltimore, Johns Hopkins UP.

262

HAZARD, P., 1935, *La crise de la conscience européenne (1680-1715)*, Paris, Boivin.

HEDENIUS, I., 1961, *Liv och Nytta*, Stockholm, Bonniers.

HEGEL, G. W. F., 1968- [1807], Gesammelte Werke, vol. IX. *Phänomenologie des Geistes*, BONSIEPEN W. and HEEDE, R. (eds.), Hamburg, Felix Meiner.

HEGEL, G. W. F., 1970, *Werke in zwanzig Bänden*, MOLDENHAUER, E. and MICHEL, K. M. (eds.), Frankfurt, Suhrkamp.

HEGEL, G. W. F., 1977 [1807], *Phenomenology of Spirit*, Miller, A. V. (trans.), Oxford, Clarendon Press.

HELLER, E., 1988, The *Importance of Nietzsche: Ten Essays*, Chicago and London, University of Chicago Press.

HENSHALL, N., 1992, *The Myth of Absolutism: Change and Continuity in Early Modern European Monarchy*, London, Longman.

HEIDEGGER, M., 1991 [1934], *Kant und das Problem der Metaphysik*, Heidegger Gestamtausgabe, vol. 3, Frankfurt, Klostermann.

HEILBRON, J. *et al.* (eds), 1998, "The Rise of the Social Sciences and the Formation of Modernity", *Sociology of the Sciences Yearbook* 20 (1996).

HILBERG, R., 1985, *The Destruction of the European Jews*, New York, Holmes and Meier.

HINDUS, M., 1931, *Red Bread*, New York, Jonathan Cape and Harrison Smith.

HIRDMAN, Y., 1989, *Att lägga livet till rätta – studier i svensk folkhemspolitik*, Stockholm, Carlssons.

HIRDMAN, Y., 1994, "Women – From Possibility to Problem? Gender Conflict in the Welfare State – The Swedish Model", *Research Report Series* No 3.

HISTORISK STATISTIK FÖR SVERIGE, 1960, Statistiska översiktstabeller, Stockholm

HOFFSTEN, N. V., 1919, *Ärftlighetslära*, Stockholm, P.A. Norstedt & Söners.

HORKHEIMER, M., 1947, *Eclipse of Reason*, New York, Oxford University Press.

HORKHEIMER, M., 1972, *Critical Theory, Selected Essays*, O'Connell, M. J. *et al.* (trans.), New York, Herder and Herder.

HORKHEIMER, M., 1978, *Dawn and Decline, Notes 1926-1931 and 1950-1969*, Shaw M. (trans.), New York, Herder and Herder.

HORKHEIMER, M., 1985 [1931-1949], Gesammelte Schriften, Volume 12: *Nachgelassene Schriften*, SCHMID NOERR G. (ed.) Frankfurt, Fischer.

HORKHEIMER, M., 1987 [1940-1950], *Gesammelte Schriften*, Volume 5: *Dialektik der Aufklärung und Schriften*, SCHMID NOERR G. (ed.) Frankfurt, Fischer.

HORKHEIMER, M., 1989 [1949-1972], *Gesammelte Schriften*, Volume 13: *Nachgelassene Schriften*, SCHMID NOERR, G. (ed.), Frankfurt, Fischer.

HORKHEIMER, M., 1995 [1937-1940], *Gesammelte Schriften*, Volume 16: *Briefwechsel*, SCHMID NOERR, G. (ed.), Frankfurt, Fischer.

HORKHEIMER, M., 1996 [1941-1948], *Gesammelte Schriften*, Volume 17: *Briefwechsel*, SCHMID NOERR, G. (ed.), Frankfurt, Fischer.

HORKHEIMER, M. and ADORNO, T. W., 1947 [1944], *Dialektik der Aufklärung: philosophische Fragmente*, Amsterdam, Querido.

Enlightenment and Genocide

HORKHEIMER, M. and ADORNO, T., 1972 [1944], *Dialectic of Enlightenment*, Cumming J. (trans.) New York, Herder and Herder.

HUIZINGA, J., 1957 [1924], *Erasmus and the Age of Reformation*, New York, Harper.

HUIZINGA, J., 1968 [1941], *Dutch Civilisation in the Seventeenth Century*, London, Collins.

HUIZINGA, J., 1990 [1924], *The Waning of the Middle Ages*, Harmondsworth, Penguin.

HYMA, A., 1965 [1924], *The Christian Renaissance*, Hamden, CTC, Archon Books.

ISAAC, J. C., 1992, *Arendt, Camus, and Modern Rebellion*, New Haven and London, Yale UP.

IZGOEV, A. S., 1923, "Piat' let v sovetskoi Rossii", *Arkhiv Russkoi Revoliutsii* 10.

JASPERS, K., 1997 [1936], *Nietzsche: An Introduction to the Understanding of his Philosophical Activity*, Wallraff, C. F. and Schmitz, F. J. (trans.) Baltimore and London, The Johns Hopkins UP.

JOHANNISSON, K., 1997, *Kroppens tunna skal, Sex essäer om kropp, historia och kultur*, Stockholm, Nordstedts.

JOHNSON, R., 1998, *Death Work: A Study of the Modern Execution Process*, Belmont, West/Wadsworth.

JONAS, H., 1984, *The Imperative of Responsibility: In Search of an Ethics for the Technological Age*, Chicago, University of Chicago Press.

KÄLVEMARK, A.-S., 1980, *More Children of Better Quality? Aspects on Swedish Population Policy in the 1930s*, Stockholm, Almqvist & Wiksell.

KARLSSON, K.-G., 1996, "Folkmordets etiologi", in GERNER, K. (ed.), *Stat Nation Konflikt, En festskrift tillägnad Sven Tägil*, Stockholm, Bra Böcker.

KASCHUBA, W, 1999, "The Emergence and Transformation of Foundation Myths" in STRÅTH, B. (ed.), *Myth and Memory in the Construction of Community*, Brussels, PIE-Peter Lang.

KAUFMANN, W., 1974, *Nietzsche: Philosopher, Psychologist, Antichrist*, 4th ed. Princeton, New Jersey, Princeton UP.

KHLEVNIUK, O. V., 1992, *1937-i: Stalin, NKVD i sovetskoe obshchestvo*, Moscow, Respublika.

KIKIN, K. K. and SENTA, N.-B. (eds), 1995, *The End of the Century: The Future in the Past*, Tokyo, New York and London, Kodansha International.

KOCH, L., 1996, *Racehygiejne i Danmark 1920-1956*, Copenhagen, Gyldendal.

KOESTLER, A., 1970, *The Trail of the Dinosaur, [and] Reflections on hanging*, London, Hutchinson.

KOONTZ, C., 1987, *Mothers in the Fatherland: Women, The Family, and Nazi Politics*, New York, St. Martin's.

KOPF, A., 1988, *Der Weg des Nihilismus von Friedrich Nietzsche bis zur Atombombe*, Munich, Minerva Publikation.

KORS, A. C. and PETERS, E. (eds), 1972, *Witchcraft in Europe 1100-1700: A Documentary History*, Philadelphia, University of Pennsylvania Press.

KOSELLECK, R., 1959, *Kritik und Krise; ein Beitrag zur Pathogenese der bürgerlichen Welt*, Freiburg, K. Alber.

KOSELLECK, R., 1985, *Futures Past: On the Semantics of Historical Time*, Cambridge, MA, The MIT Press.

KOSELLECK, R., 1988 [1959], *Critique and Crisis*, Oxford, Berg.

KOTKIN, S., 1995, *Magnetic Mountain: Stalinism as a Civilization*, Berkeley, Calif., University of California Press.

KRISTEVA, J., 1988, *Étrangers à nous-mêmes*, Paris, Fayard.

LANDAU, R. S., 1998, *Studying the Holocaust: Issues, Readings, and Documents*, London and New York, Routledge.

LANG, B., 1990, *Act and Idea in the Nazi Genocide*, Chicago, Univ. of Chicago Press.

LEMKIN, R., 1944, *Axis Rule in Occupied Europe, Laws of Occupation, Analysis of Government, Proposals for Redress*, Washington, Carnegie Endowment for International Peace.

LEVI, P., 1987, *If This is a Man*, London, Abacus.

LEYPOLD, D., 1989, *Le Ban de la Roche au Temps des Seigneurs de Rathsamhausen et de Veldenz (1489-1630): Une Seigneurie Alsacienne au Tournant du "Siècle d'Or"*, Lutz, R. (preface), Strasbourg, Librairie Oberlin.

LIEDMAN, S.-E., 1997 (ed.), *The Post-modernist Critique of the Project of Enlightenment*, Amsterdam, Atlanta, Ga., Rodopi.

LIFTON, R. J., 1986, *The Nazi Doctors: Medical Killing and the Psychology of Genocide*, New York, Basic Books.

LINDQUIST, B., 1991, *Förädlade svenskar – drömmen om att skapa en bättre människa*, Stockholm, Alfabeta Bokförlag.

LIPPMAN, W., 1929, *A Preface to Morals*, New York, MacMillan.

LÖWITH, K., 1995, *Martin Heidegger and European Nihilism*, Steiner G. (trans.), New York, Columbia University Press.

LUNDBORG, H., 1927, *Svensk raskunskap*, Uppsala, Almqvist & Wiksell. German translation *Rassenkunde des schwedischen volkes*, Iena, Gustav Fischer Verlag, 1928.

MACINTYRE, A., 1981, *After Virtue: A Study in Moral Theory*, London, Duckworth.

MALCOMSON, S. L., 1998, "The Varieties of Cosmopolitan Experiences" in CHEAH, P. and ROBBINS, B. (eds.), *Cosmopolitics. Thinking and Feeling beyond the Nation*, University of Minnesota Press, Minneapolis.

MARTIN, G. T., 1989, *From Nietzsche to Wittgenstein: The Problem of Truth and Nihilism in the Modern World*, New York, Peter Lang.

MARX, K., 1978 [1872], *The Marx-Engels Reader*, 2nd ed., TUCKER R. C. (ed.), New York, W. W. Norton.

MCALLISTER, T. V., 1996, *Revolt against Modernity: Leo Strauss, Eric Voegelin and the Search for a Postliberal Order*, Lawrence, Kansas, University of Kansas Press.

MCAULEY, M., 1989, "Bread without the Bourgeoisie," in KOENKER, D. P., ROSENBERG, W, G. and SUNY, R. G. (eds.), *Party, State, and Society in the Russian Civil War*, Bloomington, Ind., Indiana University Press.

MEDVEDEV, R. A., 1989, *Let History Judge: The Origins and Consequences of Stalinism. Revised and expanded edition*, SHRIVER, G. (ed. and trans.), New York, Columbia University Press.

MELGOUNOV, S. P., 1925, *The Red Terror in Russia*, London, Dent.

MELSON, R., 1992, *Revolution and Genocide: On the Origins of the Amenian Genocide and the Holocaust*, Chicago, University of Chicago Press.

MESTROVIC, S., 1997 (ed.), *The Conceit of Innocence*, Texas, Texas A&M Univ. Press.

MILLER, J., 1964, "Soviet Planners in 1936-1937," in DEGRAS, J. and NOVE, A. (eds.), *Soviet Planning: Essays in Honour of Naum Jasny*, Oxford, England, Blackwell.

MOORE, R. I., 1987, *The Formation of a Persecuting Society: Power and Deviance in Western Europe, 950-1250*, Oxford, England, Blackwell.

MOSSE, G., 1975, *The Nationalisation of the Masses, Political Symbolism and Mass Movements in Germany from the Napoleonic Wars through the Third Reich*, New York, Howard Fertig.

MYRDAL, A., 1968 [1941], *Nation and the Family. The Swedish Experiment in Democratic Family and Population Policy*, Cambridge, Mass. and London, The M.I.T. Press.

NEHAMAS, A., 1996, "Nietzsche, Modernity, Aestheticism" in *The Cambridge Companion to Nietzsche*, MAGNUS, B. and HIGGINS, K. M. (eds.), Cambridge, New York, Cambridge University Press.

NIETZSCHE, F., 1966 [1886], *Beyond Good and Evil*, Kaufmann, W. (trans.) Vintage Books.

NIETZSCHE, F. 1967- [1885-1887], "Nachgelassene Fragmente 1885-1887", in COLLI, G. and MONTINARI, M. (eds.) *Kritische Studienausgabe*, vol., 12.

NIETZSCHE, F., 1967 [1887], *On the Genealogy of Morals, On the Genealogy of Morals and Ecce Homo*, Kaufmann, W. and Hollingdale R. J. (trans.), New York, Vintage.

NIETZSCHE, F., 1968, *Basic Writings*, KAUFMANN, W. (ed.), New York, Modern Library.

NIETZSCHE, F., 1968 [1901], *The Will to Power*, Kaufmann, W. and Hollingdale, R. J. (trans.), New York, Vintage.

NIETZSCHE, F., 1969 [1883-85], *Thus Spoke Zarathustra*, Hollingdale, R. J. (trans.), London, Penguin.

NIETZSCHE, F., 1974 [1882], *The Gay Science*, Kaufmann, W. (trans.), New York, Vintage.

NIETZSCHE, F., 1989 [1886], *Beyond Good and Evil: Prelude to a Philosophy of the Future*, Kaufmann, W. (trans.), New York, Vintage Books.

NIETZSCHE, F., 1996 [1887], *On the Genealogy of Morals*, Smith, D. (trans.), Oxford, Oxford UP.

NIETZSCHE, F., 1997 [1887], *Daybreak: Thoughts on the Prejudices of Morality*, CLARCK, M. and LEITER, B. (eds), Hollingdale, R. J. (trans.), Cambridge, New York, Cambridge UP.

NIETZSCHE, F., 1998 [1889], *Twilight of the Idols or How to Philosophize with a Hammer*, Lange, D. (trans.), Oxford, New York, Oxford UP.

NILSSON, G. B., 1995, "Kapitalismens värderingar. De harmoniliberala genombrottsåren i Sverige och Norge 1849-1879" in ANSHELM, J. (ed.), *I tider av uppbrott. Värderingar och värdeförändringar i det moderna samhället*, Stockholm, Brutus Östlings Bokförlag Symposion.

OESTREICH, G., 1982, *Neostoicism and the Early Modern State*, Cambridge, Cambridge University Press.

ORTEGA Y GASSET, J., 1987, *La deshumanización del arte y otros ensayos de estética*, Madrid, Editorial Espasa Calpe.

PAPPE, I., 1999, "Challenging Israel's Foundation Myths: The Construction of a Constructive Mythology?" in STRÅTH, B. (ed.), *Myth and Memory in the Construction of Community*, Brussels, PIE-Peter Lang.

PATOCKA, J., 1996, *Heretical Essays in the Philosophy of History*, DODD, J. (ed.) Chicago, Open Court.

PEUKERT, D., 1989, *Max Webers Diagnose der Moderne*, Göttingen, Vandenhoeck & Ruprecht.

PIPPIN, R. B., 1996, "Nietzsche's Alleged Farewell: The Pre-Modern, Modern and Post-Modern Nietzsche" in MAGNUS B. and HIGGINS, K. M. (eds.), *The Cambridge Companion to Nietzsche*, Cambridge, Cambridge UP.

PLESSNER, H., 1974 [1935], *Die verspätete Nation*, Frankfurt, Suhrkamp.

PRYCHODKO, N., 1952, *One of the Fifteen Million*, Boston, Little, Brown.

QVARSELL, R., 1991, *Vårdens idéhistoria*, Stockholm, Brutus Östlings.

RADKEY, O. H., 1976, *The Unknown Civil War in Soviet Russia: A Study of the Green Movement in the Tambov Region 1920-1921*, Stanford, CA, Hoover Institution Press.

RADZINSKY, E., 1996, *Stalin: The First In-depth Biography Based on Explosive New Documents from Russia's Secret Archives*, Willetts, H. T. (trans.), New York Doubleday.

RANCOUR-LAFERRIERE, D., 1995, *The Slave Soul of Russia: Moral Masochism and the Cult of Suffering*, New York, New York University Press.

RAUSCHNING, H., 1939 [1938], *Germany's Revolution of Destruction*, Dickes E. W. (trans.), London and Toronto, William Heinemann.

RAUSCHNING, H., 1954, *Masken und Metamorphosen des Nihilismus: Der Nihilismus des XX. Jahrhunderts*, Frankfurt am Main and Vienna, Humboldt-Verlag.

RIALS, S., 1988, *La Déclaration des droits de l'homme et du citoyen*, Paris, Hachette.

RIES, N., 1997, *Russian Talk: Culture and Conversation during Perestroika*, Ithaca, NY, Cornell University Press.

ROHDE, D., 1997, *Endgame, the Betrayal and Fall of Srebrenica*, New York, Farrar, Straus and Giroux.

ROSEN, S., 1989, *The Ancients and the Moderns*, New Haven, Yale UP.

ROSENBERG, G., 1994, *Da Capo al Fine*, Stockholm, Moderna Tider.

Enlightenment and Genocide

ROTHSTEIN, B., 1994, *Vad bör staten göra? Om välfärdsstatens moraliska och politiska logik*, Stockholm, SNS.

RUNCIS, M., 1998, *Steriliseringar i folkhemmet*, Stockholm, Ordfront.

SAID, E. W., 1979, *Orientalism*, New York, Vintage.

SARTRE, J.-P., 1964 [1938], *Nausea*, Alexander, L. (trans.), New York, New Directions Publishing Corporation.

SCAFF, L., 1984, "Weber before Weberian Sociology", in *The British Journal of Sociology* 35(2).

SCAFF, L., 1989, *Fleeing the Iron Cage*, Berkely, University of California Press.

SCHLUCHTER, W., 1989, *Rationalism, Religion and Domination: A Weberian Perspective*, Berkeley, University of California Press.

SCOTT, J., 1973 [1942], *Behind the Urals: An American Worker in Russia's City of Steel*, Bloomington, IN, Indiana University Press.

SELLS, M., 1996, *The Bridge Betrayed, Religion and Genocide in Bosnia*, Berkely, Univ. of California Press.

SEWARD, D., 1995, *The Monks of War*, Harmondsworth, Penguin.

SMITH. J. Z., 1985, "What a Difference a Difference Makes," in NEUSNER, J. and FRERICKS, E. S. (eds.), *"To See Ourselves as Others See Us": Christians, Jews, "Others" in Late Antiquity*, Chico, Calif., Scholars Press.

SÖDERBLOM, T., 1992, *Horan och batongen. Prostitution och repression i folkhemmet*, Gidlund, Stockholm.

SOLZHENITSYN, A. I., 1973, *The Gulag Archipelago 1918-1956: An Experiment in Literary Investigation*, Whitney T. P. (trans.), New York, Harper & Row.

SOROKIN, P., 1950, *Leaves from a Russian Diary-and Thirty Years After*, Boston, Beacon.

STAROBINSKI, J., 1989, "Le mot civilisation" in STAROBINSKI, J., *Le remède dans le mal: critique et légitimation de l'artifice à l'âge des Lumières*, Paris, Gallimard.

STAUTH, G. and TURNER, B. S., 1988, *Nietzsche's Dance: Resentment, Reciprocity, and Resistance in Social Life*, Oxford, Blackwell.

STERN, F., 1987, *Dreams and Delusions: National Socialism in the Drama of the German Past*, New York, Vintage.

STRÅTH, B., 2000a, "Poverty, Neutrality and Welfare: Three Key Concepts in the Modern Foundation Myth of Sweden" in STRÅTH, B. (ed.), *Myth and Memory in the Construction of Community*, Brussels, PIE-Peter Lang.

STRÅTH, B., 2000b, "The Swedish Image of Europe as the Other" in STRÅTH, B. (ed.), *Europe and the Other and Europe as the Other*, Brussels, PIE-Peter Lang.

STRÅTH, B. 2000c (ed.), *After Full Employment, European Discourses on Work and Flexibility*, Brussels, PIE-Peter Lang.

STRAYER, J. R., 1970, *On the Medieval Origins of the Modern State*, Princeton, NJ, Princeton University Press.

STROMBERG, R., 1982, *Redemption by War: The Intellectuals and 1914*, Lawrence, Regents Press of Kansas

STRONG, T. B., 1975, *Friedrich Nietzsche and the Politics of Transfiguration*, London, University of California Press.

SVENSSON, B., 1995, *Bortom all āra och redlighet. Tattarnas spel med rättvisan*, Stockholm.

SWANSON, R. N., 1995, *Religion and Devotion in Europe, c., 1215-c., 1515*, Cambridge, England, Cambridge University Press.

SZAKOLCZAI, A., 1997, "Norbert Elias and Franz Borkenau: Intertwined Life-Works", in *EUI Working Paper*, SPS No. 97/8 (forthcoming in Theory, Culture and Society).

SZAKOLCZAI, A., 1998a, *Max Weber and Michel Foucault: Parallel Life-Works*, London, Routledge.

SZAKOLCZAI, A., 1998b, "Reflexive Historical Sociology", in *The European Journal of Social Theory* 1, 2.

TALMON, J., 1952, *Origins of Totalitarian Democracy*, London, Secker & Warburg.

THOMAS, K., 1971, *Religion and the Decline of Magic: Studies in Popular Beliefs in Sixteenth and Seventeenth Century England*, London, Weidenfeld and Nicolson.

THURSTON, R., 1996, *Life and Terror in Stalin's Russia, 1934-1941*, New Haven, Conn., Yale University Press.

TIMASHEFF, N., 1946, *The Great Retreat: The Growth and Decline of Communism in Russia*, New York, E. P. Dutton.

TOLER, J., 1992, *Per Jönson Rösiö: "The Agrarian Prophet" : A Charismatic Leader's Attempt to Rejuvenate Small Agriculture and Create a Commitment to a Cultural Revolt against Industrialism in Sweden, 1888-1928*, Stockholm, Almqvist & Wiksell International.

TOSCANO, R., 1998, "The Face of the Other, Ethics and Intergroup Conflict", in WEINER, E. (ed.), *The Handbook, of Interethnic Coexstance*, New York, Continuum.

TRAVERSO, E., 1996, *L'histoire déchirée*, Paris, Cerf.

TROMBLEY, S., 1993, *The Execution Protocol: Inside America's Capitol Punishment Industry*, New York, Anchor Books.

TURNER, V., 1967, "Betwixt and Between: The Liminal Period in Rites de Passage", in TURNER, V., *The Forest of Symbols aspects of Ndembu ritual*, New York, Cornell University Press.

TYDÉN, M., "Rasbiologi och andra rasismer" in *Folkets historia*, No.3-4, 1996.

ULAM, A. B., 1973, *Stalin: The Man and His Era*, New York, Viking.

ULLMANN, V., 1993 [1944], *Viktor Ullmann: 26 kritiken über musikalische Veranstaltungen in Theresienstadt*, SCHULTZ, I. (ed.), Hamburg, von Bockel Verlag.

U.N.T.S., 1951, No.1021, vol. 78.

VENARD, M., 1993, *Réforme protestante, réforme catholique dans la province d'Avignon (XVIe siècle)*, Paris, Cerf.

VETLESEN, A. J., 1994, *Perception, Empathy, and Judgement*, University Park, PA, Penn State Press.

VETLESEN, A. J., 1998, "Impartiality and Evil", in *Philosophy & Social Criticism*, 24-5, pp. 1-35.

VETLESEN, A. J., 1999, "Genocide: A Case for the Responsibility of the Bystander", in *Journal of Peace Research*, No.1.

VIOLA, L., 1996, *Peasant Rebels under Stalin: Collectivization and the Culture of Peasant Resistance*, New York, Oxford University Press.

VOEGELIN, E., 1952, *The New Science of Politics*, Chicago, Chicago University Press.

VOEGELIN, E., 1956, *Order and History, Israel and Revelation*, Vol., 1, Baton Rouge, Louisiana State University Press.

VOEGELIN, E., 1957a, *Order and History, The World of the Polis*, Vol. 2, Baton Rouge, Louisiana State University Press.

VOEGELIN, E., 1957b, *Order and History, Plato and Aristotle*, Vol. 3, Baton Rouge, Louisiana State University Press.

VOEGELIN, E., 1968, *Science, Politics and Gnosticism*, Chicago, Henry Regnery.

VOEGELIN, E., 1974, *Order and History, The Ecumenic Age*, Vol. 4, Baton Rouge, Louisiana State University Press.

VOEGELIN, E., 1994, *Das Volk Gottes*, Munich, Wilhelm Fink Verlag.

VOLKOGONOV, D., 1991, *Stalin: Triumph and Tragedy*, SHUKMAN H. (ed. and trans.), London, Weidenfeld and Nicolson.

VOLTAIRE, 1733, *Letters Concerning the English Nation*, London, C. Davis and A. Lyon.

VRANIC, S., 1996, *Breaking the Walls of Silence: The Voices of Raped Bosnia*, Zagreb, Aktant.

WAGNER, P. and WITTROCK, B., 1992, "Policy Constitution through Discourse: Discourse Transformations and the Modern State in Central Europe", in ASHFORD, D. E. (ed.), *History and Context in Comparative Public Policy*, Pittsburgh, University of Pittsburgh Press.

WEBER, M., 1948a [1915], "The Social Psychology of the World Religions", in GERTH, H. H. and MILLS C. W. (eds.), *From Max Weber: Essays in Sociology*, London, Routledge.

WEBER, M., 1948b [1915], "Religions Rejections of the World and Their Directions", in GERTH, H. H. and MILLS C. W. (eds.), *From Max Weber: Essays in Sociology*, London, Routledge.

WEBER, M., 1976 [1904-1905], *The Protestant Ethic and the Spirit of Capitalism*, London, Allen and Unwin.

WEBER, M., 1978a [1921-1922], *Economy and Society*, Berkeley, University of California Press.

WEBER, M., 1978b [1910], "Anticritical Last Word on The Spirit of Capitalism", in *American Journal of Sociology* 83 (5).

WEBER, M., 1981 [1920], *General Economic History*, New York, Transaction Books.

WEBER, M., 1988 [1920-1921], *Gesammelte Aufsätze zur Religionssoziologie*, 3 vols, Tübingen, J.C.B. Mohr.

WEBSTER'S 1982, *New World Dictionary of the American Language*, 2nd College ed., New York, Simon and Schuster.

WHEATCROFT, S. G., 1993, "More Light on the Scale of Repression and Excess Mortality in the Soviet Union in the 1930s", in GETTY, J. A. and MANNING, R. T. (eds), *Stalinist Terror: New Perspectives*, London, Cambridge University Press.

WIGGERSHAUS, R., 1994, *The Frankfurt School: Its History, Theories, and Political Significance*, Robertson, M. (trans.), Cambridge, MA, MIT Press.

WOKLER, R., 1994, 'Projecting the Enlightenment', in HORTON, J. and MENDUS, S. (eds.), *After MacIntyre*, Cambridge: Polity Press.

WOLFF, L., 1994, *Inventing Eastern Europe: The Map of Civilization on the Mind of the Enlightenment*, Stanford, Calif., Stanford University Press.

WOODWARD, C. V., 1974, *The Strange Career of Jim Crow*, 3rd revised ed., New York, Oxford University Press.

YOUNG, J., *The Exclusive Society: Social Exclusion, Crime and Difference in Late Modernity*, MS.

ZAREMBA, M., 1999, *De rena och de andra: om tvångssteriliseringar, rashygien och arvssynd*, Stockholm, DN.

Contributors

Zygmunt Bauman is Professor of Sociology at the University of Leads. He has published widely on issues of culture, modernity and post-modernity. The most recent of his numerous publications include *Culture as Praxis* and *Globalization: The Human Consequences.*

Stefan Elbe is a doctoral candidate in the Department of International Relations at the London School of Economic and Political Science. He is currently completing a thesis critically examining the philosophical foundations of the political project of Europe.

Elin Frykman is a researcher at the Department of Technology and Social Change, Linköping University, Sweden. Her research is centred around technology and culture as they can be understood through the practice of medical experimentation.

James Kaye is currently a researcher at the European University Institute in Florence. His research addresses discourses of the home comparatively in Austria and Sweden between the latter half of the 19th and former half of the 20th century.

Göran Rosenberg studied mathematics, philosophy, political science and journalism at the University of Stockholm. Since 1970 he has been working as a journalist and correspondent for major Swedish newspapers and Swedish Television. In 1990 he founded the Swedish monthly magazine of essays and opinions, *Moderna Tider*, which he edited until 1999. Among his books are *Friare kan ingen vara, den amerikanska idén från Revolution till Reagan* and *Det förlorade landet, en personlig historia* (a personal history of Zionism, Messianism and the State of Israel).

James Schmidt is Professor of Political Science and Sociology at Boston University. He is the author *of Maurice Merleau-Ponty: Between Phenomenology and Structuralism* and the editor of *What is Enlightenment? Eighteenth-Century Answers and Twentieth-Century Questions*. He is currently completing a study of German criticisms of the idea of enlightenment.

Bo Stråth is Professor of Contemporary History in the Department of History and Civilisation/Robert Schuman Centre at the European University Institute Florence. He has published widely on political and economic processes. His research focuses comparatively on modernisation and democratisation processes in Northern and Western Europe.

Arpád Szakolczai is Professor of Sociology at University College in Cork. His current research is on the common problematics of the works of Weber, Nietzsche, Elias and Foucault; it also investigates empirically the establishment of the new systems of local government in Hungary and the Czech and Slovak Republics, and attempts to situate these changes with reference to the broad history of the emergence of the modern state in Western Europe.

Robert Thurston is Professor of History at Miami University, Oxford, Ohio. He has most recently edited and contributed to *The People's War: Responses to World War II in the Soviet Union* and is the author of *Life and Terror in Stalin's Russia, 1934-1941*. His current research involves a comparison of the European witch hunts, American lynching, and Soviet terror.

Arne Johan Vetlesen is Professor of Philosophy at the University of Oslo. His publications include *Perception, Empathy, and Judgment, An Inquiry into the Preconditions of Moral Performance* and *Closeness an Ethics* (ed. with H. Jodalen).

Robert Wokler is Reader in the History of Political Thought at the University of Manchester. His most recent publications include *Rousseau's Enlightenment: The Historical Context of his Social Thought, The Cambridge History of Eighteenth-Century Political Thought* (ed. with M. Goldie) and *The Enlightenment and Modernity* (ed. with N. Geras).

Series "Philosophy & Politics"

Open to thinkers from all countries and cultures who are not limiting their efforts to understand the processes of social institutions, but are raising questions about their goals and meaning, this series hopes to contribute to a renewal of political philosophy. Beyond the different disciplines of social sciences, ideological commitments and the limits of "national schools", philosophy is bound to pursue its universal enquiry on human wisdom in a world chaotically pushed towards greater unity.

Series directed by Gabriel Fragnière